FAREWELL,

GODSPEED

FAREWELL,

GODSPEED

The Greatest Eulogies of Our Time

edited by CYRUS M. COPELAND

Harmony Books
NEW YORK

Published by Harmony Books, New York, New York.
Member of the Crown Publishing Group,
a division of Random House, Inc.
www.randomhouse.com

HARMONY BOOKS is a registered trademark and the
Harmony Books colophon is a trademark of Random House, Inc.

Printed in the United States of America

Design by Lynne Amft

Library of Congress Cataloging-in-Publication Data
Farewell, godspeed : the greatest eulogies of our time / edited by
Cyrus M. Copeland.—1st ed.
1. Eulogies. I. Copeland, Cyrus. M.
    CT105.F28 2003
    811'.508—dc21   2003008226
            ISBN 1-4000-4946-6

            10   9   8   7   6   5   4   3   2   1

                    First Edition

For my mother, who taught me reverence

I am not dead. I have only become inhuman. That is to say, undressed myself of laughable prides and infirmities, but not as a man undresses to creep into bed, but like an athlete stripping for the race. The delicate ravel of nerves that made me a measurer of certain fictions called good and evil, that made me contract with pain and expand with pleasure, fussily adjusted like a little electroscope, that's gone it's true. (I never miss it, if the universe does. How easily replaced!) But all the rest is heightened, widened, set free. I admired the beauty while I was human. Now I am part of the beauty. I wander in the air being mostly gas and water, and flow in the ocean. Touch you and Asia at the same moment. I have a hand in the sunrises and the glow of this grass. I left the light precipitate of ashes to Earth for a love-token.

> ROBINSON JEFFERS
> *Inscription for a Gravestone*

Contents

Captains of Industry

Matinee Idols

Explorers & High Fliers

Tunesmiths & Troubadours

Movie Moguls

Wordsmiths

Introduction

A curious thing happens when we die: we become Celebrities. People appear to say how much we *meant* to them. We are regaled and wept over and cherished. There are speeches and fanfare. Suddenly our favorite charity is awash in donations. Finally, our fifteen minutes have arrived.

But what happens when our icons die? Do they become more human?

"They made him a legend when he would have preferred to be a man," Jackie said upon JFK's death. Thirty years later at her own memorial, Ted Kennedy echoed, "Jackie would have preferred just to be herself, but the world insisted that she be a legend too. She never wanted public notice—in part, I think, because it brought back painful memories of an unbearable sorrow, endured in the glare of a million lights."

Jackie and JFK. Einstein and Ellington. Our legends live and die on the world stage. When the spotlight clicks off and the curtain falls, we scan their reviews—respectful obits polished to a glossy shine. Marriages, jobs, awards, degrees, divorces, survivors . . . the essentials are all there.

But what of their essence?

Tucked away in a cathedral somewhere, or a theater, or an airport hangar, a crowd of intimates gathers to hear tributes of a different nature. The words are personal and profound. They are spoken by those who watched from behind the spotlight. John John's uncle. Einstein's assistant. Ellington's pal. These are the witnesses who walked alongside our icons, called them by nicknames, and who—at this final moment—trade in their private recollections for a public good-bye. Their eulogies offer something far greater than a synopsis of our icons' lives: they are proof of their humanity.

Culled from the intimacies behind the image, *Farewell, Godspeed* is their loving testimony.

Here is Andy Warhol's close friend describing his hidden spirituality. Who knew the Big Apple Pop Art Iconographer spent hours in church and working in soup kitchens? Here is Lillian Hellman remembering her lover Dashiell Hammett. From her we learn Hammett, like his literary creation Sam Spade, could see through lies and never tell one. Here is Albert Einstein's assistant describing the dilemma of one of the twentieth century's great humanists: the relentless pursuit of scientific discovery that led, among other places, to that Strangelovian nightmare, the A-bomb. And here is Neil Simon, prolific master of the Broadway comedy, distilling his memories of director/choreographer Bob Fosse into a "Ten Best" list. Bits of humanity that escape the spotlight's gaze. In their recounting, we glimpse what made our icons *real*— their fragile lives reconstructed as their vulnerabilities and nuances come to surface. Death warps celebrity. Like Alice down the rabbit hole, they become bigger *and* smaller. More iconic. More human.

"We are always saying farewell in this world," Adlai Stevenson observed at Eleanor Roosevelt's memorial, "always standing at the edge of loss attempting to retrieve some memory, some human meaning, from the silence—something which is precious and gone."

Here also is a reminder of the heights of human accomplishment, told in the poetry of loss. Many of these eulogies are gems of oratory, luminous writing to honor great living. And occasionally, dramatic dying.

"Shoot, you are only going to kill a man," Che Guevara taunted a Bolivian soldier—who immediately complied. In his eulogy, Fidel Castro lionized Che's contempt for danger and absence of ego. "If we want to say how we want our revolutionary fighters, our militants, our men to be, we should say without hesitation: Let them be like Che!"

Guevara wasn't the only one to die sadly, boldly, in a blaze of color and conviction. Ryan White, Isadora Duncan, Martin Luther King,

Gianni Versace, Virginia Woolf, the *Challenger* Astronauts, Timothy Leary, JFK, Malcolm X . . . all passed from this world in remarkable ways. In death as in life, they left their mark. Their send-offs are all found here.

Director William Richert on his friend River Phoenix: "I think he wanted to touch danger, and the artist he was felt he could handle death, perhaps even collaborate with it and play out a scene or two. This time however, he opened the one door from which he could never return." Phoenix's death on a sidewalk outside Hollywood's Viper Room, on Halloween, age 23, a speedball coursing through his veins, was a sad sequel in the tradition of screen rebels. Forty years earlier, age 24 and astride a spectacularly brief career, James Dean died en route to race his Porsche. Speed kills—on the road *or* in the veins. But in Hollywood the compulsion to live, and die, with abandon continues.

A great eulogy is both art and architecture—a bridge between the living and the dead, memory and eternity. Here are 64 bridges to cross. Strung together with words, they survive by the sheer force of their beauty. There is something timeless about a well-worded good-bye, and as I crossed these bridges, I found the veil between worlds would lift. Scientists, actors, writers, visionaries, politicians, musicians—a stream of ethereal guests came to visit, their souls hovering as their eulogies made their way into this book.

Here then is a netting of great souls—bound by this book, and their imprint on our lives. Whether to art or to music, to business or science, or to the evolving social conscience, their contributions marked a century's progress—a century that saw gigantic leaps forward in all directions. Their accomplishments became ours. We continue to watch them on screen, read their stories, our lives made better by their inventions.

They are gone, and the world weighs less. But what an impression they left.

So welcome to their memorial. Pull up your front row seat. Here, from those who watched in the spotlight's shadow, are the final tributes. Here is how we remember—and thank—them.

ISADORA DUNCAN
1878-1927

By MAX EASTMAN, *political sympathizer and friend*

Written on the occasion of her death

ISADORA DUNCAN WAS THE LAST FRIEND I SAW WHEN I LEFT Europe this spring. She stood in the little crowd on the platform at the Gare Saint Lazare. I was standing at the car window, laughing and half crying at the sadly funny excitement of people parting with their friends, and suddenly I heard her voice calling my name and "Goodbye!" She raised her hand when I caught sight of her, and stood still with it raised in the air and moving slowly in a serene and strong benediction. A great beam of that energetic and perfectly idealistic light shone out of her eyes to me. She looked very great. She looked like a statue of real liberty.

It made me sad for a long time, because greatness in this little world is sad. Greatness coming to an unhappy end is almost unendurable, and I had felt that Isadora was coming to an unhappy end. I felt it underneath all the delightful bubbling of her mirth when I saw her during the winter in Cannes. It was at the house of our friend Lucien Monod, a Communist and an artist. She had just received a cablegram that money would be forwarded for her memoirs, and she was full of laughing joy—that wild, reckless, witty joy that all her friends remember. Isadora could sprinkle the whole world with her wit and make it shine.

Isadora Duncan was one of the great men and women—more indubitably so, I think, than any other artist who has lived in our time. They speak of Duse and Sarah Bernhardt and Isadora as a trio of great women, but Isadora was incomparably above the other two. She was not only a supreme artist as they were, endowed by nature with momentous power and the perfect gift of restraining it, but she was also a great mind and a moral force. She used her momentous power, as the giants of mankind have always done, not only to entertain the world but to move it.

And she did move it. It is needless to tell how she changed the art of dancing. She was a revolution in that art, and so to some extent in the whole art of theater. All the civilized world acclaimed her, and recognized in that young brave girl's beautiful body, running barefoot and half-naked, running and bending and pausing and floating in a stream of music, as though the music had formed out of its own passion a visible spirit to live for a moment and die when it died—all the world recognized in that an artistic revolution, an apparition of creative genius, and not merely an achievement in the established art of the dance.

But I think few people realized how far beyond the realm of art—how far out and how deep into the moral and social life of our times—the influence of Isadora Duncan's dancing extended. All the bare-legged girls, and the poised and natural girls with strong muscles and strong, free steps wherever they go—they all owe more to Isadora Duncan than to any other person. And the boys, too, they have a chance to be unafraid of beauty, to be unafraid of the natural life and free aspiration of an intelligent animal walking on the earth—all who have in any measure escaped from the rigidity and ritual of our national religion of negation, all of them owe an immeasurable debt to Isadora Duncan's dancing. She did not only go back into the past to Athens to find that voluntary restraint in freedom that made her dancing an event in the history of art. She went forward into the future—farther, I suppose, than Athens—to a time when man shall be cured altogether of civilization, and return, with immunity to that disease if with few other blessings, to his natural home outdoors on the green surface of the earth. That made her dancing an event in the history of life.

Isadora was exiled—banished by more than an accident of the marriage law—from America. But nevertheless Isadora was very American. The big way in which she conceived things, and undertook them, and the way she succeeded with them, was American. Even her faults were American—her passion for "pulling off stunts"—"gestures" is the way she would say it—was American. She made a grand sport of her public position and character. She played with publicity like a humorous Barnum. Even her extravagant and really bad irresponsibility, which went almost to the point of madness in later years, was in the reverse sense an American trait. It was an exaggerated reaction against America's "righteousness." *Wrongtiousness* is what you would have to call it if you wished to appraise it with a sense of its origin.

America fighting the battle with Americanism—that was Isadora. From that battle incomparable things are to come—things that will startle and teach the world. And Isadora led the way into the fight all alone, with her naked and strong body and her bold character, vivid as an Amazon. If America triumphs over greed and prudery, intellectual and moral cowardice, Isadora Duncan will be sculptured in bronze at the gate of the Temple of Man in the new day that will dawn. She will stand there, poised in terrible impatience, knee raised and arms tensely extended as in the *March Militaire* of the Scythian warrior's dance— beautiful—a militant and mighty woman, the symbol and the veritable leader of those who put on their courage like armor and fought for the affirmation of life in America.

1878	Born in San Francisco, the youngest of four children. Despite financial struggle, Isadora's childhood is filled with literature, classical music, and especially dance—courtesy of a cultured pianist mother. Learns to "listen to the music with your soul."
1890	Gives dance lessons to neighboring children, age 12.

1895   Cast in *A Midsummer Night's Dream*, the 17-year-old Duncan and
        her family move to New York, where she is hailed as a child
        with the wisdom of ages, and accepted into New York society—
        its newest star. Then promptly forgotten. Broke, she packs her
        veils and sails for England.

1898   Barefoot and wearing a Grecian gown, she debuts at London's
        Lyceum, where she proceeds to startle with her freestyle chore-
        ography, incorporating everyday motions like skipping and run-
        ning. Success follows rapidly, and news of Duncan travels to the
        Continent.

1903   In Greece, she teaches a group of children ancient Byzantine
        dances. They frolic from village to village in sandaled feet. The
        consensus? Duncan is mad. And broke again.

1904   Founds a school for poor children in Germany, establishing a cur-
        riculum that includes art, culture, movement, and spirituality.
        From the group of students, Duncan adopts six daughters—dubbed
        "the Isadorables" by the press—who tour the world with her.

1905   Meets and falls in love with Gordon Craig. She bears him a child,
        but is unprepared for "the chains of marriage." Goes on to have
        another child with lover Paris Singer.

1909   Unprepared for her radical politics and see-through costumes,
        American audiences are appalled—and enthralled—with her
        flouting of Victorian mores. In one performance, she bears her
        breasts to protest the corset. Duncan: "My body is the temple of
        my art."

1913   Dancing to Chopin's *Funeral March* in Paris, Duncan has a vision
        of her children's demise, only to have her vision materialize days
        later when they are drowned in the Seine.

1921   Due to her leftist politics, Duncan finds her U.S. citizenship re-
        voked. She briefly marries Russian poet Sergei Esenin, and upon
        their return to America is detained under suspicion of being a
        "Bolshevist agent."

1927 Dies in a freak auto accident (a trailing veil catches the wheel and breaks her neck) at age 49, in France—bequeathing a blueprint for freedom of movement in dance and life. "The Mother of Modern Dance" is cremated and entombed in Le Père Lachaise cemetery in Paris.

BOB FOSSE

1927–1987

By NEIL SIMON, *collaborator and longtime friend*

Delivered at memorial service, October 30, 1987

The Palace Theater, New York City

THE FIRST TIME I MET BOB FOSSE, A REAL-ESTATE AGENT WAS taking me through an apartment I was interested in renting. As I came out of the bedroom into the living room, Bob Fosse and another agent were going from the living room to the bedroom. It was one of those Hollywood "meet cute" situations. We met and instantly fell in love. It lasted almost thirty years. We had our fights, our squabbles, our reconciliations, and we even had our children together. . . . Well, at least they were born a few months apart.

To talk about Bob Fosse as a great director and choreographer is almost superfluous at this gathering. You don't have to tell anyone Babe Ruth was a great hitter. Bob Fosse the man interested me every bit as much as Bob Fosse the talent.

A few months ago I started to make notes on a play I wanted to write called *The Hampton Boys*. It was about and based on my impressions of Bob Fosse. When I first started writing plays, a first-rate producer once told me, Never start with story, always begin with good characters. You couldn't find a better one than Bob. The play concerned a man who was celebrating his fiftieth birthday—that's Bob—and he decides to invite his ten best male friends out to East Hampton on a bitter cold day in February, to a rather run-down rented house, short on heat and amenities, without a phone or television, and have them spend the weekend together, while the Fosse character instigated fights, made them play truth games (that he loved so much), each man getting as his roommate the one man he liked the least, and by Sunday night, when everyone was ready to leave, they had not only had a harrowing experience, but they felt, in some measure, they all had made a breakthrough in their preconceived ideas of each other . . . and they left, not only closer in their friendships, but with a new awareness even of themselves. That's what Bob could do to you: He could put you through the wringer, and make you test yourself to the limit, because that's what he was always doing to himself.

He was one of those people who you had to gear yourself up to be with because you always wanted to be at your best. If you were going to have lunch with him, you had to go out and have lunch someplace else first, just to break in your conversation.

When I heard of his passing, which I don't think any of us believes yet, my mind wandered back to all the times I spent and worked with him, and my biggest regret is that in these last few years, there wasn't enough of that time spent together. And to share this time and my thoughts today, I started to make a list of the most vivid and memorable times I spent with Bob. It's my Ten Best Bob Fosse list.

1. A day in Philadelphia when we were trying out *Little Me*. A terrific song, "Real Live Girl," just wasn't working as it should. Bob disappeared for the day, and that night he called me, Cy Coleman, Carolyn Leigh, Cy Feuer, and Ernie Martin into an empty rehearsal studio. There was, as I recall, just a pianist, Bob, and a few props. And Bob proceeded to do the new version of the song, as fourteen soldiers would be doing it. Bob sang and danced not as one person, but as fourteen, making them all so vivid and clear and different that you didn't know which guy you liked best. They were all funny and some of them were touching. I think I said to Cy Feuer, "Wow. We've got a great cast. . . ." Needless to say, the number became a showstopper.

2. In that same show, Bob and I were sitting together in the second row at the Erlanger Theatre watching a runthrough. At the end of the

performance, the sound of two women in the back of the house applauding. It was Gwen and my wife, Joan, both in full pregnancy. The show and the babies opened just about the same time. I am happy to say that today, Nicole Fosse and Nancy Simon remain the best of friends.

3. A day of auditions, either for *Charity* or *Little Me*. It was the dancers' call and there were easily two hundred dancers to see that day. Bob sat on a stool at the center of the stage, his back to the orchestra seats, where I was sitting alone, watching. Each dancer would put his or her dance bag at the side of the stage, then when called by name, would simply come out, do a long run, a leap, a twist, and a jump in the air. Maybe more, but not much . . . And Bob would either say, and always graciously, "Please stand with the group on the right" or "Thank you very, very much." After about a hundred dancers had leapt across the stage, one very attractive but very nervous young lady came out, prepared, and then did her run, leap, twist, and jump and landed with a great smile on her face, looking at Bob for approval and a contract. Bob said, again graciously, "Thank you very much." The girl stood stunned. She didn't move, literally, for minutes. There was dead silence in the theater. She walked over quietly, picked up her dance bag, and said to Bob, "No one ever says thank you to me"—and proceeded to pummel Bob with her heavy dance bag, hitting him so hard, she knocked him off the stool. Two stagehands pulled her away into the wings. Bob got back on the stool, smoothed back his hair, and said, "Ladies, no more dance bags onstage, please."

4. The opening night of *Little Me* in New York. I was standing with Bob and Cy Coleman at the back of the house, and Sid Caesar, who otherwise gave a brilliant performance, coughed on each of his first three laugh lines—causing, obviously, no one to laugh on his first three laugh lines. I looked at Cy, Cy looked at me, and then we both looked at Bob. Bob very simply put his arms down at his sides, closed his eyes,

and fell backward, every part of his body hitting the floor simultane-ously—a perfect ten at any Olympics. He hardly moved on the floor, except to moan very quietly. And then a few minutes later, a very hos-tile and inebriated man got out of his seat, walked up the aisle on his way to the men's room, turned to us and said angrily, "This is the worst goddamned show I've seen since *My Fair Lady*." Bob laughed until he cried.

5. Playing croquet on a bumpy lawn at his house in the Hamptons. Bob was the most notorious and blatant cheater I ever saw. The won-derful thing is, he never did anything sneaky or surreptitious. If you were winning, he would simply kick your ball into the bushes in full view of everyone. If your ball was heading into the wire hold for the winning shot, he would simply pick up the wire before your ball got through it and announce, "Lunch." Or sometimes he would just pick up the wire and the wicket and just place it an inch away from wher-ever his ball was. And then he'd smile and say, "What's wrong?" His philosophy was that what he was doing was right. They just forgot to write "Cheating allowed" into the rule book.

6. Bob's appreciation for the written word. I loved watching his face when I brought in new pages for a scene that needed reworking. He'd put on the glasses that dangled on a strap around his neck, read them, and then throw back his head and laugh and say, "Gee, Doc. That's really great." And then add, "Would you like to choreograph the next number?"

7. A night in early September in the Hamptons, when the autumn chill was first in the air and the sunsets were more glittering than ever. Gwen and Joan did the cooking and Bob and I and the kids played touch football in the back of the house. If his team was losing by thirty-one points, he would grab the ball out of my hand, run for a touch-down, and say, "Touchdowns now count for thirty-two points." We

had lobster, corn on the cob, and cold wine, and that's all there was to it, but it's a day I can never get out of my head.

8. Watching him make acceptance speeches for all the awards he won. He *never* said a wrong word.

9. His birthday was June 23 and mine was July 4. He was eleven days older than me and it was a constant source of kidding. I'd say things like, "I always look up to you, Bob, and want to be just like you when I get to be your age." Or when he came into a room, I'd get up and give him my seat. I'd say, "It's okay, Bob. I understand. The legs are the first things that go." And he'd say to me, "In the first eleven days of my life before you were born, I had more girls than you'd ever have in all your life."

10. One of the last memories was a party Bob gave out at Quogue about a year ago for the entire company of the new *Sweet Charity*. It was crowded with dancers and actors and was, like all Fosse parties, fun and games. He and I played each other Ping-Pong and the winner was to be designated the youngest forever. He and I finally sat down alone over a glass of wine and reminisced about our lives. He looked at me with a big smile on his face and said to me so sweetly and sincerely, "It was great, wasn't it?" And Bob won the game. He'll be the youngest forever.

1927	Born Robert Louis Fosse in Chicago, the son of a vaudevillian.
1940	Tours with his own dance act at the age of 13, earning over $100/week.
1942	At 15, Robert is already choreographing for a nightclub, instructing dancers how to strategically place their ostrich feathers for Cole Porter's "That Old Black Magic."

1945 Fosse enlists in the navy. Onstage in the Pacific, he learns how to juggle his performer/director/choreographer duties. "I never knew I could handle anything like that until I tried it on Okinawa. From then on, I knew what I wanted and where I wanted to go."

1950 Debuts on Broadway in *Dance Me a Song.*

1953 Hollywood beckons. Fosse signs with MGM and begins to choreograph for the screen. When his career stalls, he returns to Broadway to choreograph *The Pajama Game.* His groundbreaking staging of "Steam Heat" is the talk of New York, previewing the Fosse style: disjointed steps, precision choreography down to a suggestively lifted eyebrow, scintillating slow-motion segments. Fosse wins a Tony.

1954 . . . and another Tony for *Damn Yankees,* where he meets his third and final wife, actress/dancer Gwen Verdon. She subsequently becomes the leading lady in almost all his shows.

1956 Fosse and Verdon reach their pinnacle with *Sweet Charity.*

1972 Fosse's finest year. Wins Best Director Oscar for *Cabaret,* a Tony for *Pippin,* and an Emmy for *Liza with a Z.* But the heavy workload catches up: The following year while working on *Chicago,* he suffers a heart attack. Fosse tempers his drinking and smoking—but not his womanizing.

1979 Directs *All That Jazz,* an unsparing autobiographical look into his life. The film is nominated for nine Oscars.

1987 Dies of cardiac arrest moments before the curtain rises on his revival of *Sweet Charity,* at age 60. On his own ending: "I always thought I would be dead at 25. It was romantic. People would mourn me. *Oh, that young career.*"

KEITH HARING

By KAY A. HARING, *sister*

Delivered at memorial service, May 4, 1990

St. John's Cathedral, New York City

KEITH WAS MY BIG BROTHER. OVER THE YEARS PEOPLE HAVE often questioned me: What was it like, growing up with Keith? What is it like to have a brother who is famous? Was he always like this?

My memories of growing up with Keith are like remembering him just yesterday.

I remember when we were kids, every summer we'd have penny-fairs in our backyard. We'd invite the whole neighborhood, charge admission, and run carnival games and contests. At the end of the day, we'd divide our profits, and while my sisters and I were thinking of saving our money for future goals, Keith was inviting all the neighborhood kids to come downtown with us, and he'd treat everyone at the local ice cream shop.

I remember that Keith was always the leader in our latest exclusive "club," where we'd make up secret coded messages, have meetings, and plan ways to upset our parents.

I remember that on Tuesday nights our church youth group would drive to a nearby city and spend the evening at a drop-in center for city kids, just hanging out with them, playing games, and helping with art projects.

I remember that Keith was always drawing—it was his hobby, his pastime, his vehicle of expression, his very being.

So you see, it has always seemed to me that the brother who I grew up with is the same brother all of you know. Only the neighborhood get-togethers became the Manhattan club scene, the art projects with kids grew to include thousands and thousands of youth, his generous nature reached to touch virtually millions, and the canvas on which he drew became the whole world.

I learned a lot from my big brother: That a wall was meant to be drawn on. A Saturday night was meant for partying. And that life is meant for celebrating.

Keith introduced me to designer clothes, New York City, the art world, sushi, and as a young teenager I learned that the only way to listen to the Grateful Dead and the Beatles was with the volume turned *all* the way up.

Keith showed me that it is possible to live what you believe. He covered hundreds of walls with his art, he made friends and partied around the world, and every year he had the most elaborate birthday celebrations, which he so appropriately named his "Party of Life."

Keith taught me strength in the face of death. And humor.

He had an IV hooked up to him constantly during the last few weeks, and he nicknamed the milky-white fluid flowing into his arms his "slime." And I can't tell you how many times I caught him making faces at the nurses behind their backs.

Keith's battle with AIDS taught me that *every* day is worth living. When he tested HIV-positive, instead of complaining about the burden of the disease and in answer to a comment on how hard it must be to live with that knowledge, he replied, "No, it just makes everything that happens now so much better. 'Cause you never know when you're doing something for the last time, so you live each day like it is the last."

My life changed after that.

And Keith continued to draw, filling every space before him, leaving his mark like there was no tomorrow.

Two days before he died, Keith was lying on the edge of his bed, and the window was open so you could see the city rooftops all the way out to the Empire State Building. Keith couldn't hold a marker anymore, so he took my hand, and with those smooth, graceful strokes we all know so well, we painted in the sky with all of New York City as our backdrop.

And all that I can think now is that wherever Keith is, he's leaving those wonderful graffiti-chalk drawings all around him, and today, on the thirty-second birthday of our brother Keith, I'm sure there is the biggest "Party of Life" happening up in heaven right now.

1958	Born in Reading, PA, the eldest of four siblings. His penchant for art shows up early: "My father made cartoons. Since I was little, I had been creating characters and stories. In my mind, though, there was a separation between cartooning and being an 'artist.' "
1977	Moves to New York to attend the School of Visual Arts. The manic, multicultural city agrees with Haring—a place to explore his gay identity and artistic inspirations. His initial canvas is the subway station, where he experiments with drawing lighthearted silhouettes. "It was this chalk-white fragile thing in the middle of all this power and tension and violence that the subway was." Spontaneous, hip, and at least initially underground, Haring's style is established.
1981	Paints, prints, and distributes 20,000 free posters for an anti-nukes rally in New York City.
1982	His art gets bigger. Murals on buildings in New York, Wisconsin, Rio de Janeiro—and later, Germany, Brazil, India, and Holland—all sport his fun, politicized expressions.
1983	Designs watch faces for Swiss company Swatch.
1984	Opens Pop Shop in New York City, a way to distribute his art

without having to deal with traditional art galleries. "Those prices meant that only people who could afford big art prices could have access to my work. The Pop Shop makes it accessible." Later that year, he paints a 300-foot mural on the Berlin Wall.

1987   Continuing in the tradition of projects to benefit children, Haring paints outdoor mural on a children's hospital in France. (Years before, he had designed the United Nations stamp commemorating the Year of the Child.)

1988   Diagnosed with AIDS, Haring maintains a characteristically philosophical outlook. "All of the things you make are a kind of quest for immortality. . . . They don't depend on breathing, so they'll last longer than any of us will. Which is sort of an interesting idea, that it's extending your life to some degree." Opens another Pop Shop, in Tokyo.

1989   Keith Haring Foundation is established to spread his work, and fund AIDS and children's organizations.

1990   Dies of AIDS, age 32, leaving a multitude of murals in the subways and on walls across the world.

JEROME ROBBINS

By MIKHAIL BARYSHNIKOV, *friend and protégé*

Delivered at memorial service, November 16, 1998

Lincoln Center, New York City

A N EMPTY STUDIO. WINDOWS HIGH, NEAR THE CEILING, through which soft gray light makes geometric lines on the floor. A ballet barre. Mirrors on the wall repeat this scene but with softer edges. The sun's projection on the window slowly crawls from one side of the room to the other. The wail of a passing siren momentarily reveals the reality of time and place, and a cloud, moving slowly somewhere eastward, blurs the image of the window on the door.

Will he return? Or has he never left? This is more a plea than a question.

He is here. Standing, turned away from the mirror. The body slightly askew, leaning forward. One hand on his hip, the other reflectively stroking his perfectly clipped, regal beard. His chin is down, *that gaze* fixed diagonally to the floor.

For a brief moment a shard of amberlike rosin lies ignited by the sunlight, only to revert in shadow to its humble purpose. Begging to be crushed, to be useful.

The silence is broken by the squeak of his sneakers. A muted but impatient whistle cuts off the musical phrase. His look is cold and penetrating, not pleased. Is he searching for himself or something within him? Suddenly his mood brightens. Is it satisfaction? Or is it the memory of the first crocus at Sneeden's Landing or that glass of the wine in the piazza in Spoleto that lifts his spirit?

Just like that he is somber again. What is it that bothers him so? Maybe remembering how the work came so easily for that other person [Balanchine], that person whom he worshiped.

And again, a glance into the mirror. The light whistle and the soft squeak of his shoes against the floor.

He is now standing in the middle of the space. The space that he has tamed, that he owns. Like a noble old man standing in the holiest of places, proudly revealing the sum total of his life. Supremely confident and yet vulnerable. Knowing how very much has been good, extremely good—and what could have been better.

So, too, with him. Standing in the space. Awaiting the judgment of the people he gave the best part of his life to. His public.

Yes, he has wounded some but enriched many. Changing their hearts. Opening their eyes. Making them better.

This is what this man loved to do here—where now the shaft of evening sunlight has passed, leaving the space in peace, until that time when we again hear his sneakers on the floor like the chirp of a lone bird gliding fitfully toward the horizon over Long Island Sound.

1918	Born Jerome Rabinowitz in New York City to Polish immigrant parents.
1935	Enrolls in New York University, but the Depression deepens and Jerome (already failing two courses) is forced to drop out. Unwilling to work in his father's corset factory, he apprentices at a dance center—changing his name to Robbins.
1940	Accepted to the American Ballet Theater, he quickly advances to solo roles. Appearing as the tragic puppet in *Petroushka,* Robbins attracts notice.
1944	Dreams up a show about three sailors on leave in New York, en-

listing the services of the unknown composer Leonard Bernstein. (Robbins: "Why can't we do ballets about our own subjects, meaning our life here in America?") In December, *On the Town* opens on Broadway to exuberant reviews.

1945   Follows up with *Billion Dollar Baby*, then *High Button Shoes*.

1949   Joins George Balanchine's newborn New York City Ballet. Robbins dances numerous roles, but it is as a choreographer that he makes his mark. Balanchine nourishes his genius, and Robbins lends his all-American sassiness to the company.

1953   Robbins stuns the theatrical community: Called before the House Un-American Activities Committee, he admits to membership in the Communist Party during the 1930s—then names eight other members. Excoriated, he refuses to apologize, except to say that he "made a great mistake in entering the Communist Party." Unlike other McCarthy victims, Robbins goes on to even greater success, directing such outings as *The Pajama Game, Peter Pan,* and *Bells Are Ringing.*

1957   The pinnacle: Re-teams with Leonard Bernstein on Broadway's *West Side Story*. With electrifying Sharks vs. Jets choreography, the show establishes Robbins as a perfectionistic talent and taskmaster. He subsequently wins Oscars for the filmed version— both for Best Director and Best Choreography.

1966   Disappointed with the trend toward rock spectacles like *Hair,* Robbins launches the American Theater Lab. He rejoins the New York City Ballet three years later, recharged, and stays for the rest of his career—his future tied to Balanchine.

1989   Takes a leave of absence to stage *Jerome Robbins' Broadway*, a resounding critical success.

1994   Collaborates with Mikhail Baryshnikov on *A Suite of Dances.*

1998   Despite declining health, Robbins insists on staging *Les Noces* for the New York City Ballet. Two months later, he suffers a massive stroke and dies in New York, age 80. That evening, the lights of Broadway dim in recognition.

GIANNI VERSACE

By MADONNA, *longtime friend*

Written on the occasion of his death

I SLEPT IN GIANNI VERSACE'S BED. OF COURSE, HE WASN'T in it at the time, but I couldn't help feeling that I was soaking up some of his aura. I believe that when we sleep, our soul leaves our body to be rejuvenated. Powerful and profound things happen to us in our bed at night, and energy accumulates and hovers above it.

There was a lot of nervous energy around Gianni's bed, and I must say I never slept very well in it. I kept wanting to leap out of the bed and do things: write poetry, smell the gardenias and jasmine that surrounded the house, gaze out my window at the magnificent lake, and press my face onto the cool marble of any number of naked-men statues that filled his bedrooms. I didn't know who they were. They could have been important Greek gods or just your standard Roman hunks, but they were lovely to look at and very distracting. There were ancient books to comb through, Old Master paintings to study, and local architecture to marvel at. I was in heaven, but more important, I was envious of a person who had the courage to live life so luxuriously. I'm too practical for that.

I had been invited to stay in Gianni's villa in Lake Como after shooting my second Versace campaign in Milan. I was thrilled to spend the Fourth of July in such a beautiful setting. I arrived with boyfriend and entourage in tow. As a special favor, I had asked Gianni if I could bring my friend Marjorie Gross, who was dying of cancer. She came along, and we all had to keep pinching ourselves to make sure we weren't dreaming. Every evening at sunset we were served fresh Bellinis, which we sipped under the giant magnolia tree at the edge of the lake. The cook prepared delicious meals, the Sri Lankan servants waited on us with white gloves, and my dog Chiquita was taken for long walks by gorgeous Italian bodyguards with walkie-talkies. The captain of a large speedboat was always on standby to take us for our daily swim in the crystal-clear waters of the lake. Dirty clothes never stayed on the floor for more than a few seconds, and beautiful Versace gowns kept arriving, a new batch every day. I even wore one to dinner. I had this fantasy that I was in an Antonioni film and the shoot was going to go on indefinitely. I felt like a spoiled princess. "The Versaces really know how to live!" We kept repeating this over and over like a mantra.

Gianni phoned regularly to make sure that everything was okay and that we were all taken care of. I thought about asking if my dog could have a manicure, but I decided against it. Even Gianni must draw the line somewhere. In retrospect I think he would have said yes, and a pet groomer would have been delivered in a matter of minutes. The only person as generous as Gianni is his little sister, Donatella, who embraces the beautiful things in life with the same fervor.

But let me be very clear. The Versaces work as hard as they play. Obviously we were enjoying the fruits of Gianni's labor. Evidence of his work ethic was all over the house. There were sketches lying around everywhere. Art books were marked or open to pages that were obviously going to show up somewhere in his new designs, and millions of magazines were piled on tables, full of articles or advertisements showing his glamorous and sexy clothes, page after page bursting with color and eroticism. This was a man with a mission—a force to be reckoned with. I was on vacation in his house. He was working.

Eventually my fantasy came to an end, and we all headed back to our lives, which seemed dull in comparison. Gianni was probably designing his next collection, editing one of his books, or building a new villa. Probably all three.

The last time I saw him was in the spring in Miami. Donatella had invited me over for a pre-Easter dinner. I went to Casa Casuarina with a few friends and found Gianni in great spirits. He was mesmerized by the blue nail polish on my daughter's toenails. After dinner his niece Allegra sat at our feet and played with Lourdes while he talked about *la dolce vita*. He had kicked cancer, he was proud of his latest collection, and life was good. That's when I launched into my speech about yoga and how good it would be for his mind, body, and soul. He seemed open, and I gave him my yoga teacher's number. I could totally imagine this extravagant Calabrian with a twinkle in his eye in the lotus position.

The great yogis believe there is no end to life. I'm inclined to agree. Even though Gianni's life on this earth has ended, his spirit is everywhere, and his soul lives forever.

I'm going to miss you, Gianni. We're all going to miss you. But I've got a pocketful of memories in my Versace jeans, and they're not going anywhere.

1946	Born in Calabria, Italy. Playing in his mother's atelier, Gianni begins his fashion career knee high, making puppets out of fabric scraps. His mother's approach to fashion is more reverential: Before she cuts, she crosses herself.
1955	Designs first dress, age 9.
1972	Absent formal training, Versace moves to Milan and takes a job designing for Genny. Six years later, he launches his own eponymous collection.
1979	Hires photographer Richard Avedon to unleash the Versace image: theatrical, bombastic, and *wildly* expensive. Drenched in klieg lights and rock music, his shows take on an equally dramatic tone. The consensus: A fashion firebrand is born.

1982   Begins designing costumes for ballet and opera. Outfitted in Versace tutus and toe shoes, the American Ballet, the New York City Ballet, and companies throughout Europe plié more color-fully.

1985   Launches Istante—a younger, more informal line. Other lines follow: Versace Jeans, Versus, Versace Sport.

1991   On a stopover to Cuba, Versace falls in love with Miami's then-downtrodden South Beach. Buys an oceanfront block. Forty million dollars later, modeled after a sixteenth-century castle, Casa Casuarina rises from the South Beach sands.

1992   Professing that "I'm a little like Marco Polo, going around and mixing cultures," Versace unveils his bondage and silk print collection. Feminists balk. Another buying frenzy begins. *National Review:* "Versace has persuaded wealthy and beautiful women to pay large sums of money to pretend to be hookers." But behind the glitz, Versace is passionately a family man, dedicated to sister Donatella and brother Santo. And a curious man: his voracious appetite for knowledge leads him to keep five libraries and a full-time librarian.

1993   Council of Fashion Designers of America bestows on him the Fashion Oscar. The same year, he battles a rare ear cancer.

1995   Profits reach $900 million/year. Versace empire now spans clothes, fragrances, china, and furnishings.

1997   Shot and killed by hustler Andrew Cunanan in front of his South Beach home. Versace's memorial service is attended by 2000 people, including supermodels, fellow fashion designers, Princess Diana, and artists Sting and Elton John, who sing the Twenty-third Psalm. The House of Versace continues under Donatella's direction.

ANDY WARHOL

By JOHN RICHARDSON, *art historian and old friend*

Delivered at memorial service, April 1, 1987

St. Patrick's Cathedral, New York City

B ESIDES CELEBRATING ANDY WARHOL AS THE QUINTESSEN-
tial artist of his time and place—the artist who held the most revealing mirror up to his generation—I'd like to recall a side of his
character that he hid from all but his closest friends: his spiritual side.
Those of you who knew him in circumstances that were the antithe-
sis of spiritual may be surprised that such a side existed. But exist it did,
and it's the key to the artist's psyche.

Never forget that Andy was born into a fervently Catholic family
and brought up in the fervently Catholic *Ruska Dolina*, the Ruthenian
section of Pittsburgh. As a youth, he was withdrawn and reclusive, devout and celibate; and beneath the disingenuous public mask, that is
how he at heart remained. Thanks largely to the example of his adored
mother, Julia, Andy never lost the habit of going to Mass more often
than was obligatory. As fellow parishioners will remember, he made a
point of dropping in on his local church, St. Vincent Ferrer, several
days a week until shortly before he died.

Although Andy was perceived—with some justice—as a passive
observer who never imposed his beliefs on other people, he could on
occasion be an effective proselytizer. To my certain knowledge, he was
responsible for at least one conversion. He took considerable pride in
financing a nephew's studies for the priesthood. And as you have
doubtless read on your Mass cards, he regularly helped out at a shelter

serving meals to the homeless and the hungry. Trust Andy to have kept these activities very, very dark.

The knowledge of this secret piety inevitably changes our perception of an artist who fooled the world into believing that his only obsessions were money, fame, glamour, and that he was cool to the point of callousness. Never take Andy at face value. The callous observer was in fact a recording angel. And Andy's detachment—the distance he established between the world and himself—was above all a matter of innocence and of art. Isn't an artist usually obliged to step back from things? In his impregnable innocence and humility Andy always struck me as a *yurodstvo*—one of those saintly simpletons who haunt Russian fiction and Slavic villages, such as Mikova in Ruthenia, whence the Warhols stemmed. Hence his peculiar, passive power over people; his ability to remain uncorrupted, no matter what activities he chose to film, tape, or scrutinize. The saintly simpleton side likewise explains Andy's ever-increasing obsession with folklore and mysticism. He became more and more like a medieval alchemist searching, not so much for the philosopher's stone as for the elixir of youth.

If in the sixties some of the hangers-on at the Factory were hell-bent on destroying themselves, Andy was not to blame. He did what he could to help, but nothing in the world was going to deter those lemmings from their fate. In any case Andy was not cut out to be his brother's keeper. That would hardly have been compatible with the existent detachment that was his special gift. However, Andy *did* feel compassion, and he *did,* in his Prince Myshkin way, save many of his entourage from burnout.

Though ever in his thoughts, Andy's religion didn't surface in his work until two or three Christmases ago, when he embarked on his series of *Last Suppers*, many of them inspired by a cheap mock-up of Leonardo's masterpiece he bought in Times Square. Andy's use of a Pop concept to energize sacred subjects constitutes a major breakthrough in religious art. He even managed to give a slogan like "Jesus Saves" an uncanny new urgency. And how awesomely prophetic is

Andy's painting—one of his very last—which announces: "Heaven and Hell Are Just One Breath Away!"

1928	Born Andrew Warhola in Pittsburgh, PA, to Czech parents.
1945	Enrolling in Carnegie-Mellon, Andrew studies painting and design. Summers are spent dressing windows at a department store.
1949	Moving to Manhattan, Warhola crops his name and freelances at *Glamour* magazine. Over the following decade, Warhol works continuously as an artist—at fashion magazines, doing covers for Columbia Records, designing Christmas cards and book jackets. He hires assistants (including his mother) to keep up with demand.
1952	*Fifteen Drawings*: Warhol's first exhibition, based on Truman Capote's writings, is shown at the Hugo Gallery in New York.
1957	Gets a nose job. Blond wig and glasses follow.
1960	Painting Campbell's soup cans, Del Monte peach halves, and Coca-Cola bottles, Warhol satirizes and glorifies commercial America—and refers to his own studio as the Factory. The Factory is anything but commercial: Doused in trippy lighting and tinfoil walls, it doubles as a mecca for bohemians.
1961	Warhol launches his silk screens of Troy Donahue, Marilyn Monroe, Elvis Presley, Elizabeth Taylor, and Marlon Brando. His response to critics who label him unoriginal? "I am not a creator of art, but a recreator."
1964	And recreational. Typical schedule: "We usually worked until around midnight, and then we'd go down to the Village. . . . I'd get home around four in the morning, make a few phone calls . . . and then when it started to get light I'd take a Seconal, sleep for a couple of hours, and be back at the Factory by early afternoon."

1965	Shows his work across Europe and North and South America.
1968	Shot by actress and hanger-on Valerie Solanis in his studio. Pronounced clinically dead, Warhol survives; Solanis is sentenced to 3 years.
1969	Shoots *Blue Movie*—130 minutes of philosophical discussion, followed by 10 minutes of action justifying the title. Ruled obscene, it is published in book form. By now Warhol is the recognized laureate of the avant-garde, pushing boundaries in several mediums.
1970	Continues painting. His portraits command $25,000 each.
1985	Campbell's Soup hires Warhol to do portraits of their soup mixes.
1987	Hospitalized for an enlarged gall bladder, Warhol has a heart attack while undergoing a routine operation and dies, age 58. He leaves behind an estate valued at half a billion dollars.

SUSAN B. ANTHONY

1820–1906

By REV. ANNA HOWARD SHAW, *close friend and fellow suffragist*

Delivered at funeral, March 15, 1906

Central Presbyterian Church, Rochester, NY

YOUR FLAGS AT HALF-MAST TELL OF A NATION'S LOSS, BUT there are no symbols and no words that can tell the love and sorrow that fill our hearts. And yet out of the depths of our grief arise feelings of truest gratitude for the beauty, the tenderness, the nobility of example, of our peerless leader's life. There is no death for such as she. There are no last words of love. The ages to come will revere her name. Unnumbered generations of the children of men shall rise up to call her blessed. Her words, her work, and her character will go on to brighten the pathway and bless the lives of all peoples. That which seems death to our unseeing eyes is to her translation. Her work will not be finished, nor will her last word be spoken while there remains a wrong to be righted, or a fettered life to be freed in all the earth.

You do well to strew her bier with palms of victory, and crown her with unfading laurel, for never did a more victorious hero enter into rest.

Her character was well poised; she did not emphasize one characteristic to the exclusion of others; she taught us that the real beauty of a true life is found in the harmonious blending of diverse elements, and her life was the epitome of her teaching. She merged a keen sense of justice with the deepest love; her masterful intellect never for one moment checked the tenderness of her emotions; her splendid self-assertion found its highest realization in perfect self-surrender; she

27

demonstrated the divine principle that the truest self-development must go hand in hand with the greatest and most arduous service for others.

Here was the most harmoniously developed character I have ever known—a living soul whose individuality was blended into oneness with all humanity. She lived, yet not she; humanity lived in her. Fighting the battle for individual freedom, she was so lost to the consciousness of her own personality that she was unconscious of existence apart from all mankind.

Her quenchless passion for her cause was that it was yours and mine, the cause of the whole world. She knew that where freedom is there is the center of power. In it she saw potentially all that humanity might attain when possessed by its spirit. Hence her cause, perfect equality of rights, of opportunity, of privilege for all, civil and political, was to her the bedrock upon which all true progress must rest. Therefore she was nothing, her cause was everything; she knew no existence apart from it; in it she lived and moved and had her being. It was the first and last thought of each day; it was the last word upon her faltering lips; to it her flitting soul responded when the silenced voice could no longer obey the will, and she could only answer our heartbroken questions with the clasp of her trembling hand.

She was in the truest sense a reformer, unhindered in her service by the narrowness and negative destructiveness that often so sadly hampers the work of true reform. Possessed by an unfaltering conviction of the primary importance of her own cause, she nevertheless recognized that every effort by either one or many earnest souls toward what they believed to be a better or saner life should be met in a spirit of encouragement and helpfulness. She recognized that it was immeasurably more desirable to be honestly and earnestly seeking that which in its attainment might not prove good than to be hypocritically subservient to the truth through a spirit of selfish fear or fawning at the beck of power. She instinctively grasped the truth underlying all great movements that have helped the progress of the ages, and did not wait for an individual or a cause to win popularity before freely extending to its struggling life a hand of helpful comradeship. She was never found in the cheering crowd that follows an already victorious standard. She left that to the time-servers who divide the spoil after they have crucified their savior. She was truly great; great in her humility and utter lack of pretension.

On her eightieth birthday this noble soul could truthfully say in response to the words of loving appreciation from those who showered garlands all about her: "I am not accustomed to demonstrations of gratitude or of praise. I have ever been a hewer of wood and a drawer of water to this movement. I know nothing, I have known nothing of oratory or rhetoric. Whatever I have done has been done because I wanted to see better conditions, better surroundings, better circumstances for women."

Speaking of her, Lady Henry Somerset said: "She has the true sign of greatness in that she is absolutely without pretension. No woman of fame has ever so thoroughly made this impression of modesty and unselfishness upon my mind." This was the impression that she made upon all who knew her, and leaving her presence one would say, "How humble she is!" Viewing her life achievements, one exclaims, "How transcendently great she is!" No wonder she has won a name and fame worldwide and that she has turned the entire current of human conviction. One indeed wrote truly who said of her: "She has lived a thousand years if achievements can measure the length of life."

She whose name we honor, whose friendship we reverence, whose love we prize as a deathless treasure, would say this is not an hour for grief or despair—"If my life has achieved anything, if I have lived to any purpose, carry on the work I have to lay down."

In our last conversation, when her prophetic soul saw what we dare not even think, she said: "I leave my work to you and to the others who have been so faithful—promise that you will never let it go down or lessen our demands. There is so much to be done. Think of it! I have struggled for sixty years for a little bit of justice and die without securing it."

Oh, the unutterable cruelty of it! The time will come when at these words every American heart will feel the unspeakable shame and wrong of such a martyrdom. She did not gain the little bit of freedom for herself, but there is scarcely a civilized land, not even our own, in which she has not been instrumental in securing for some woman that to which our leader did not attain. She did not reach the goal, but all along the weary years what marvelous achievements, what countless victories! The whole progress has been a triumphal march, marked by sorrow and hardship, but never by despair. The heart sometimes longed for sympathy and the way was long, and oh so lonely; but every step was marked by some evidence of progress, some wrong righted, some right established.

We have followed her leadership until we stand upon the mount of vision where she today leaves us. The promised land lies just before us. It is for us to go forward and take possession. Without faltering, without a desertion from our ranks, without delaying even to mourn the loss of our departed leader, the faithful host is marching on. Already the call to advance is heard along the line, and one devoted young follower writes: "There are hundreds of us now, her followers, who will try to keep up the work she so nobly began and brought so nearly to completion. We will work the harder to try to compensate the world for her loss." Another writes: "I believe as you go forth to your labors you will find less opposition and far more encouragement than heretofore. The world is profoundly stirred by the loss of our great leader, and in consequence the lukewarm are becoming zealous, the prejudiced are disarming, the suffragists are renewing their vows of fidelity to the cause for which Miss Anthony lived and died. Her talismanic words, the last she ever uttered before a public audience, 'Failure is impossible,' should be inscribed on our banners and engraved on our hearts."

She has not only blessed us in the legacy of her life and work, but she has left us the dearest legacy of her love. The world knew Miss Anthony as the courageous, earnest, unfaltering champion of a great principle, and the friend of all reforms. Those of us who knew her best knew that she was all this and more; that she was one of the most home-making and home-loving of women. To her home her heart always turned with tenderest longing, and for the one who made home possible, she felt the most devoted love and gratitude. She inscribed upon the first volume of her life history, "To my youngest sister, Mary, without whose faithful and constant home-making there could have been no freedom for the out-going of her grateful and affectionate sister."

To this home-making sister the affection of every loyal heart will turn, and we, her coworkers, will love and honor her, not alone for this devotion to her sister, but for her loyal comradeship and faithful service in our great cause. She is our legacy of love, and it will be the joy of every younger sister to bestow upon her the homage of our affection.

On the heights alone such souls meet God. In silent communion they learn life's sublimest lessons. They are the world's real heroes. Hers was an heroic life. By it she teaches us that the philosophy of the ancients is wrong; that it is not true that men are made heroic by indifference to life and death, but by learning to love something more than life. Her heroism was the heroism of an all-absorbing love, a love which neither indifference, nor persecution, nor misrepresentation, nor betrayal, nor hatred, nor flattery could quench; a heroism which would suffer her to see and to know nothing but the power of injustice and hatred to destroy, and the power of justice and love to develop, all that is best and noblest in human character. To such ends the causes which such souls espouse, "Failure is impossible." Truly did Dean Thomas say in her address at our National Convention: "Of such as you were the lines of the poet Keats written—

They shall be remembered forever,
They shall be alive forever,
They shall be speaking forever,
The people shall hear them forever."

1820	Born Susan Brownell Anthony in Adams, MA, the second of 7 children.
1838	The 1837 Depression causes her father to declare bankruptcy and the family loses their Battenville house. Susan and sister Guelma are taken out of school.
1845	The Anthonys move to Rochester, NY; their house becomes a meeting place for antislavery activists, including Frederick Douglass. The following year, Susan begins teaching at Canajoharie Academy for a yearly salary of $110.
1852	Attends her first women's rights convention.
1854	Circulates petitions for married women's property rights and woman suffrage. Refused permission to speak at the Capitol in Washington, Anthony begins her New York State campaign for woman suffrage, speaking and traveling alone.
1861	Conducts antislavery campaign from Buffalo to Albany: "No Union with Slaveholders. No Compromise."
1868	Anthony begins publication of *The Revolution*; forms Working Women's Associations for women in the publishing and garment trades.
1869	Calls the first Woman Suffrage Convention in Washington, D.C.
1872	Anthony is arrested for voting, and indicted. A year later Anthony is tried and fined $100 with costs after the judge ordered the jury to find her guilty. She refuses to pay but is not imprisoned.
1881	Anthony, Elizabeth Cady Stanton, and Matilda Joslyn Gage pub-

lish volume I of *History of Woman Suffrage,* followed over the next two decades by volumes II, III, and IV.

1895	Raising the roof on her Rochester home to create a workroom, she and Ida Husted Harper begin work on her biography. The following year, *The Life and Work of Susan B. Anthony* is published. Anthony establishes a press bureau to feed articles on woman's suffrage to the national and local press.
1900	Uses the cash value on her life insurance to fund the University of Rochester's financial requirements for the admission of women.
1905	Meets with President Theodore Roosevelt in Washington, D.C., about submitting a suffrage amendment.
1906	Impassioned to the end, Anthony attends suffrage hearings in Washington, D.C.; gives her "Failure Is Impossible" speech on her birthday; then dies at her Madison Street home, age 86.
1920	The 19th Amendment to the U.S. Constitution, also known as the Susan B. Anthony Amendment, grants the right to vote to all U.S. women over 21.

QUENTIN CRISP

1908–1999

By LOUIS COLAIANNI, *close friend and protégé*

Delivered at memorial service, March 4, 2000

Cooper Union, New York City

ALTHOUGH QUENTIN WAS A SELF-PROFESSED SINNER, HE was actually of saintly character. Like a Lower East Side Mother Teresa, he ministered to whatever person needed his attention most at the moment, loving all of humankind, but showing no preferential treatment to one individual over another. This could be worrying to his friends, whose desire for audience might at any moment be superseded by Quentin's urgent duty to meet with "a strange man in a dim cellar." In Quentin's sacred book friends were not always given a ringside seat. How could they be? It was Quentin's lofty goal to meet everyone on Earth before he died. In a sense friends were a hindrance to this ambition. "I like my friends," he would say, "but I adore strangers."

I don't mean to suggest that Quentin was unappreciative of his friends. Far from it. Although Quentin was not overtly demonstrative and was determined at all cost to remain calm, he nevertheless had ways of expressing esteem for those who were near and dear to him. To borrow from an old gospel song, Quentin Liked Me, This I Know, for His Diaries Tell Me So. I am not bragging, but merely brimming with joy when I say that Quentin wrote of our friendship. I can think of no higher compliment than to be immortally linked with Quentin through his books. I never had and never will have another friend like Quentin.

Whenever we spoke, he lifted my spirits. His patter was endless and endlessly delightful. He might regale me with the synopsis of a silent movie, recounted meticulously after a single viewing, more than seventy years ago. "Why should I see it again?" he would ask. "I shall never forget a single frame of it." Or he might gauge the talent of an actress by the number of hairstyles and costume changes she managed to cram into a single film. He might speak of God as "you know who," the Soviet Union as "you know where," and the focal point of Mr. Mapplethorpe's photographs as "you know what." His discourse included a long string of Misters. Jesus Christ is "Mr. Nazareth," the singer Sting is "Mr. Sting," and it was "Miss Wray" who was held captive atop the Empire State Building by "Mr. Kong." After more than fifteen years, I remained "Mr. Co-lai-ah-ni," intoned in a careful *bel canto*. Quentin referred to my job (that of voice and speech professor) as "teaching the world to make a loud noise for a long time." He would smirk at his own cleverness, but I would laugh out loud, often and enthusiastically. A trait which, I think, Quentin found endearingly American.

I moved from Manhattan ten years ago, and although, in Quentin's words, I "return to this enchanted isle from time to time for a breath of fresh happiness," I am now a full-time Missourian. As such, I have been promoted from the rank of prefect in Quentin's Academy of Being to that of Midwestern spy and missionary. One thing that Missouri could use more of, in my opinion, is Quentin Crisp. For as a principality of the Bible Belt, Missouri, the so-called "Show-Me" state, is lacking in first-class exhibitionists. Therefore, with Quentin's help, I created in a corner of my Kansas City apartment the Quentin Crisp Museum. It overflows with relics of Quentin, who himself generously donated books, artwork, manuscripts, his first typewriter, and even a lock of his hair.

Yes, Quentin is always with me, he is my patron saint. To honor him I composed the official Quentin Crisp Museum Prayer. He took delight in this:

Our lord Quentin,
Who art in Third Street,
Denis was thy name.
Thy kindred come,
Thy hair be done,
On Earth as it is in henna.
Give us the Cooper Square Diner's bread,
And forgive us our unworthiness,
As we forgive the roughs who attacked you in London.
Lead us with the tide (but faster),
And deliver us from the English.

For Manhattan is thy kingdom and thy profession is BEING,
For ever and ever.

Amen.

As many know, Quentin was born Denis Pratt. He was fond of saying that, like his hair, he had "dyed" his name. In closing, I would like to speculate on his choice of Crisp for a surname. Two of my favorite heroes are Quentin Crisp and Shakespeare's King Henry the Fifth. An odd pairing, for Quentin was as gentle as Henry was warlike. Henry's cause was to conquer nations through force and violence; Quentin's cause was to educate his oppressors through the art of self-expression. Yet, as different as they were, both of my heroes found themselves outnumbered and fought against the odds.

In a famous speech from Shakespeare's play, King Henry rouses his army by invoking two early Christian martyrs: Their names were Crispin and Crispian, and they were brothers. I like to think that, as a young man, Quentin, who was often beaten bloody in the city streets merely for being himself, borrowed his last name, Crisp, from these brothers, these two courageous men, whose brains were dashed out on the streets of ancient Rome because of their beliefs.

And Crispin Crispian shall ne'er go by
From this day to the ending of the world,
But we in it shall be remembered;
We few, we happy few, we band of brothers;

From this day to the ending of the world, Quentin lives on
through us. And we few here tonight, we band of brothers . . . we
carry on.

1908	Born Denis Pratt in Surrey, England, on Christmas Day. Later describes his childhood as "uneventful" and his family as "middle-class, middle-brow, middling." Gets beat up frequently in school.
1931	Changes his name and moves to London, where he tries his hand at illustration, writing, clerical jobs, and prostitution. Too flamboyantly gay, Crisp finds he cannot make a living selling his body.
1930s	Works as a commercial artist and window dresser. Mocked for his dainty ways, Crisp nevertheless chooses to live "not merely as a self-confessed homosexual, but a self-evident one." Tints his hair bright red, wears eye shadow, scarves, and silk blouses, and transforms himself into a walking, wit-dispensing objet d'art.
1941	Rejected for military service due to "sexual perversion."
1942	Tried for soliciting and acquitted.
1945	Takes up nude modeling for art students. "Posing as a profession" agrees with Crisp—he does it for the next 30 years.
1968	Pens his autobiography, *The Naked Civil Servant*. Offering blunt depictions of gay life punctuated with Crispian wit, the book does well—but the 1975 telefilm starring John Hurt vaults Crisp to minor celebrity.
1978	Launches his one-man show, *An Evening with Quentin Crisp*—a

discourse on how to live—and tours the world for the next 20 years, taking the show to Europe, Australia, and North America. Enchanted with the city's broad-minded grandeur, the "stately homo of England" moves to New York, where he enjoys a busy life as an author, columnist, actor, and East Village personality.

1981	Gets green card. Enjoys being described as a "resident alien."
1999	Dies of a massive heart attack in Manchester, on the eve of British tour. Memorial celebration is held at the Great Hall of Cooper Union in the East Village—a noted platform for free speech. Colaianni delivers his eulogy from the same lectern that Abraham Lincoln used in launching his presidential campaign. Crisp's ashes are subsequently scattered all over New York.

CHE GUEVARA

1928–1967

By FIDEL CASTRO, *fellow revolutionary*

Delivered at memorial service, October 19, 1967

Plaza de la Revolution, Havana, Cuba

CHE WAS ONE OF THOSE PERSONS WHOM EVERYBODY liked immediately because of his simplicity, because of his naturalness, because of his comradeship and personality and originality . . . even before his other singular virtues were revealed. He was the doctor of our troop, and thus our bonds and feelings came to be.

Che was impregnated with a profound hatred for imperialism—not only because of his political ideologies, but because he had had the opportunity to witness in Guatemala the imperialist intervention by mercenary soldiers who overthrew the revolution in that country. For such a man as he, arguments were not necessary. It was enough for him to know that Cuba lived under a similar situation. And so one day near the end of November 1955, he began the trip to Cuba with us. I recall that the crossing was very difficult for him because he could not even obtain the medicines that he needed [as a doctor], and he suffered a severe attack of asthma during the entire crossing without any relief, but also without a single complaint.

We arrived. We began the first marches. We suffered the first setback. And after a few weeks we met again—this small group of those who were left of the *Granma* expedition. Che continued to be the doctor of our group.

The first victorious battle was waged, and Che also became a soldier of our troop. The second victorious battle was waged and Che the soldier became the most distinguished of the soldiers in that battle—a

39

battle of extraordinary importance. The situation was difficult: We were going to attack a strongly defended position in full daylight, at the edge of the sea. We had enemy troops at our rear. Che, who was still the doctor, asked for three or four men and quickly assumed command of the attack. He was not only a fighter but also a doctor, giving assistance to the wounded comrades and caring for wounded enemy soldiers. And when it was necessary to abandon that position and begin a long march besieged by various enemy forces, it was necessary for somebody to stay with the wounded. El Che stayed with the wounded, caring for them.

That was one of his outstanding characteristics—immediate willingness, instantaneous readiness to volunteer for the most dangerous mission. Naturally this elicited admiration, double admiration for the comrade who fought beside us, who was not born in this land, who was a man of profound ideas, who was a man who dreamt of struggle in other parts of the continent—and yet that altruism, to risk his life constantly. In this way Che became major and commander of the second column in the Sierra Maestra. His prestige grew. His fame as a magnificent fighter grew—and carried him to the highest ranks during the war. Che was an unbeatable soldier. From a military standpoint, he was an extraordinarily capable man, extraordinarily brave and aggressive. If he had an Achilles' heel as a guerrilla, it was his aggressiveness, his absolute disregard for danger. The enemies try to draw conclusions about his death. But Che was a master of war. . . .

We not only admire the warrior in El Che, but how he faced—with just a handful of men—an entire army trained by Yankee advisers, supplied by Yankee imperialism, supported by the oligarchies of neighboring nations. That was an extraordinary feat. In the pages of history, one couldn't find a case in which somebody with such a small number of men embarked on such a struggle. It is proof of his self-confidence. His confidence in the people. In the capacity of men for combat. One may seek in the pages of history, and nothing comparable will be found.

The enemy may believe they have defeated his ideas and guerrilla concepts. What they gained with a lucky blow to eliminate his physical life.

The death of Che is a hard blow—a tremendous blow to the revolutionary movement because it deprives it of its most capable and experienced chief. But they who sing victory are mistaken. They are mistaken who believe that his death is the defeat of his ideas, his tactics, his guerrilla concepts, his thesis, because that man who fell as a mortal man, a man who exposed himself many times to enemy fire, a military man, a chief, he was a thousand times more capable than those who with one stroke of luck killed him.

Che had another quality: heart. He was an extraordinarily humane man, extraordinarily sensitive. A rare man—equal parts action and thought, a man of shining revolutionary virtue and human sensitivity.

A tireless worker in the years that he was at the service of our country, he did not know a single day of rest. Many responsibilities were assigned to him—the presidency of a national bank, the directorship of the planning board, the Ministry of Industry, as a commander of military regions. His multifaceted intelligence was capable of understanding any task, in any field, in any way of thinking. For him there were no days of rest, no hours of rest. If we looked at his office window, the lights burned until late at night. He was a tireless reader. His thirst for knowledge was practically insatiable, and the hours he did not sleep, he studied.

As a communist revolutionary, he had infinite faith in moral values and in the conscience of man. He saw that morality was the fulcrum for communism.

He thought, developed, and wrote about many things. And there is something that ought to be said on a day like today: It is that Che's writings, his political and revolutionary thoughts, will have a permanent value in the Cuban—indeed, Latin American—revolutionary process. . . . This is the weak side of the imperialist enemy, thinking that, along with the physical man, they have liquidated his example.

And they do not hesitate in publishing in such an impudent manner the circumstances in which he was executed by them, after having been seriously wounded in battle. They have not even reflected on the loathsomeness of the action. And they have publicized, as the right of thugs, they have reported, as the right of oligarchs and mercenaries, how they fired at a revolutionary fighter who was seriously wounded.

And they explain why they did it—claiming that it would have required an overwhelming process to try Che, claiming that it would have been impossible to place such a revolutionary in the dock of a court. Not only that, but they have also not hesitated in hiding his remains. In cremating his body, they demonstrate their fear, their belief that by liquidating the physical life of a fighter, they liquidate his ideas and his example.

How should we view Che's example? Do we believe we have lost him? It is true that we will never again see new writings. It is true that we will never again hear his voice. But Che left the world a patrimony: He left us his revolutionary thoughts. His revolutionary virtues. His character, his will, his tenacity, his spirit for work. He left us his example. And Che's example should be a model for our people. Che's example should be the ideal model for our people.

If we want to say how we want our revolutionary fighters, our militants, our men to be, we should say without hesitation: Let them be like Che.

If we want to say how we want the men of future generations to be, we should say: Let them be like Che.

If we want to say how we want our children to be educated, we should say without hesitation: We want them to be educated in Che's spirit.

In his mind and in his heart, the flags, the prejudices, the chauvinisms, the egoism had disappeared. He was willing to shed his blood for the fortune of any people. He was ready to shed it freely, instantly. And so his blood was shed in this land, where he was wounded in battle. His blood was shed in Bolivia for the redemption of the exploited and the oppressed, the humble and the poor. That blood was shed for all the exploited and oppressed. That blood was shed for all the peoples of America, and it was shed for Vietnam, because he knew that in fighting against imperialism there, he was offering Vietnam the highest expression of solidarity.

That is why we, on this night, after this demonstration which shows that we are a sensitive people, an appreciative people, which shows that we know how to pay homage to the memory of courageous men who fall in battle, how we support the revolutionary struggle, how we raise and will always keep high the revolutionary banners and principles—that is why today we shall elevate our thoughts and, with optimism about the final victory of the peoples, tell Che and the heroes who fought and fell with him: To victory always!

Fatherland or death, we shall win!

1928	Born Ernesto Guevara Lynch de la Serna, to a middle-class family in Argentina.
1938	At 10, Ernesto is already an avid reader of Marx and Freud.
1946	Attends medical school in Buenos Aires, initially hoping to understand his asthma condition.
1949	Exploring Argentina on bicycle, Ernesto encounters extreme poverty. Convinced he doesn't want to be a middle-class general practitioner, he returns home to continue his medical studies with a focus on dermatology. Later doctors for a leper colony in Peru.
1953	In Guatemala, an itinerant, penniless Ernesto participates in the overthrow of President Arbenz and witnesses the CIA's counter-revolutionary tactics. His anti-imperialist ideas take root.

1954	Meets Fidel Castro. Convinced that revolution will solve Latin America's social inequities, Ernesto joins his unit. Becomes known as Che—or "chum."
1956	Che, Castro, and 81 other rebels set out for Cuba on the rickety ship *Granma*. Only 16 survive the initial skirmish. Taking refuge in the Sierra Maestra mountains, they fight to overthrow Cuban dictator Batista. The revolution rages for three years.
1957	Doctor Che is appointed major.
1959	The rebels take Havana. Che becomes (1) a citizen of Cuba, (2) a husband, marrying Aledia March, and (3) Director of the National Bank of Cuba, where he is instrumental in cutting Cuba's economic ties with the U.S. and redirecting trade to the Communist Bloc. A strong opponent of U.S. influence in the Third World, Che now guides the Castro regime on its leftward path.
1960	Publishes *Guerilla Warfare*. Advocating peasant revolution, the book is immediately censored throughout Latin America.
1964	Heads the Cuban delegation to the United Nations.
1965	Focusing on exporting revolution to Latin America and Africa, Che falls out of favor with the Castro regime. He renounces his Cuban citizenship, writes farewell letters to his parents, children, and Fidel Castro—then disappears. "I have fulfilled the part of my duty that tied me to the Cuban revolution . . . and I say good-bye to you, to the comrades, to your people."
1967	Leads a guerrilla unit in Bolivian jungles. Betrayed by a peasant woman, Che is captured and killed by the Bolivian army. His last words: "Shoot, you are only going to kill a man." Dead at 39, he is immediately vaulted to legendary status as the incendiary guerrilla with a star on his beret.
1997	His remains are discovered and returned to Cuba for proper burial.

HELEN KELLER

1880–1968

By SEN. LISTER HILL, *Alabama*

Delivered at memorial service, June 5, 1968

Washington Cathedral, Washington, D.C.

MAY I SAY HOW PRIVILEGED I FEEL TO PAY TRIBUTE AT this hour to Helen Keller. I would that all the world could know the deep sense of pride that we of Helen Keller's native state, Alabama, feel in this remarkable and gentle lady.

We call to mind at this hour the story of the infant girl made blind and deaf by disease, imprisoned at the very early age of nineteen months; imprisoned, as she called it, in a "no world." All of us remember the challenging story of how this pitiful child, with the help of her devoted teacher, Anne Sullivan Macy—who was partially blind herself—emerged from hopeless childhood into a remarkable womanhood; how, through her own determination and faith, and through the patience and understanding of Anne Sullivan, who to Miss Keller was "eyes to the blind and feet to the lame," she won her magnificent victory over darkness.

After learning the first hand signals at the age of eight, she soon became fluent in using sign language, and mastered the Braille alphabet. In writing of those first stammering starts at sign language, she said, "There was a strange stir within me. When I understood that it was possible for me to communicate with other people by these signs, a delicious sensation rippled through me, and sweet, strange things that were locked up in my heart began to sing." And then, through almost miraculous efforts, she learned to speak.

In considering this miraculous achievement, we must remember that Miss Keller deeply felt her handicaps. In her earlier years, she wrote:

> *Sometimes, it is true, a sense of isolation enfolds me like a cold mist as I sit alone and wait at life's shut gate. Fate, silent, pitiless, bars the way. Fain would I question his imperious decree; for my heart is still undisciplined and passionate; but my tongue will not utter the bitter, futile words that rise to my lips, and fall back into my heart like unshed tears. Silence sits immense upon my soul.*

She attended the Horace Mann School for the Deaf in Boston, and then she entered the Perkins Institution for the Blind. She told her teacher she wanted to go to college, and she entered Radcliffe in Cambridge, Massachusetts, where in 1904 she graduated cum laude. At Radcliffe, Helen Keller wrote her first book, her autobiography, entitled *The Story of My Life*. The book became standard reading in schools throughout the country. Before her writing career was over, Miss Keller wrote eleven books, the last of which was *Let Us Have Faith*.

Miss Keller's personal victory over darkness and despair turned her life and ambitions to the service of others. With energy and stamina that were almost limitless, she dedicated her life to others. She gave of herself unceasingly—speaking, writing, traveling, working constantly to improve the conditions of deaf and blind people. She was the moving spirit that led to a new era of work for the blind of the world. Tirelessly she strove to fulfill her dream, "that every blind child have an opportunity to receive an education . . . and every blind adult, a chance for training and useful employment."

As she has written:

> *Many persons have a wrong idea of what constitutes true happiness. It is not attained through self-gratification but through fidelity to a worthy purpose. Happiness should be a means of accomplishment, not an*

end in itself. The more we try to help each other and make life brighter, the happier we shall be.

With this guiding philosophy, Helen Keller employed the symbol of her own courage and faith to the benefit of millions of her fellow handicapped in America and throughout the world. As a counselor to the American Federation of the Blind, she guided programs to advance economic, cultural, and social opportunities of deaf and blind persons throughout the United States. Through the Helen Keller World Crusade for the Blind, she inspired programs for the education and re-habilitation of blind persons around the globe. She learned to speak seven languages and she lectured in thirty-five countries on all five continents. In her 75th year, Miss Keller embarked on a 40,000-mile journey to promote services for the blind throughout Asia. Two years later, she made a similar mission to the Scandinavian countries.

Wherever she went, she was received with a massive outpouring of love and admiration; she was honored by heads of state; she was ac-claimed by all. She was decorated in almost as many countries as she visited. She received the Order of St. Sava of Yugoslavia in 1931 and an honorary doctor of laws degree in Glasgow in 1932. She was named Chevalier of the Legion of Honor of France in 1952 and received the Southern Cross of Brazil in 1953. The great warmth of her person-ality particularly attracted children, whom she loved deeply and by whom she was constantly surrounded.

Famous and important people thronged to meet her and enjoy her company. They found her a witty and interesting conversationalist, well informed on matters of interest at the time. She was truly a citi-zen of the world. She came to know famous men such as Oliver Wendell Holmes, Mark Twain, Albert Einstein, John Greenleaf Whittier, Andrew Carnegie, and Alexander Graham Bell, who did much to counsel and help her.

Helen Keller has truly "lighted a candle of understanding in our hearts which shall not be put out." She will live on, one of the few, the immortal names not born to die. Her spirit will endure as long as man can read and stories can be told of the woman who showed the world that there are no boundaries to courage and faith, which she so devoutly and beautifully expressed when she said:

> *What is so sweet as to awake from a troubled dream and behold a beloved face smiling upon you? I have to believe that such shall be our awakening from earth to heaven. My faith never wavers that each dear friend I have "lost" is a new link between this world and the happier land beyond the morn. My soul is for the moment bowed down with grief when I cease to feel the touch of their hands or hear a tender word from them; but the light of faith never fades from my sky.*

Although she was denied the light of day, Helen Keller cast more of the radiance of heaven than any person on this earth. Within this radiance and the light and example of her life, may we carry on in our troubled world, worthy of her deeds, her hope, and her faith—a faith of which the Lord spoke in His words, "Then the eyes of the blind shall be opened, and the ears of the deaf unstopped."

1880	Born in small rural town in Alabama with full sight and hearing.
1882	Falls dramatically ill. When fever breaks, her mother reports that Helen no longer responds to the dinner bell—or shows recognition when she waves. She is deaf and blind.
1887	Anne Sullivan is hired as governess. Sullivan struggles to control Helen—who throws dishes and tantrums with regularity—while teaching her to finger-spell. Sullivan's breakthrough comes during a visit to the water pump, spelling out "water." Helen later writes, "I felt a misty consciousness as of something forgotten, a thrill of returning thought, and somehow the mystery of language was revealed to me." Thereafter her progress is astonishing.

1900   Accepted to Radcliffe—the first deaf-blind person to enroll in college. With Sullivan's help she graduates with honors.

1902   Publishes *The Story of My Life*.

1916   Falls in love with family employee Peter Fagan. Romance is curtailed by Helen's mother, who believes Fagan's character flawed. A flurry of follow-up letters follows in Braille, but the romance eventually dies. Keller goes on lecture tours with Sullivan, who interprets sentence by sentence. Together they earn up to $2000/week.

1917   Keller joins a vaudeville show, depicting her first understanding of "water." Dark and cynical, the show is a huge success.

1918   Campaigns to alleviate the living and working conditions of the blind, many of whom are confined to asylums.

1931   Sullivan dies. On her deathbed: "Thank God I gave up my life so that Helen might live. God help her to live without me when I go." Helen's secretary, Polly Thompson, takes Sullivan's place. After World War II they travel the world raising money for the American Foundation for the Blind—venturing to Japan, Europe, Australia, South America, and Africa.

1953   *The Unconquered,* a documentary about Helen's life, wins an Academy Award.

1960   Thompson dies. Her ashes are buried next to Anne Sullivan's at the National Cathedral in Washington, D.C.

1964   Keller is awarded the Presidential Award of Freedom—the highest award bestowed on a civilian—by Lyndon Johnson. Begins to retire from public life.

1968   Dies peacefully during a summer nap. Her funeral is held at the National Cathedral, and her ashes are placed next to those of Anne Sullivan and Polly Thompson.

MARTIN LUTHER KING JR.

1929–1968

By BENJAMIN E. MAYS, *President of Morehouse College, longtime friend and mentor*

Delivered at memorial service, April 9, 1968

Morehouse College, Atlanta, GA

To GIVE THE EULOGY AT THE FUNERAL OF DR. MARTIN Luther King Jr. is like eulogizing one's deceased son—so close and so precious was he to me. Our friendship goes back to his student days at Morehouse College. It is not an easy task; nevertheless I accept it, with a sad heart and with full knowledge of my inadequacy to do justice to this man. It was my desire that if I predeceased Dr. King, he would pay tribute to me on my final day. It was his wish that if he predeceased me, I would deliver the homily at his funeral. Fate has decreed that I eulogize him. I wish it might have been otherwise, for, after all, I am three score years and ten and Martin Luther is dead at thirty-nine.

How strange. God called the grandson of a slave on his father's side, and the grandson of a man born during the Civil War on his mother's side, and said to him: "Martin Luther, speak to America about war and peace; about social justice and racial discrimination; about its obligation to the poor; and about nonviolence as a way of perfecting social change in a world of brutality and war."

Here was a man who believed with all of his might that the pursuit of violence at any time is ethically and morally wrong; that God and the moral weight of the universe are against it; that violence is self-defeating. And that only love and forgiveness can break the vicious cycle of revenge.

He had faith in this country. He died striving to desegregate and integrate America to the end that this great nation of ours, born in revolution and blood, conceived in liberty and dedicated to the proposition that all men are created free and equal, will truly become the lighthouse of freedom where none will be denied because his skin is black and none favored because his eyes are blue; where our nation will be militarily strong but perpetually at peace; economically secure but just; learned but wise; where the poorest—the garbage collectors—will have bread enough and to spare; where no one will be poorly housed; each educated up to his capacity; and where the richest will understand the meaning of empathy. This was his dream, and the end toward which he strove. As he and his followers often sang: "We shall overcome someday; black and white together."

Let it be thoroughly understood that our deceased brother did not embrace nonviolence out of fear or cowardice. Moral courage was one of his noblest virtues. As Mahatma Gandhi challenged the British Empire without a sword and won, Martin Luther King Jr. challenged the interracial wrongs of his country without a gun. And he had the faith to believe that he would win the battle for social justice. I make bold to assert that it took more courage for King to practice nonviolence than it took his assassin to fire the fatal shot. The assassin is a coward; he committed his dastardly deed and fled. When Martin Luther disobeyed an unjust law, he accepted the consequences of his actions. He never ran away and he never begged for mercy. He returned to the Birmingham jail to serve his time.

Perhaps he was more courageous than soldiers who fight and die on the battlefield. There is an element of compulsion in their dying. But when Martin Luther faced death again and again, and finally embraced it, there was no external pressure. He was acting on an inner compulsion that drove him on. More courageous than those who advocate violence as a way out, for they carry weapons of destruction for defense, but Martin Luther faced the dogs, the police, jail, heavy criticism, and finally death. And he never carried a gun, not even a knife to defend himself. He had only his faith in a just God to rely on, and the belief that "thrice is he armed who has his quarrels just."

Coupled with moral outrage was Martin Luther King Jr.'s capacity to love people. Though deeply committed to a program of freedom for Negroes, he had love and concern for all kinds of peoples. He drew no distinction between the high and the low; none between the rich and the poor. He believed especially that he was sent to champion the cause of the man farthest down. He would probably say that if death had to come, I am sure there was no greater cause to die for than fighting to get a just wage for garbage collectors. He was suprarace, supranation, supradenomination, supraclass, and supraculture. He belonged to the world and to mankind. Now he belongs to posterity.

But there is a dichotomy in all this. This man was loved by some and hated by others. If any man knew the meaning of suffering, King knew. House bombed; living day by day for thirteen years under constant threats of death; maliciously accused of being a Communist; falsely accused of being insincere and seeking the limelight for his own glory; stabbed by a member of his own race; slugged in a hotel lobby; jailed thirty times; occasionally deeply hurt because friends betrayed him—and yet this man had no bitterness in his heart, no rancor in his soul, no revenge in his mind; and he went up and down the length and breadth of this world preaching nonviolence and the redemptive power of love. He believed with all his heart, mind, and soul that the way to peace and brotherhood is through nonviolence, love, and suffering. He was severely criticized for his opposition to the war in Vietnam. It must be said, however, that one could hardly expect a prophet of Dr. King's commitments to advocate nonviolence at home and violence in Vietnam. Nonviolence to King was total commitment not only in solving the problems of race in the United States but in solving the problems of the world. . . .

We all pray that his assassin will be apprehended and brought to justice. But make no mistake: The American people are in part responsible for Martin Luther King Jr.'s death. The assassin heard enough condemnation of King and of Negroes to feel that he had public support. He knew that millions hated King.

The Memphis officials must bear some of the guilt for Martin Luther King's assassination. The strike should have been settled several weeks ago. The lowest-paid men in our society should not have to strike for a more just wage. A century after emancipation, and after the enactment of the Thirteenth, Fourteenth, and Fifteenth Amendments, it should not have been necessary for Martin Luther King Jr. to stage marches in Montgomery, Birmingham, and Selma, and go to jail thirty times trying to achieve for his people those rights that people of lighter hue get by virtue of being born white. We, too, are guilty of murder. It is time for the American people to repent and make democracy equally applicable to all Americans. What can we do? We, and not the assassins, represent America at its best. We have the power—not the assassins—to make things right.

If we love Martin Luther King Jr. and respect him, as this crowd surely testifies, let us see to it that he did not die in vain; let us see to it that we do not dishonor his name by trying to solve our problems through rioting in the streets. Violence was foreign to his nature. He warned that continued riots could produce a fascist state. But let us see to it also that the conditions that cause riots are promptly removed, as the president of the United States is trying to get us to do. Let black and white alike search their hearts, and if there be prejudice in our hearts against any racial or ethnic group, let us exterminate it. And let us pray, as Martin Luther King Jr. would pray if he could: Father, forgive them, for they know not what they do. If we do this, Martin Luther King Jr. will have died a redemptive death from which all mankind wil benefit.

I close by saying to you what Martin Luther King Jr. believed: If physical death was the price he had to pay to rid America of prejudice and injustice, nothing could be more redemptive. And, to paraphrase the words of the immortal John Fitzgerald Kennedy, permit me to say that Martin Luther King Jr.'s unfinished work on earth must truly be our own.

1929	Born Michael Luther King in Atlanta, GA, to a religious family headed by Rev. Martin Luther King Sr. Later renamed after his father.
1943	Age 14, Martin wins a speaking contest sponsored by the Negro Elks Society. On the bus ride home, he is forced to relinquish his seat to a white person and stand for the duration of the 90-mile trip. Later recalls, "I don't think I've ever been so deeply angry in my life."
1948	Upon graduating from Morehouse College, King is admitted to Crozer Theological Seminary in Chester, PA, where he is ordained as a Baptist minister at age nineteen.
1953	Marries Coretta Scott. Four children follow.
1954	Moves to Montgomery, AL, to preach at Dexter Avenue Church. Avoiding the religious emotionalism of gospel churches ("The shouting and stomping . . . it embarrassed me"), King views the church as an instrument of social change.
1955	Seamstress Rosa Parks refuses to relinquish her bus seat to a white man in Montgomery. King leads a boycott of Montgomery buses. The civil rights movement begins.
1957	Delivers 208 speeches, developing exceptional oratorical skills.
1958	Publishes his first book, *Stride Toward Freedom,* an account of the Montgomery bus boycott. While promoting his book in a Harlem bookstore, King is stabbed by an African-American woman.
1959	Visits India to study Mahatma Gandhi's methods of nonviolent protest. Upon his return, King resigns from Dexter Avenue Church to focus on civil rights full-time. "Get the weapon of nonviolence, the breastplate of righteousness, the armor of truth," he tells his demonstrators in Alabama, "and just keep marching."
1960	King family moves to Atlanta, where King and his father become co-pastors of Ebenezer Baptist Church.
1963	Jailed for the thirteenth time during a march in Birmingham, AL, a burgeoning battleground for civil rights. In jail, King writes

Letter from a Birmingham Jail, asserting civilians have a moral duty to disobey unjust laws. *Letters* becomes a civil rights classic. Later that year, delivers his "I Have a Dream" speech at civil rights demonstration in Washington.

1964   Receives Nobel Peace Prize at age 35—the youngest recipient ever. Although he has been stabbed, has been physically attacked, and has had his house bombed three times, King remains resolutely committed to nonviolence.

1968   Marches in support of sanitation workers in Memphis. Delivers his last speech, "I've Been to the Mountaintop." The next day, he is shot and killed at the Lorraine Hotel in Memphis by petty criminal James Earl Ray. His coffin is taken to the funeral atop a farm wagon pulled by two mules, in recognition of King's association with the poor. Despite pleas for nonviolence, there are resulting riots and disturbances in 130 American cities, and 20,000 arrests.

1986   The third Monday in January is proclaimed a national holiday in King's honor.

KARL MARX

1818 – 1883

By FRIEDRICH ENGELS, *collaborator and friend*

Delivered at funeral, March 17, 1883

Highgate Cemetery, London

O N THE FOURTEENTH OF MARCH, AT A QUARTER TO THREE in the afternoon, the greatest living thinker ceased to think. He had been left alone for scarcely two minutes, and when we came back we found him in an armchair, peacefully gone to sleep—but forever.

An immeasurable loss has been sustained both by the militant proletariat of Europe and America, and by historical science, in the death of this man. The gap that has been left by the death of this mighty spirit will soon enough make itself felt.

Just as Darwin discovered the law of evolution in organic nature, so Marx discovered the law of evolution in human history; he discovered the simple fact, hitherto concealed by an overgrowth of ideology, that mankind must first of all eat and drink, have shelter and clothing, before it can pursue politics, science, religion, art, etc. . . .

But that is not all. Marx also discovered the special law of motion governing the present-day capitalist method of production and the bourgeois society that this method of production has created. The discovery of surplus value suddenly threw light on the problem [for] which all previous investigators, both bourgeois economists and socialist critics, had been groping in the dark.

Two such discoveries would be enough for one lifetime. Happy the man to whom it is granted to make even one such discovery. But in every single field that Marx investigated—and he investigated very many fields, none of them superficially—in every field, even in that of mathematics, he made independent discoveries.

Such was the man of science. But this was not even half the man. Science was for Marx a historically dynamic, revolutionary force. However great the joy with which he welcomed a new discovery in some theoretical science whose practical application perhaps it was as yet quite impossible to envisage, he experienced a quite other kind of joy when the discovery involved immediate revolutionary changes in industry and in the general course of history.

For Marx was before all else a revolutionary. His real mission in life was to contribute in one way or another to the overthrow of capitalist society and of the forms of government that it had brought into being, to contribute to the liberation of the present-day proletariat, which he was the first to make conscious of its own position and its needs, of the conditions under which it could win its freedom. Fighting was his element.

And he fought with a passion, a tenacity, and a success such as few could rival. His work on the first *Rheinische Zeitung,* the Paris *Vorwärts,* the Brussels *Deutsche Zeitung,* . . . the *New York Tribune,* and in addition to these a host of militant pamphlets, work in revolutionary clubs in Paris, Brussels, and London, and finally, crowning all, the formation of the International Workingmen's Association—this was indeed an achievement of which Marx might well have been proud, even if he had done nothing else.

And consequently Marx was the best hated and most calumniated man of his times. Governments, both absolutist and republican, deported him from their territories. The bourgeoisie, whether conservative or extreme democrat, vied with one another in heaping slanders upon him. And now he has died, beloved, revered, and mourned by millions of revolutionary fellow workers—from the mines of Siberia to California, in all parts of Europe and America—and I make bold to say that though he may have many opponents, he had hardly one personal enemy.

His name and his work will endure through the ages.

1818	Born in Prussia to a middle-class family.
1835	Enters Bonn University to study law, but seduced by a "metropolis of intellectuals," he spends the next five years steeping himself in philosophy. His education concludes six years later with a doctoral thesis on the philosophy of Epicurus, whose freedom-from-fear gospel strikes a chord with Marx.
1842	Publishes articles in radical newspaper *Rheinische Zeitung*. Later becomes editor. Focusing on protecting rights of the working masses, Marx reshapes the paper into an increasingly revolutionary and democratic vehicle, until it buckles under opposition and is shut down by the police.
1843	Marries Jenny von Westphalen after a seven-year engagement fraught with parental opposition. They move to Paris, where he immerses himself in the study of utopian socialists. The following year, Jenny gives birth to the first of six children.
1844	Meets Friedrich Engels, beginning their lifelong friendship.
1845	Under pressure from the Prussian government, Marx is ordered to leave France. Upon settling in Belgium, he renounces his Prussian citizenship.
1848	Publishes his seminal work, *The Communist Manifesto*, urging all workers to unite in revolution. Later that year, revolutionary events flare up in Vienna, Berlin, and Budapest. Marx and Engels start a daily newspaper in Cologne, using it as a platform to support the workers' struggle in Bohemia, Italy, Poland, and other countries.
1849	Marx and Engels are tried for subversion but successfully defend their newspaper and freedom of the press. Disenchanted with the German revolutionaries, Marx eventually relocates to London, where he lives in poverty while developing his economic theories.
1851	Begins contributing articles to the *New York Daily Tribune*, covering the European political beat. Continues writing for the paper for 10 years.

1864   Founds the International Workingmen's Association to battle appalling working conditions and unlivable minimum wages.

1867   Publishes *Capital: A Critique of Political Economy,* one of the first works to explore the relationship between capital and labor with a scientific eye.

1881   Wife Jenny dies after a long illness, devastating Marx. With his own health rapidly deteriorating, he journeys to Algeria, southern France, and finally Switzerland for a long rest.

1883   His favorite daughter, Jenny, dies from cancer. Marx succumbs weeks later and dies, age 65. His funeral is a small affair—eight friends follow the coffin to his grave, where Marx is buried alongside wife Jenny. Though he doesn't live to see the workers' revolution that he wrote passionately about, few social uprisings since have escaped his influence.

ELEANOR ROOSEVELT
1884–1962

By ADLAI STEVENSON, *friend and political ally*

Delivered at memorial service, November 17, 1962

Cathedral of St. John the Divine, New York City

ONE WEEK AGO THIS AFTERNOON, IN THE ROSE GARDEN at Hyde Park, Eleanor Roosevelt came home for the last time. Her journeys are over. The remembrance now begins.

In gathering here to honor her, we engage in a self-serving act. It is we who are trying, by this ceremony of tribute, to deny the fact that we have lost her, and, at least, to prolong the farewell, and possibly to say some of the things we dared not say in her presence, because she would have turned aside such testimonial with impatience and gently asked us to get on with some of the more serious business of the meeting.

A grief perhaps not equaled since the death of her husband seventeen years ago is the world's best tribute to one of the great figures of our age—a woman whose lucid and luminous faith testified always for sanity in an insane time and for hope in a time of obscure hope—a woman who spoke for the good toward which man aspires in a world that has seen too much of the evil of which man is capable.

She lived seventy-eight years, most of the time in tireless activity, as if she knew that only a frail fragment of the things that cry out to be done could be done in the lifetime of even the most fortunate. One has the melancholy sense that when she knew death was at hand, she was contemplating not what she achieved, but what she had not quite managed to do. And I know she wanted to go—when there was no more strength to do.

Yet how much she had done, how much still unchronicled. We dare not try to tabulate the lives she salvaged, the battles, known and unrecorded, she fought, the afflicted she comforted, the hovels she brightened, the faces and places near and far that were given some new radiance, some sound of music, by her endeavors. What other single human being has touched and transformed the existence of so many others? What better measure is there of the impact of anyone's life?

There was no sick soul too wounded to engage her mercy. There was no signal of human distress that she did not view as a personal summons. There was no affront to human dignity from which she fled because the timid cried "Danger." And the number of occasions on which her intervention turned despair into victory we may never know.

Her life was crowded, restless, fearless. Perhaps she pitied most not those whom she aided in the struggle, but the more fortunate who were preoccupied with themselves and cursed with the self-deceptions of private success. She walked in the slums and the ghettos of the world, not on a tour of inspection, nor as a condescending patron, but as one who could not feel complacent while others were hungry, and who could not find contentment while others were in distress. This was not sacrifice. This for Mrs. Roosevelt was the only meaningful way of life.

These were not conventional missions of mercy. What rendered this unforgettable woman so extraordinary was not merely her response to suffering; it was her comprehension of the complexity of the human condition.

Not long before she died, she wrote that "within all of us there are two sides. One reaches for the stars, the other descends to the level of beasts." It was, I think, this discernment that made her so unfailingly tolerant of friends who faltered and led her so often to remind the smug and complacent that "there but for the grace of God."

But we dare not regard her as just a benign incarnation of good works. For she was not only a great woman and a great humanitarian but a great democrat. I use the word with a small d—though it was, of course, equally true that she was a great Democrat with a capital D. When I say she was a great small-d democrat, I mean she had a lively and astute understanding of the nature of the democratic process. She was a master political strategist with a fine sense of humor. And, as she said, she loved a good fight.

She was a realist. Her compassion did not become sentimentality. She understood that progress was a long labor of compromise. She mistrusted absolutism in all its forms—the absolutism of the word and even more the absolutism of the deed. She never supposed that all the problems of life could be cured in a day or a year or a lifetime. Her pungent and salty understanding of human behavior kept her always in intimate contact with reality. I think this was a primary source of her strength, because she never thought that the loss of a battle meant the loss of a war, nor did she suppose that a compromise that produced only part of the objective sought was an act of corruption or of treachery. She knew that no formula of words, no combination of deeds, could abolish the troubles of life overnight and usher in the millennium.

The miracle, I have tried to suggest, is how much tangible good she really did; how much realism and reason were mingled with her instinctive compassion; how her contempt for the perquisites of power ultimately won her the esteem of so many of the powerful; and how, at her death, there was a universality of grief that transcended all the harsh boundaries of political, racial, and religious strife and, for a moment at least, united men in a vision of what their world might be.

We do not claim the right to enshrine another mortal, and this least of all would Mrs. Roosevelt have desired. She would have wanted it said, I believe, that she knew well the pressures of pride and vanity, the sting of bitterness and defeat, the gray days of national peril and personal anguish. But she clung to the confident expectation that men could fashion their own tomorrow if they could only learn that yesterday can be neither relived nor revised.

Many who have spoken of her in these last few days have used a word to which we all assent, because it speaks a part of what we feel. They have called her a lady, a great lady, the First Lady of the world. But the word *lady*, though it says much about Eleanor Roosevelt, does not say all. To be incapable of self-concern is not a negative virtue; it is the other side of a coin that has a positive face—the most positive, I think, of all the faces. And to enhance the humanity of others is not a kind of humility; it is a kind of pride—the noblest of all the forms of pride. No man or woman can respect other men and women who does not respect life. And to respect life is to love it. Eleanor Roosevelt loved life—and that, perhaps, is the most meaningful thing that can be said about her, for it says so much beside.

It takes courage to love life. Loving it demands imagination and perception and the kind of patience women are more apt to have than men—the bravest and most understanding women. And loving it takes something more beside—it takes a gift for life, a gift for love.

Eleanor Roosevelt's childhood was unhappy—miserably unhappy, she sometimes said. But it was Eleanor Roosevelt who also said that "one must never, for whatever reason, turn his back on life." She did not mean that duty should compel us. She meant that life should. "Life," she said, "was meant to be lived." A simple statement. An obvious statement. But a statement that by its obviousness and its simplicity challenges the most intricate of all the philosophies of despair.

Many of the admonitions she bequeathed us are neither new thoughts nor novel concepts. Her ideas were, in many respects, old-fashioned—as old as the Sermon on the Mount, as the reminder that it is more blessed to give than to receive, as the words of St. Francis that she loved so well: "For it is in the giving that we receive."

She imparted to the familiar language—nay, what too many have come to treat as the clichés—of Christianity a new poignancy and vibrance. She did so not by reciting them, but by proving that it is possible to live them. It is this above all that rendered her unique in her century. It was said of her contemptuously at times that she was a do-gooder, a charge leveled with similar derision against another public figure one thousand nine hundred and sixty-two years ago.

We who are assembled here are of various religious and political faiths, and perhaps different conceptions of man's destiny in the universe. It is not an irreverence, I trust, to say that the immortality Mrs. Roosevelt would have valued most would be found in the deeds and visions her life inspired in others, and in the proof that they would be faithful to the spirit of any tribute conducted in her name.

And now one can almost hear Mrs. Roosevelt saying that the speaker has already talked too long. So we must say farewell. We are always saying farewell in this world—always standing at the edge of loss attempting to retrieve some memory, some human meaning, from the silence—something which is precious and gone. Often, although we know the absence well enough, we cannot name it or describe it even. What left the world when Lincoln died: Speaker after speaker in those aching days tried to tell his family or his neighbors or his congregation. But no one found the words, not even Whitman. "When lilacs last in the dooryard bloomed" can break the heart, but not with Lincoln's greatness, only with his loss. What the words could never capture was the man himself. His deeds were known; every schoolchild knew them. But it was not his deeds the country mourned; it was the man—the mastery of life which made the greatness of the man.

It was always so. On that April day when Franklin Roosevelt died, it was not a president we wept for. It was a man. In Archibald MacLeish's words: "Fagged out, word down, sick. With the weight of his own bones, the task finished, the war won, the victory assured, the glory left behind him for the others. . . ."

It is so now. What we have lost in Eleanor Roosevelt is not her life. She lived that out to the fullest. What we have lost, what we wish to recall for ourselves, to remember, is what she was herself. And who can name it? But she left "a name to shine on the entablatures of truth, forever."

We pray that she has found peace, and a glimpse of the sunset. But today we weep for ourselves. We are lonelier. Someone has gone from one's own life—who was like the certainty of refuge. And someone has gone from the world—who was like a certainty of honor.

1884	Born Anna Eleanor Roosevelt in New York City. Openly disappointed with Eleanor's lack of a pretty face, her mother is aloof. Her father—though loving—drinks heavily and is banished from the family home.
1886	Meets distant cousin Franklin Delano Roosevelt for the first time.
1899	An orphan since age 10, Eleanor attends a girls' school in England. Develops her first taste of self-confidence, studying languages and literature. Summers are spent on the Continent. Writes, "No matter how plain a woman may be, if truth and loyalty are stamped upon her face all will be attracted to her."
1902	Returns for her debut. "It was simply awful," she later says.
1904	Meets and becomes engaged to Franklin Delano Roosevelt.
1905	Marries Roosevelt. They live in Manhattan while FDR studies law at Columbia. Over the next 11 years, she bears six children, one of whom dies in infancy. "For ten years, I was always just getting over having a baby or about to have another one, so my occupations were restricted."
1910	Franklin Roosevelt elected to the New York State Senate.
1918	Discovers FDR's love affair with Lucy Mercer. "The bottom dropped out of my own particular world. I faced myself, my surroundings, my world, honestly for the first time." Her mother-in-law persuades her to stay in the marriage.
1928	FDR stricken with polio. Eleanor tends devotedly to him, becoming "his eyes and ears." Later elected governor, he finds Eleanor a trusted and tireless partner.
1932	FDR elected to White House. Eleanor transforms role of First

Lady, becoming the first woman to speak in front of a national convention, earn money as a lecturer, write a daily syndicated column, and hold press conferences. Restricts press conferences to female reporters, knowing news organizations will be forced to hire women. (She is less successful at entertaining. When the king and queen of England visit, she arranges a much-criticized menu of hot dogs and hamburgers, served picnic style.)

1939	Inspecting New Deal programs in the South, she is stunned to find lingering prejudice against blacks and petitions her husband, who eventually signs an executive order banning discrimination. During her 12 years in the White House she becomes an object of almost universal respect.
1945	FDR dies. She tells reporters, "The story is over." But the following year she begins a new position as the first U.S. Delegate to the United Nations. Travels the world tirelessly, working to secure rights for the poor and oppressed.
1952	Stumps for Adlai Stevenson. When he runs again in 1956, she campaigns again, cementing their friendship.
1962	Dies of tuberculosis, in New York City, age 78. Among the scores of world leaders attending her funeral are recent or future presidents Kennedy, Johnson, Truman, Eisenhower, and Hoover. Roosevelt is buried next to her husband at their estate of Hyde Park.

RYAN WHITE

1971–1990

By REV. DR. RAY PROBASCO, *pastor and good friend*

Delivered at funeral, April 11, 1990

Second Presbyterian Church, Indianapolis, IN

H E WAS DIFFERENT FROM THE REST OF US, EVEN THEN. Born with an affliction called hemophilia—an illness that separated him from the other children—he couldn't go out and play. No climbing trees, running fast, or playing baseball in the park. One day he asked his grandmother, "Why can't I play like [my sister]?" And his grandmother said, "Ryan, you just need to take life slower than the others. You get to appreciate the good things in life—birds, trees, flowers. Try it and you'll see." And he looked up and said, "You'd better tell Andrea to slow down so that she can appreciate the good things in life, too."

There was never a day that Ryan was not in pain. Many days his joints would ache, but he would never complain—a characteristic that would serve him well throughout his shortened life. Ryan had little time to waste. He learned even then to make the best of every day.

In December 1984, Ryan was diagnosed with a little-understood disease called AIDS. There were few drugs at first and very little information about the illness, so very quickly a great deal of fear permeated Ryan's community. After he contracted AIDS, Ryan's struggle to live life as an "ordinary" kid become more intense because he wanted to go to school. The details of this struggle are well documented, but what most people don't know is this: There wasn't a person who knew Ryan who could ever hate him. People hated and feared the disease that had taken over his body. They hated the disease—just as Ryan did.

At first Ryan and the disease were perceived as one and the same, and as we all discovered, they were so very far apart.

It was Ryan who first humanized the disease called AIDS. He allowed us to see the boy who just wanted more than anything else to be like other children, and to be able to go to school. Many of us marvel at the ability of one so young to be able to communicate so articulately the way he felt, thought, and believed. He didn't want to be labeled the "AIDS boy," and often remarked to his family that "if others wouldn't keep telling me I had it, I'd forget all about it."

When first diagnosed, he was told that he would live only a short time. It was then that Ryan's faith in God began to take root and bloom. He was prayed for by his church, and then one community after another, until there was prayer that circled the globe—from Spain to the Philippines, and from New Zealand to Great Britain. The world prayed and God responded.

Experimental drugs were discovered and Ryan received them. A dedicated and devoted doctor named Martin Kleiman came forward to treat Ryan. Nurses and more doctors, researchers and technicians helped care for him. And there was still a world praying.

Children began asking, "Ryan, are you afraid to die?" And Ryan responded—and I quote: "Everybody is going to die. If I die, I'm going to a better place."

Ryan and his family always believed there would be a miracle, that God would heal Ryan right here on earth, and not wait until he was received in heaven. But that didn't happen. I believe God gave us that miracle in Ryan. He healed a wounded spirit and made it whole.

Many of you who are in this beautiful room of our Lord's house are very successful by the world's standards. Your life is filled with glamour and fame. Yet you brought Ryan and his cause into your life and aided him in his mission and showed us how to do the same. Now I challenge all of you to accept Ryan's faith. Ryan was successful, too—getting all of us involved. He helped us to care and to believe that with God's help nothing is impossible, even for a kid.

Ryan's life reminds me of a little poem taken from the children's story about Daniel and the Lion's den:

> *Dare to be a Daniel*
> *Dare to stand alone*
> *Dare to have a purpose*
> *Dare to make it known*

Ryan did, and we, too, have chosen to stand, standing and struggling to find a cure. And with God's help, and each of yours, we'll make AIDS a disease—not a dirty word.

1971	Born a hemophiliac in Kokomo, IN, Ryan's otherwise normal childhood is interrupted by frequent visits to the doctor.
1981	AIDS is first diagnosed in America.
1984	Battling pneumonia, Ryan has surgery to remove part of his left lung. Doctors discover that he has contracted AIDS from a tainted blood product. He is given six months to live.
1985	14-year-old Ryan is banned from school. Brings a discrimination case against school officials. Eventually settles on separate restrooms and disposable silverware in the cafeteria—but the community's fears are not allayed. Students harass him. A bullet is fired into his home. The fight to stay in school pushes the reluctant Ryan into the limelight and transforms him into an eloquent spokesperson for AIDS patients. His focus: education to combat discrimination and slow the disease's progress.
1987	Family moves to Cicero, IN. At Hamilton Heights High School, Ryan is treated like any other student—except for the fact that he's internationally famous for his battle and educational efforts.

1989   ABC dramatizes his life in *The Ryan White Story,* starring Judith
       Light and Lukas Haas.

1990   Dies of complications from AIDS, age 19, with his mother and
       family friend Elton John at his side. Funeral attendees include
       Barbara Bush, Phil Donahue, Michael Jackson, and Elton John.
       Months later, the Ryan White CARE Act is passed by Congress
       to help uninsured people with AIDS. At the time, there are more
       than 150,000 reported cases of AIDS in the U.S.

MALCOLM X

1925–1965

By OSSIE DAVIS, *longtime friend*

Delivered at memorial service, February 27, 1965

Faith Temple Church of God, Harlem, NY

HERE—AT THIS FINAL HOUR, IN THIS QUIET PLACE— Harlem has come to bid farewell to one of its brightest hopes, extinguished now and gone from us forever. For Harlem is where he worked and where he struggled and fought—his home of homes, where his heart was, and where his people are—and it is, therefore, most fitting that we meet once again, in Harlem, to share these last moments with him. For Harlem has ever been gracious to those who have loved her, have fought for her, and have defended her honor even to the death.

It is not in the memory of man that this beleaguered, unfortunate, but nonetheless proud community has found a braver, more gallant young champion than this Afro-American who lies before us—unconquered still. I say the word again, as he would want me to: Afro-American. Afro-American Malcolm, who was a master, was most meticulous in his use of words. Nobody knew better than he the power words have over the minds of men.

Malcolm had stopped being a "Negro" years ago. It had become too small, too puny, too weak a word for him. Malcolm was bigger than that. Malcolm had become an Afro-American and he wanted so desperately that we, that all his people, would become Afro-Americans, too.

There are those who will consider it their duty, as friends of the Negro people, to tell us to revile him, to flee, even from the presence

71

of his memory, to save ourselves by writing him out of the history of our turbulent times. Many will ask what Harlem finds to honor in this stormy, controversial, and bold young captain—and we will smile. Many will say turn away—away from this man, for he is not a man but a demon, a monster, a subverter, and an enemy of the black man—and we will smile. They will say that he is of hate, a fanatic, a racist who can only bring evil to the cause for which you struggle! And we will answer and say to them: Did you ever talk to Brother Malcolm? Did you ever touch him or have him smile at you? Did you ever really listen to him? Did he ever do a mean thing? Was he ever himself associated with violence or any public disturbance? For if you did, you would know him. And if you knew him, you would know why we must honor him.

Malcolm was our manhood, our living, black manhood! This was his meaning to his people. And in honoring him, we honor the best in ourselves. Last year, from Africa, he wrote these words to a friend: "My journey," he says,

> is almost ended, and I have a much broader scope than when I started out, which I believe will add new life and dimension to our struggle for freedom and honor and dignity in the States. I am writing these things so that you will know for a fact the tremendous sympathy and support we have among the African States for our Human Rights struggle. The main thing is that we keep a United Front wherein our most valuable time and energy will not be wasted fighting each other.

However we may have differed with him—or with each other about him and his value as a man—let his going from us serve only to bring us together now. Consigning these mortal remains to earth, the common mother of all, secure in the knowledge that what we place in the ground is no more now a man but a seed which, after the winter of our discontent, will come forth again to meet us. And we will know him then for what he was and is—a prince, our own black, shining prince!—who didn't hesitate to die because he loved us so.

1925	Born Malcolm Little in Omaha, NE. Parents, the Rev. Earl and Louise Little, belong to Universal Negro Improvement Association, advocating black independence from whites. KKK and other white supremacist groups continually threaten the family.
1928	The Littles' house is destroyed by arson.
1931	Earl Little found dead on town's trolley tracks.
1939	Louise Little suffers complete nervous breakdown. Declared insane, she is committed to a state mental hospital, where she remains for 26 years. Malcolm drops out of school and wanders the Boston underworld, consorting with thieves, hoodlums, drug dealers, and pimps.
1948	Doing eight-to-ten years' hard labor for armed robbery, Malcolm encounters the Nation of Islam, a group preaching racial separation as the path to black freedom. He converts.
1952	Released on parole. Adds X in place of his surname and travels the country promoting Nation of Islam. For 12 years Malcolm preaches that "the white man" is the devil and that Nation of Islam founder Honorable Elijah Muhammad is God's messenger.
1958	Marries Betty Shabazz. Five daughters follow.
1959	A three-week tour of the Middle East and Africa as Elijah Muhammad's emissary.
1963	Continues public appearances—speaking on radio, television, even granting an interview to *Playboy*. Delivers "The Black Revolution" speech in Harlem, NY.

1964   A packed year. Withdraws from the Nation of Islam: "I feel like a
        man who has been asleep somewhat and under someone else's
        control. I feel what I'm thinking and saying now is for myself."
        Following a pilgrimage to Mecca, renounces racial separatism:
        "True Islam taught me that it takes all of the religious, political,
        psychological, and racial ingredients to make the human family
        and the human society complete." And has sense of his demise:
        "It is anybody's guess which of the extremes . . . might meet a
        fatal catastrophe first: 'nonviolent' Dr. King, or so-called 'violent'
        me."

1965   Assassinated at 39 by three Black Muslims during a Harlem
        rally—alleged work of Nation of Islam.

LUCILLE BALL

1911–1989

By DIANE SAWYER, *longtime admirer*

Delivered at memorial service, May 16, 1989

St. Ignatius Loyola Church, New York City

I'VE BEEN TOLD THAT THERE IS A DEBATE THAT IS ONE OF the longest-running minor theological arguments in Christianity. A debate that has engaged everybody from dusty, old scholars in the Medieval Ages to Baudelaire. The issue is this: Is there laughter in heaven?

Now, one school says: Of course there is no laughter in heaven, because the whole point of heaven is serene contemplation of the truth. But the other school says that there must be laughter in heaven, because laughter is the best x-ray to determine what is true.

I suppose it's not an issue likely to be solved by scientific minds, unless someone returns with an audio recording one day. But until that time, I would just like to submit, if I could, one more argument for the School of Heavenly Laughter. That argument, in the form of a woman, sometimes with pie in her face, sometimes with chocolates under her hat, and sometimes engaged in a polysyllabic fight to the finish with Vegameatavitamins. She is a woman who showed us the spiritual power of laughter. Of laughter that could travel as fast as the speed of light, and still drop gently onto a single human heart.

Lucille Ball told a friend of hers once that the essence of her comedy was to take the unbelievable and make it believable and true. And what she came up with was so true that people in eighty-three countries felt that she was giving them a revelation about their lives. Laughter of that kind, it seems to me, is not just unifying, it is humanity's holiday. It's a kind of spiritual bench along the path, a place where we gather together and say, in the quiet moment of laughter revealed, we are all alike. We are, in fact, just guests here on this planet, at this one moment in time.

I don't know about you, but I found myself intrigued by a kind of paradox of memory in the last few weeks, as I've been thinking about Lucy. I find that when I remember back to the time when I was growing up, and watching her on television, I can barely remember anything about my real life. I remember a couple of things. I remember when the bird died, and I remember when I put pickles down the shirt of a little boy with freckles who was standing in front of me. But, I promise you, I can't remember a thing about my real life, compared to what I can remember about the Ricardos. I find I can remember where every piece of furniture was in the living room. And do you remember the stove in the kitchen? I can remember that, too. And it seems to me that maybe that's because I had this sense, as I was sitting home laughing, that there were other people in their houses, sitting home and laughing, too. And the power of that connection was what made it stay in my mind.

I have this honor tonight because of Lucille Ball's family. A friend of hers told me that sometimes she would watch me on the news, I guess as I was slogging through the jungles and across the deserts in pursuit of a story. I just wish that I could have told her, even just once, how much I think she did to inspire women of my age to get out there.

Do you remember back then? Back in the 1950s when on television Mrs. Cleaver and Mrs. Anderson were telling you that the very important things were to make sure you didn't sweat? I remember thinking that someone pushing the outer edge of propriety was that "career woman," Betty Crocker.

And streaking through all of that unrelenting politeness back in the 1950s was a woman with red hair. How I admired her bravery. Because it wasn't the kind of courage that it takes to go out and fight a war, or to go in and slay some bears in the forest. It was the kind of courage that it takes every day just to get through life. The courage that it takes to make an all-out defense of a friend, no matter what happens. And the courage that it takes sometimes to risk your dignity just to see a little bit beyond the horizon.

There was Lucy Ricardo doing everything I wanted to do, and a lot of things I was afraid I would do, and surviving it. And I guess we all knew back then, too, that there was another Lucy. Someone behind that Lucy we saw on the screen. In some ways, on occasions, I'm told they were not that dissimilar. Once a friend recalls she was on the telephone and discovered that her bathtub was overflowing while she was talking on the telephone, and set about in her wacky, domestic way, trying to clean it up with a Dustbuster.

And there was the other time she told about when she emptied the entire contents of a saltshaker onto the top of the chopped liver she was going to serve to her guests, so as they were driving up the driveway, she was trying to hold the liver under the faucet to rinse the salt off.

But then there was a Lucy not like that one at all. The tough, resilient professional in a brutal industry. Someone who spent twenty-five years on television and then, as she must have, had the challenge of living with a legend that she created. Someone who must have, at times at least, looked at the Lucy preserved, agelessly, in the celluloid amber on the screen, and then had to go back and look in the mirror and see that she was getting older.

And yet, through it all, she was still giving her costars the credit for doing all the really funny things. She was still giving Desi Arnaz the credit for putting it all together, she was giving Gary Morton the credit for keeping her together, and she was, with gruff and tough and tender attention, giving her children and grandchildren and friends the credit for the main accomplishment in her life.

But at least, there at the end, we all got to tell her. We got to speak to her, and tell her about the circles of laughter she sent rippling out, that go rippling out still. In a way, hundreds of millions of us were all able to gather there at the foot of her bed in the hospital, to remind her and ourselves about the way she united us in the redeeming acts of laughter. The moments that recall to us again that we are just guests on this planet. And if life is a sometimes thrilling, sometimes disturbing, difficult party on this planet, it was to say to her again that she was the life of that party.

So let the scholars, if they will, argue about it for five hundred centuries more. I just know this: It may be that during "business hours" God and the angels only sit around watching six-part documentaries and Bill Moyers. But back in the "family quarters" I bet they switch to *I Love Lucy*. And that's how I know there is laughter in heaven. Because a God who would have created her would never let her laughter be far from home.

1911	Born in Jamestown, NY, to Desiree Hunt, a pianist, and Henry Ball, a telephone lineman.
1926	Leaves home at age 15 to enroll in drama school but is dismissed because she has "no talent." She adopts the alias Diane Belmont and begins a modeling career.
1933	Cast as one of 12 slave girls in the MGM film *Roman Scandals*.
1938	Becoming a veritable Queen of the B Movies, going on to star in more than 60 films during her 20-year reign, Ball is frustrated with playing nurse, clerk, or college girl: "I never cared about the movies because they cast me wrong." But her comedic talents begin to attract notice. Raves *The New York Times*: "She is rapidly becoming one of our brightest comediennes."
1940	Weds Desi Arnaz. They have a volatile marriage with frequent separations and reconciliations.
1949	Pitches a show about zany housewife and her Cuban bandleader husband (played by Arnaz), but TV executives balk. The couple produces a pilot with $5000 of their own money.

1951   *I Love Lucy* premieres on CBS. As the elastic-faced housewife
        who lands in highly implausible situations, Ball rockets the show
        to number one—and revolutionizes television in the process.
        I Love Lucy is one of the first shows to be filmed, and the
        resulting high-quality prints eventually air in over 100 countries.
        Ball's transformation from platinum blonde to wisecracking
        redhead is complete.

1952   Wins the first of four Emmy Awards.

1953   Gives birth to her second child the same night that her character
        gives birth on television. 53 million people welcome Little
        Ricky—more than watch Eisenhower's inauguration.

1960   After 20 years of marriage, Lucy and Desi call it quits. Ball:
        "He was the love of my life, but I just couldn't take it anymore."
        The following year, she marries former nightclub comic
        Gary Morton.

1962   Buys Arnaz out of their jointly owned, highly successful produc-
        tion company, Desilu, becoming the first woman to head a major
        television production studio. Proceeds to produce a curriculum
        of TV's greatest hits: *Our Miss Brooks, The Dick Van Dyke Show,*
        Star Trek, and *Mission Impossible.* Ball eventually sells Desilu to
        Gulf and Western for $17 million.

1984   Becomes the first woman inducted into the Television Academy
        Hall of Fame.

1989   Dies from a ruptured aorta, age 77. The title and heart-shaped
        logo of her show prove prescient: Half a century after its intro-
        duction, *I Love Lucy* continues to showcase Ball's deft pantomime
        and impeccable timing in reruns.

JACK BENNY

1894–1974

By BOB HOPE, *longtime friend and colleague*

Delivered at memorial service, December 12, 1974

Forest Lawn Cemetery, Hollywood Hills, CA

IT IS SAID THAT A MEMORIAL SERVICE IS FOR THOSE WHO are left behind, for those who mourn the loss of a loved one. If that is the case, then this service is for the world, because last Thursday night the world lost somebody it loved a lot.

When Benny Kubelsky was born, who in their wildest dreams would imagine that eighty years later at the event of his passing every television program, every radio show would stop, and that every magazine and newspaper would headline it on their front pages? The millions of people who had never met him, who had only seen or heard him, would feel the pain of a very personal loss.

The void that is left with us at Jack's passing is quickly filled with the happy memories that we have of him. That's the way Jack would like it to be. He wants us to remember the happiness we shared with him rather than the sadness of losing him. Any path that Jack Benny crossed was left with more laughter, not less.

How do you say good-bye to a man who was not just a good friend but a national treasure? It's hard to say that no man is indispensable. But it's true just the same that some are *irreplaceable*. No one has come along to replace Jolson, or Bogart, or Gable, or Will Rogers, or Chevalier. I think it's a safe bet that no one will ever replace Jack Benny. Jack had that rare magic—that indefinable something called genius. Picasso had it. Gershwin had it. And Jack was blessed with it. He didn't just stand on a stage . . . he owned it.

For a man who was the undisputed master of comedy timing, you'd have to say that this was the only time when Jack Benny's timing was all wrong. He left us much too soon.

He was stingy to the end. He gave us only eighty years, and it wasn't enough.

And it's an amusing footnote that the penny-pinching cheapskate we all knew and loved was portrayed by a man who gave so much of himself to all of us. Though the idol of millions, he remained modest. Though the homes of the great were open to him, he remained a simple man. Though blessed with a sharp wit, he never used it to injure or belittle.

Admired by presidents and royalty, he never lost the humble, down-to-earth quality of Benny Kubelsky from Waukegan. Kings and porters, they were all the same to Jack. He gave the same smile to everybody. He was getting ready to do a picture called *The Sunshine Boys*. But then Jack was always getting ready to do something, whether a concert, a television show, or a benefit, and besides, he was always a Sunshine Boy. He brought more sunshine to this world than Easter morning.

Jack Benny long ago ceased to be merely a personality and became an institution. If there's a Mount Rushmore for humanitarians, that first stone face might easily resemble him. And if stone could talk, it would say . . . "Well!"

Jack was one of the richest men I know. He was happy with who he was. He was happy with what he was. He was happy with where he was. Few are as rich as that.

Jack Benny, a gentle man, crossed all barriers, all boundaries, all countries, all races, all creeds. I'll never forget in 1958 when I made my first trip to Moscow and it was announced in the papers that America's leading comedian was visiting. That night I went to Ambassador Thompson's home and Mrs. Thompson met me at the door and said, "How wonderful that you should come. Did you bring your violin?"

His first love was the violin . . . which proves once again, as Jack used to say, you always hurt the one you love. And yet with that violin, Jack raised more money and benefited more worthwhile causes and charities than a dozen violin virtuosos. His technique wasn't much, but God sure loved his tone.

It is a cliché to say that in times of darkness, Jack Benny brought light with his gift of laughter, making us forget our troubles. For Jack was more than an escape from life. He *was* life—a life that enriched his profession, his friends, his millions of fans, his family, his country.

Perhaps what made Jack Benny such a great laugh-maker was that he himself loved to laugh. He was the greatest audience a comedian could ever want, and all of us would play jokes on him just to break him up and hear him laugh. I know it might sound corny, but there will be times from now on when the lightning will crackle with a special kind of sound, or thunder will peal with a special roar, and I'll think to myself that Cantor or Fields or Fred Allen must have told Jack a joke.

Jack had another quality that's become as rare as nickel candy bars: taste. When Jack was on the tube, you didn't have to chase the kids out of the room. And he was a perfectionist, a meticulous craftsman. His radio show was classic, a masterpiece of ensemble playing.

I think: How many generations grew up to the sound of Jack Benny? To the names of Mary Livingstone, Don Wilson, Dennis Day, Rochester, Phil Harris, Anaheim, Azusa, Cucamonga? For over forty years, first on radio, then on television, Jack was a pioneer, ever extending the frontiers of humor. He was one of the first, if not the first, to have great film stars on his show, playing themselves and getting big laughs. The Ronald Colemans, the Jimmy Stewarts, the Greg Pecks— they went on for Jack because they trusted him and his superb sense of what was exactly right.

Jack knew that the best laughs were the ones you worked the hardest for. He and Mary felt the same way about friends. They both cultivated lasting friendships because they were friends in return. This is the kind of love that surrounds Mary now, and will surround her for as long as people remember Jack Benny and Mary Livingstone. That is the best definition of eternity that I know of.

When a man can leave as much of himself as Jack left us, then he can never be truly gone. He has to be immortal.

In his book *You Can't Go Home Again*, Thomas Wolfe might have written these words about any of us:

> *If a man has talent and cannot use it*
> *He has failed.*
> *If a man has talent and uses only half of it*
> *He has partly failed.*
> *If he has talent and learns somehow to use the whole of it*
> *He has gloriously succeeded*
> *And won a satisfaction and a triumph*
> *Few men ever know.*

Jack had a great talent, and he learned somehow to use the whole of it. In his beautiful, full lifetime, Jack succeeded—gloriously. Jack found a great joy in the joy he brought to others. I cannot say it better than these words:

> *His life was gentle*
> *And the elements so mixed in him*
> *That nature might stand up and say to all the world:*
> *This was a man!*

God keep him. Enjoy him. We did for eighty years.

1894	Born Benjamin Kubelsky in Waukegan, IL, on Valentine's Day.
1910	Having flunked out of high school, Ben plays violin for the Barrison Theater. After two years in the orchestra pit, he goes on tour with pianist Cora Salisbury, countering her heavy concertos with comedic flourish. Changes his name to Ben K. Benny.
1916	Joins the navy. One night, after playing a classical piece on his violin, which invites ridicule, Ben sets down "the fiddle" and starts telling jokes. A solo act is born.
1920	Changes his name to Jack Benny to avoid confusion with another talk-and-fiddle act. By 1921 he has evolved into a successful vaudevillian—"Jack Benny: Aristocrat of Humor."
1927	Falls in love with hosiery saleswoman Sadie Marks. They marry.
1928	Appears in his first film, *Bright Moments,* followed by *Hollywood Revue* and *Chasing Rainbows* in 1929. Goes on to make several films for Paramount over the next two decades.
1932	Guests on Ed Sullivan's radio show. Benny: "Ladies and gentlemen, this is Jack Benny talking. There will be a slight pause while you say, 'Who cares?' " Evidently, enough listeners to net him a contract. Offered *The Jell-O Program Starring Jack Benny,* Benny rides the radiowaves to stardom. Vain, stingy, and eternally 39, he is the bachelor who stoically suffers through life's little tragedies, surrounded by an endlessly ribbing entourage. (Wife Sadie plays Mary Livingstone. The character is so popular that she changes her own name to Mary.)
1934	Adopts baby Joan.
1944	During the war, Benny broadcasts from military bases across the U.S. Promoting an "I Can't Stand Jack Benny Because . . ." contest, the show receives 277,000 entries. Benny is thrilled and slightly miffed.
1950	Launches *The Jack Benny Program,* a TV show built on the same persona. The show lasts for 15 years, attracting an average of 18 million viewers a week.

1954   Begins violin lessons at age 60. In subsequent concerts, he donates his fee to the symphonies he works with; one such concert saves Carnegie Hall from demolition.

1965   After retiring from television, Benny continues performing with symphonies and makes numerous live appearances.

1974   Dies of pancreatic cancer, age 80, while working on his "Third Farewell Special" for NBC. His funeral is attended by more than a thousand people. In his will, he leaves instructions with a florist to deliver a red rose to his wife every day until her death. Benny's epitaph? "A Gentle Man."

STAN LAUREL

1 8 9 0 – 1 9 6 5

By DICK VAN DYKE, *longtime friend and admirer*

Delivered at funeral, February 26, 1965

Forest Lawn Memorial Park, Glendale, CA

THIRTY YEARS AGO WHEN THE LATEST LAUREL AND HARDY movie played in my hometown in Illinois, I attended the Saturday matinees. That is to say, from about eleven A.M. to maybe nine or ten P.M.—or whenever my mother and father came to drag me home.

From then on, and for the rest of the week, my parents were entertained, regaled, as were my friends at school, by my impressions of Stan Laurel. But nobody really paid a lot of attention because every other kid on the block was doing his impressions of Stan Laurel. You would have to go to a far corner of the world to find somebody who doesn't do an impression of Stan Laurel.

There are hundreds of millions of people all over the world who felt the pang of sorrow when Stan left us, and it's impossible for anyone to speak for all of those people. All I can do is speak for myself and say how I felt about him. Stan's influence inspired me to go into show business in the first place, and his influence molded my point of view, my attitude about comedy. I had never met the man, but four years ago when I came to California I meant to meet Stan Laurel by hook or crook, and I wangled for a year, any way I could, to get his phone number, his address—anything that could put me in touch with him. Do you know where I finally found it? In the phone book, in a West Los Angeles phone book: Stan Laurel, Ocean Avenue, Santa Monica. I picked up the phone and received an invitation to come up there and visit.

When Stan passed away, his little desk there was awash with fan mail that had been pouring in from all over the world, as it had been during most of his later life. He insisted on sitting there at that little portable typewriter and answering every one of them, personally, and of course he was so far back—months and months behind in the answering—but he wouldn't give up. He never gave up on anything; he never gave up on life, and most of all, he never gave up that God-given mirth that he had.

In the wee hours of one of his last mornings on earth, a nurse came into Stan's room to give him emergency aid. Stan looked up and said, "You know what? I'd lot rather be skiing." The nurse said, "Do you ski, Mr. Laurel?" He said, "No! But I'd lot rather be skiing than doing this."

Stan once remarked that Chaplin and Lloyd made all the big pictures and he and Babe made all the little cheap ones. "But they tell me our little cheap ones have been seen by more people through the years than all the big ones. They must have seen how much love we put into them."

And that's what put Stan Laurel head and shoulders above all the rest of them—as an artist, and as a man. He put into his work that one special ingredient. He was a master comedian and he was a master artist—but he put in that one ingredient that can only come from the human being, and that was love. Love for his work, love for life, love for his audience—and how he loved that public. They were never squares or jerks to Stan Laurel.

Some of his contemporaries didn't criticize Stan favorably back in the thirties. Some of his contemporaries took great delight in showing their tools, and their skills, their methods on the screen; they were applauded because the audience could see their art. Stan was never really applauded for his art because he took too much care to hide it, to conceal the hours of hard creative work that went into his movies. He didn't want you to see that—he just wanted you to laugh, and you did!

You could never get him to pontificate about comedy. He was asked thousands of times, all through his life, to analyze comedy.

"What's funny?" he was always asked, and he always said: "How do I know? Can you analyze it? Can anybody? All I know is just how to make people laugh." That's all he knew!

Stan always believed that no comedy could depend merely on the spoken word, and all over the world, millions of people have laughed at Stan, who never understood one word he ever said.

His sense of humor was clean and it was kind. The worst things that ever happened in a Laurel and Hardy movie happened to Stan Laurel.

Stan was the creative one of the team, and the Babe liked that very much. His leisure hours were spent on the golf course. He was an easygoing, extroverted, happy man, and that was the way Ollie liked it. Stan found his fulfillment in the free hours that he spent at the studio—he loved working on new gags, on new ideas for comedy. Comedy was his whole life. Ollie had one well-known answer when anybody asked him about any of their current projects. He always said: "Ask Stan."

And that's a piece of advice that was still being taken during the last few years by every great comedian in the country, and all the other countries around the world. They all came to "ask Stan." That living room in that small apartment had been graced in the last few years by Jerry Lewis, Danny Kaye, Marcel Marceau, Red Skelton, and dozens and dozens of others who just came up to "ask Stan." They all recognized him as the greatest of them all. His sweetness to me, I'll never forget. Stan didn't let them down either when they went up there. He was just as aware of the world around him in 1965 as he was at any other time in his life, and he knew what was funny about it. And he could be the greatest today all over again.

I once tried to do an impression of Stan Laurel on my television show and I took meticulous care to get just the right kind of hat, the right kind of clothes, and to get everything down right. I put it on the air, and in a fever after the show, I called him up and said, "What did you think?" He said, "It was just fine, Dicky, but . . . ," and for the next forty minutes, he gave me a list of details that I had done wrong. He was a perfectionist. And then he just said, "God bless," and hung up. I wish I had a tape of that phone call: He said more things in there than I'll ever learn about my business, or the importance of human beings being able to laugh at themselves. A man like Stan Laurel taught millions and millions of people to laugh at themselves. Somehow when we lose a great leader, a great scientist, a great teacher, there always seems to be somebody to take their place. But the loss that we had with a man like Stan Laurel is a deep one because there doesn't seem to be anybody to take his place. He won't happen again because the world's a different place now.

Three generations of people found his comedy equally human, warm, and funny through his films, which he never owned. Maybe future generations will. But he will never happen again and the world seems to know it. Telegrams and phone calls poured in from almost every country in the world, expressing love and affection and grief at the news that Stan Laurel had left us.

There were some strange places that Stan and Ollie went—they never took a vacation for a long time, but once they took a tourist vacation and went to China. They were in the deepest part of the interior of China and, as tourists, they visited a Buddhist temple there. They were invited to come in and look at the altar, and there on the altar was a tremendous blowup in color of Ollie and Stan.

Once when they were in England, on a tour, they were surprised to find that wherever they went, they were mobbed by crowds of people. They didn't realize how much everyone loved them so. They were hiding in Cobh, Ireland, to get some quiet, and suddenly the churchbells of Cobh began to ring—playing "The Cuckoo Song." Stan said, "We both cried at that time, because of the love we felt coming from everyone."

Stan spent the last years of his life with a serious illness. Those were years shared by his wonderful wife, Ida. She was the only one who really knew about the pain and suffering that was behind that famous smile, that wonderful high-pitched giggle he had. She shared his memories with him. He has a daughter, Lois, and a son-in-law, Rand, and two grandchildren who had a better grandfather than Santa Claus could have been.

Stan and Ollie are both gone now, and I feel the halls of heaven must be ringing with divine laughter at that sweet pair. . . .

A number of years ago I found a poem that I liked very much, and after I got to know Stan, I sent it to him a couple of Christmases ago as a card, and he called me and said how much he loved it and he was going to keep it. It's called "A Prayer for Clowns."

God bless all clowns
Who star in the world with laughter
Who ring the rafters with flying jest,
Who make the world spin merry on its way
And somehow add more beauty to each day.

God bless all clowns
So poor the world would be
Lacking their piquant touch, hilarity,
The belly laughs, the ringing lovely mirth
That makes a friendly place of this earth.

God bless all clowns—
Give them a long good life.
Make bright their way—they're a race apart!
Alchemists most, who turn their hearts' pain
Into a dazzling jest to lift the heart.
God bless all clowns.

I'd just like to say to Stan what he always said to all of us when we took his leave: God bless.

1890	Born Arthur Stanley Jefferson in Ulverston, England. Son of a showman, Stan is raised in the English music halls.
1896	At 6, Stan is already doing comedy onstage in Wales.
1910	Tours America as Charlie Chaplin's understudy, but Chaplin's hardy constitution prevents him from once taking the stage. Decides to try his luck with vaudeville.
1917	Adopts "Laurel"—bestowed by actress/girlfriend Mae Dahlberg. The two have a tumultuous relationship; the abrasive Dahlberg becomes a prototype for a string of unsuitable women for Laurel.
1926	Signs with famous movie director Hal Roach to write and direct, but Roach has other plans, introducing him to Oliver "Babe" Hardy. The duo Laurel and Hardy is born. As "the thin one," Laurel develops well-known mannerisms—scratching his head when in doubt, crying when in trouble—to counter Hardy's beefy, exasperated persona. As the hands-on creative partner, Laurel writes, directs, and edits many of their movies.
1928	The duo receive their first star billing in *From Soup to Nuts.* They go on to do more than 100 films together.
1929	With fine voices, Laurel and Hardy make the successful transition to talkies. Behind the scenes, however, a frustrated Laurel has numerous run-ins with Roach over his low-budget approach to their movies.
1932	*The Music Box* earns the duo an Oscar for Best Short Subject.
1935	Divorces first wife Louis Neilson. Three more follow.
1940	Tired of cost-cutting, Laurel and Hardy leave Roach in search of greater creative control. They are given even less at Fox and MGM. Eventually they form their own production studio but are unable to replicate the success they enjoyed with Roach's guidance.

1946	Laurel marries fourth and final wife, Ida Kitaeva.
1956	Hardy suffers a massive stroke, which leaves him unable to speak. When visiting, Laurel doesn't speak either, amusing him with silly facial expressions. When Hardy dies the following year, an inconsolable Laurel stops performing but continues to write until his death.
1961	Receives a special Oscar for creative pioneering in comedy.
1965	Dies of a heart attack at 74, after warning his friends, "If anyone at my funeral has a long face, I'll never speak to him again."

GILDA RADNER

1946–1989

By ALAN ZWEIBEL, *longtime friend and writing partner*

Delivered at memorial service, June 1, 1989

Lorimar Studios, Culver City, CA

ABOUT FOURTEEN YEARS AGO I WAS HIDING BEHIND A potted plant and this girl asked if I could help her be a parakeet, and I've been smitten with Gilda ever since. When we met, we were just these two kids in a big city and, because we made each other laugh, people invited us places we never got to go before. And now? Well, I haven't mourned, and I haven't even cried yet, because even though she's dead, I just don't want her to die. I don't know why God makes people and then takes them back while they're still having fun with the life he gave them in the first place. Just like I don't know if I'm supposed to celebrate the fact that Gilda was in my life, or feel cheated that she's not here anymore. But even though her body grew to betray her, spirits just don't die. And that's what Gilda was. Even as an adult, she was still a little girl who believed in fairy tales and that if she said "Bunny Bunny" on the first day of every month, it would bring her love, laughter, and peace. Well, Gilda, this is June 1, and if you're in a place where you can't say it, I'll say it for you—"Bunny Bunny"—and I hope you're okay. I'm gonna miss you, Gilbert.

1946   Born in Detroit. Named after glamorous title character in Rita Hayworth's film, Gilda is re(nick)named Little Ham.

1960   Her father dies of brain cancer. Devastated, Gilda begins a life-long battle with eating disorders.

1966   Drops out of college and moves to Toronto, where she joins Second City troupe. In castmates John Candy, Dan Aykroyd, and John Belushi she finds fertile ground—honing her biting humor and improvisation skills. Television and film roles follow.

1974   Briefly meets Gene Wilder on the set of *Blazing Saddles*.

1975   Producer Lorne Michaels picks Radner to join *Saturday Night Live;* her audition consists of recounting her amazing Bingo skills (allegedly, Radner plays 14 cards at once). For five seasons, she introduces America to a host of striking characters and soon-to-be household mottoes: "That was so funny I almost forgot to laugh" and "It's always something!" At *SNL*, Radner tops the ratings and popularity surveys.

1977   Wins Emmy for her performance on *Saturday Night Live*.

1979   Launches hit show *Gilda Radner—Live from New York!*

1984   Marries Gene Wilder in South of France. The relationship had kindled on the set of *Hanky Panky* two years earlier.

1986   Diagnosed with ovarian cancer. Losing her hair, she opts for gravity-defying Roseanne Roseanna-Danna's wig—and co-opts Roseanna's catchphrase *It's Always Something* for her autobiography.

1988   Final TV performance on *The Gary Shandling Show*, where she cracks jokes about her condition (when Shandling asks where she's been, she ripostes, "I've had cancer. What's your excuse?").

1989   Dies in her sleep, age 42, on a Saturday night. Six years later, Radner's friends open the first Gilda's Club in New York City, offering free cancer support and laughter to all who enter its red door.

CHARLES SCHULZ

1922-2000

By CATHY GUISEWITE, *friend and colleague*

Delivered at memorial service, February 21, 2000

Burbank Center, Santa Rosa, CA

IT'S NIGHT. SNOOPY BAMS ON THE DOOR. CHARLIE BROWN gets out of bed, opens the door, and crouches down next to Snoopy on the porch. "Are you upset, little friend?" he asks. "Have you been lying awake, worrying? Well, don't worry. I'm here. I'm here to give you reassurance. Everything is all right. The floodwaters will recede. The famine will end. The sun will shine tomorrow and I will always be here to take care of you. Be reassured." Snoopy walks back to his doghouse. Charlie Brown gets in bed, pulls the covers up to his face, looks out, and asks, "Who reassures the reassurer?"

The world has lost the most beloved cartoonist of all time. The cartoonists of the world have lost our guiding light—our reassurer. Our amazing gentle hero, who made us want to drop to our knees and worship him at the same time he made us want to put our arms around him and tell him everything would be okay. That he wasn't really a failure. That for most people, raising five wonderful children, two stepchildren, and eighteen grandchildren who were totally devoted to you would kind of take you out of the loser category.

The most inspirational moment of my life was the day I was spiraling into my weekly creative coma and Sparky called me on the phone. The fact that he called, of course, was inspiring enough, because I'd never actually even recovered from the fact that Charles Schulz would speak to me, let alone that he would consider me part of the same profession he was in.

He said, "Hi, this is Sparky. I can't think of anything today."

I said, "What are you talking about? You're Charles Schulz."

"I just keep staring at these four miserable blank boxes. I can't think of anything."

"You're Charles Schulz," I said. "You're not me. Of course you can think of something."

He said, "I'm just like you. I can't think of anything, either."

What he did for me that day, he did for millions of others in zillions of ways. He gave us characters who knew exactly how we *felt*. Who made us feel we were never alone. And then he gave cartoonists himself and made us feel we were never alone. I think in the same way that he never forgot the exact moment when he dropped the ball in a baseball game sixty-nine years ago, he never forgot what it felt like to be a new cartoonist on the brink of global rejection, so he called us up. He looked at our work. He encouraged us, commiserated with us. He made us feel he was exactly like us.

And he was, except for a couple of little differences. . . .

Sparky had the exact same deadlines we all do, except he had no assistants on the comic strip. Also, he had 25 zillion licensed products, forty-something animated specials, a Saturday-morning TV series, four feature films, a Broadway hit, fourteen hundred books, part of a theme park, thousands of pieces of mail a week, five children, two stepchildren, and eighteen grandchildren to worry about.

While the rest of us stuff down junk food at our drawing boards, screaming that we can't take the pressure, Sparky found time to walk over to the ice arena each day for a nice lunch! While some of us begged for vacations because we were cracking under the stress, Sparky worked three months ahead of his strip so he could have heart surgery without missing a day.

While some of us whine about the shrinking space for comics, Sparky was given a smaller space than any other cartoonist in 1950, and created a new style of art and writing so eloquent and perfect that every single one of us has tried to copy something from it.

While some of us insist on pushing the boundaries of subject matter to keep our work fresh, Sparky drew a personal code of ethics for himself, stricter than an editor would have, and brilliantly stayed within his own lines for more than eighteen thousand strips.

He worked in handsome slacks and nice sweaters and never got ink all over himself. He wrote about doomed romances, D-minuses, and emotional disasters, and took the millions of dollars that he could have spent on therapy and quietly gave it away to causes that mattered to him and to his family.

He elevated our profession with his gracious, dignified manner. Raised our standards with his astounding consistency and commitment. Made us proud of what we do. Everyone in the room always felt more important when Sparky was in it.

Several years ago, a group of us was invited to visit some underprivileged children. We sat at a long table with paper and markers, and the kids immediately hurried past me and the other cartoonists to form a line in front of Sparky. I remember wondering what it must feel like to know you've touched so many people in such a profound way that everyone, from grandparents to tiny children, just wanted something to prove they'd been in your presence.

I remember watching in awe as the first little boy stepped up to Sparky to get his autograph. Sparky leaned down and asked the little boy what he'd like him to draw. And I remember this sweet, shy little face looking up at Sparky and answering, "Popeye. Can you draw Popeye?"

Sparky, of course, could.

And somewhere out there, someone owns a fabulous Popeye signed by Charles Schulz.

Sparky loved comic strips more than anyone I ever met. He left his mark on the comic pages not just with his characters, but with all the characters created by those who were inspired and encouraged by him, who would never have done this for a living if it weren't for him.

Many cartoonists will spend the rest of their lives defining success by whether or not Sparky would have liked the strip we drew that day. We'll write about the insecurities because he paved the way. We'll draw in simple lines because he taught us how. We'll wail "aaugh" and "bleah" and "rats" because he did it first.

And on those days when it all seems so useless and demoralizing, when we're disgusted and frustrated and out of hope, we'll sit quietly, look at a *Peanuts* comic strip, and receive Sparky's eternal gift to all of us: We'll be reassured.

1922	Born in Minneapolis, MN, the only child of Dena and Carl Schulz. Nicknamed Sparky by an uncle.
1934	Gets Spike, "the smartest and most uncontrollable dog I have ever seen"—and later the inspiration for beloved cartoon beagle Snoopy.
1943	Drafted, Schulz serves as squad leader in Germany, Austria, and France, but sees little combat. Once refuses to attack an artillery encampment because he sees a dog wander inside. "The army taught me all I needed to know about loneliness."
1947	Draws *L'il Folks* panel cartoon for local paper.
1950	After multiple rejections, Schulz sells his strip to United Feature Syndicate—they rename it *Peanuts* (a title he hates). Based on a round-headed Charlie Brown and his existential beagle Snoopy, *Peanuts* debuts in seven papers. Schulz is paid $90/week.
1951	Marries Joyce Halverson.
1953	*Peanuts* is a bona fide hit, earning Schulz $30,000/year. "Good grief" and "security blanket" enter the lexicon. Schulz on the strip's appeal: "All the loves are unrequited; all the baseball games are lost; all the test scores are D-minuses; the Great Pumpkin never comes; and the football is always pulled away."
1960	*A Charlie Brown Christmas* debuts on television, winning an

Emmy the next year and immortality in reruns. Despite success, Schulz is plagued by panic attacks and chronic depression.

1972   Divorces Joyce. "I don't think she liked me anymore, and I just got up and left one day." The following year, he meets Jeannie Clyde in an ice rink and marries her.

1975   *Peanuts'* 25th anniversary: The sage comic is now read by 355 million people around the world, in 2,600 papers, in 21 languages—and brings Schulz endorsements of $1 billion a year.

1981   Undergoes quadruple bypass surgery.

1986   Inducted into Cartoonist Hall of Fame.

2000   Diagnosed with colon cancer, Schulz lays down his pen, swearing that *Peanuts* won't be drawn by anyone else. "This is my excuse for existence. No one else will touch it." Just hours before the Sunday papers carry his last strip, Schulz dies in his sleep. At 18,250 strips, the saga of Charlie Brown becomes the longest story ever told by one human being.

ANDREW CARNEGIE

1835–1919

By JOHN H. FINLEY, *friend and golf partner*

Delivered at memorial service, April 20, 1920

Engineering Societies Building, New York City

HE WAS A WEAVER'S LAD—THIS BOY BEARING THE NAME of the practical disciple, Andrew, who became the patron saint of Scotland. I say "practical," for it was Andrew who said when asked how the thousands on the shores of Galilee were to be fed: "There is a lad here which hath five barley loaves and two small fishes, but what are they among so many?" And had this disciple beheld, in the year of his Lord 1847, in the land to which he had become patron saint, the want and misery due to the stopping of the hand looms by the coming of steam machines, and had then seen this wee Dunfermline lad, he might have made much the same remark: "There's a lad here wi' his five senses and twa' sma' han's, but what are they amang sae mony?"

We say that it was a miracle that was performed on the shores of Galilee, when the boy's meager store was suddenly multiplied to feed the thousands. Was it not as great a miracle that the seemingly petty store of the weaver's lad was transformed (in what is but a moment of time in His sight, to whom a thousand years are but as yesterday)—transformed not only into food, but books and music and pictures and other human blessings, and not for a few thousands only, but for millions?

In this miracle the Scotch lad had, to be sure, an active, aggressive, shrewd part, but it was no less a miracle, and it was one (and I say it in all reverence) that could not have been wrought even by the Almighty with the aid of this eager lad anywhere else than in the free air of America.

I am informed that there are mysterious substances known to chemists as "catalysts," which have such potency that they bring into solution elements before seemingly insoluble and yet are themselves apparently unchanged—substances often so infinitesimal in relation to the effects they produce that it is as if you were to dissolve a whole island by throwing a few crystals upon it. So the catalytic, robust, sunny spirit of this youth, who never grew old, did incomparable, incommensurate things in the earth.

It was not merely nor chiefly that he touched the ore that was lying in the far hills beyond Superior, and transferred it from there into a girder, a bridge, a steel rail, a bit of armor plate, a beam for a skyscraper, and in utter silence, as I have witnessed the process in the flaming shreds of Pittsburgh, with the calm pushing and pulling of a few levers, the accurate shoveling by a few hands, and the deliberate testing by a few eyes—wonderful as that all was and is.

And it was not even that in every luminous, white-hot ingot swung in the steel mills in the smoky valley of the Youghiogheny there was something for the pension of a university professor, something for an artist in New York or Paris, something for an astronomer on a California mountain, something for a mathematician over his computations, something for the historian over his archives, something for the teacher in the school upon the hill above, something for every worshiper in hundreds of kirks and churches, something for every one of hundreds of thousands of readers in libraries from Scotland to California, as a result of the multiplication of the childish store in his hands as he stood an immigrant lad on the shores of America, with a "fair and free field" before him. For besides those there were gifts to millions more than were reached directly and indirectly by the steel ingots. These were gifts of the alchemy of his personality that touched the spirits and imaginations of men. The material gifts were like those of Prometheus, who bestowed upon mortal man the "bright glory of fire that all arts spring from." His supreme gifts to mankind were, however, not those of a demi-god, a Titan, working with the elements of the earth and looking down upon them as inferior creatures for whom he had made sacrifices. They were those of a very human mortal man who loved his fellowmen, who suffered and fought and wept and rejoiced with them as one of them.

He no doubt would not wish me to trace the name Andrew, which his Scotch mother gave him, back to the Greek, but it was in its origin Greek nonetheless, the Greek name for "man," and he might have belonged to any age of men beginning with that of Moses or Pericles. He could have stood unembarrassed before any ruler from Pharaoh to Napoleon, and did so stand before the emperors, kings, and presidents of his own day. Long before he became famous for his wealth, I have read, he was a personal friend of Gladstone, Matthew Arnold, Herbert Spencer, John Morley, and James Bryce. And after he had become a world figure, he was still the friend of the lowliest and the poorest.

He was a triumphant democrat with a genius for friendships, a passionate love for America—with an international mind having an orbit of concern for the cosmos (but with Dunfermline and Pittsburgh as its two foci), and with a love for all things beautiful, but with a preordained taste for that which had a Caledonian form or fragrance or melody in it: the "auld gray toon"; the abbey bell sounding the curfew; the scent of the heather; "songs possessed of souls caught from living lips"; the Scotch mist, even, which served to remind him "of the mysterious ways of Providence."

And yet he was not servile to his ancestry, the strain of whose thoughts had run through the "radical breasts" (a phrase he has himself used) of his parents. In his love for the voice of the organ, for example, he doubtless shocked many of his psalm-singing compatriots as did David when he danced before the ark of the Lord. And how pleased Mr. Carnegie would be with the program of this afternoon, dominated by music and crowned by an oratorio, of which he expressed such discerning appreciation in his delightful story of his travels in Great Britain, for he once said that those who thought music an unworthy intruder in the domains of sacred dogma "should remember that the Bible tells us that in heaven music is the principal source of happiness—the sermons seem nowhere—and it may go hard with such as fail to give it the first place on earth."

He has unwittingly, no doubt, made the best characterization of himself in the definition of every Scotchman, who is "two Scotchmen":

As his land has the wild, barren, stern crags and mountain peaks around which the tempests blow, and also the smiling valleys below where the wild rose, the foxglove and the bluebell blossom, so the Scotchman, with his rugged and hard intellect in his head above, has a heart below capable of being touched to the finest issues. . . . Poetry and Song are part of his nature. Touch his head and he will begin and argue with you to the last; touch his heart and he falls upon his breast.

These two men did not struggle against each other in the one energetic, restless body, but helped each other. The poet enhanced the deed (for as Mr. Carnegie said, "To do things is only one half the battle; to be able to tell the world what you have done—that is the greater accomplishment"). And the hardheaded man put the poetry into everyday life, with an enchanting book, or the celestial voice of an organ, or an illuminating statistic, or an eternal truth for the first time discovered, or a telescope revealing the differing glory of the stars, or the stirring voice of the bagpipes making the day, or a symphony ending it.

The Scotch minister whom I heard preach this morning referred to a little shop in Edinburgh in whose window little figures of kings and queens and princes and others were displayed, with the sign (which has given title to one of Robert Louis Stevenson's essays), "A Penny Plain, Twopence Colored." Mr. Carnegie's figures were all colored—colored by his generous, warm heart.

The two Scotchmen in him were held together in happy partnership by an American tolerance, a New World breadth of generosity (which is not usually associated with the Scotch), and a Western humor which had, however, a tang of the moors in it, and was overconscious of the ethics of the golf links. I have a vivid memory of one characteristic bit of his kindly, quiet wit at my own expense. We had played a few holes in my first game of golf with him, when my conscience, beginning to trouble me, provoked me to question whether I ought to be out in the country away from my work playing golf with him. "Oh," he said, quick as a flash, "Pritchett and I will both certify that you are not playing golf."

And when we played our last game together, it was out by the Dornoch Firth, in the first days of the Great War in August of 1914. After he had finished the game, which he must have divined would be his last, he gave me his putter with this inscription in his own hand: "A very close game: couldn't have been closer so equally and badly we play."

Ah! If we could all but play the game of life as manfully and cheerfully, as eagerly, as fearlessly, as hopefully, and with as kind a heart as he, we might be proud of our score, even though he, a Scotchman, would go no farther than to admit of his own "it micht ha' bin waur."

> *Beyond the dark Brook of the Shadow he's gone*
> *On over the hills and the moors toward the dawn,*
> *This Laird o the castle by Dornoch's gray Firth*
> *To find the Great Palace he had sought for the earth.*

1835   Born in Dunfermline, Scotland, to a working-class family. When his father loses his weaving job to steam-powered looms, his mother opens a small grocery shop to support the family.

1848 Hoping for deliverance from their poverty, Andrew's mother borrows 20 pounds to pay their fare to America.

1849 Andrew secures work as a messenger boy in Pittsburgh. On his rounds, he meets Thomas Scott, a railroad executive. Scott later offers Andrew $35/month to be his private secretary. Andrew: "I couldn't imagine what I could ever do with so much money."

1859 Carnegie is promoted to superintendent of the Pennsylvania Railroad.

1865 Guided by what he calls "flashes," Carnegie founds the Keystone Bridge Company, which builds bridges with iron rather than wood. A year later he founds the Keystone Telegraph Company.

1872 Visiting Bessemer steel plants in England, Carnegie realizes the commercial potential of steel.

1875 Opens his first steel plant, Edgar Thomson Works, named for the president of the Pennsylvania Railroad. Unsurprisingly, his first order for 2000 rails is placed by the Railroad.

1886 Marries 37-year-old Louise Whitfield.

1886 Writes and publishes "The Gospel of Wealth," suggesting that the wealthy have a moral obligation to society.

1892 In a move that would haunt him, Carnegie helps beat down the Homestead Strike by hiring Pinkerton thugs to intimidate strikers. Ten people are killed in the ensuing battle. Carnegie's reputation as champion of the worker is irreparably tarnished.

1899 Organizes several of his companies into Carnegie Steel.

1901 J. P. Morgan buys Carnegie Steel for $480 million. "Congratulations," Morgan says, "you are now the richest man in the world."

1902 Believing "he who dies rich, dies disgraced," Carnegie begins giving his fortune away. Two decades of philanthropy ensue, focused on institutions like libraries, universities, and world peace organizations. Struggling scientist Marie Curie receives a grant.

1919 Dies at his estate in Massachusetts, age 84, having given away $350 million and spawned the growth of a nation. His gravestone simply reads "Andrew Carnegie."

HENRY FORD

1863 – 1947

By EDGAR A. GUEST, *longtime friend*

Delivered on a national radio broadcast, October 1, 1947

I WOULD LIKE TO TELL YOU ABOUT A TRULY GREAT FRIEND of mine and a benefactor of all mankind, known to presidents, potentates, princes, and the humble peoples of every land upon the earth, as Henry Ford.

Among those of us who knew him well he will walk no more, but so long as human achievements are cherished and remembered, his name will be a living force and an inspiration to all the generations to follow.

Henry Ford has been called in the midst of his eighty-third year to join the great of the earth. Tonight he knows the answer to the mystery of life and death of which he often thought and talked. Life to him was a thrilling experience; a never-ending struggle for the perfection of the human soul. Among the few who have come closest to attaining that perfection in a single lifetime, his name must be recorded.

We are all his debtors now. There is none of us—rich or poor, in humble or high place—whose life has not been bettered by his labor. He came into the world when the backs of men were weary and heavy-laden. By the dreams he had, pursued, and achieved, the burdens of drudgery were taken from the shoulders of the humble and given to steel and wheel.

He would not have us mourn for him too deeply. He knew that his loved ones and friends would be saddened by his absence, but as he was often heard to say: "There is too much to do in a day to spend minutes of it in the futility of grief."

Once when he was asked by one who now and then walked the woods with him in springtime if he had not wished that his mother could have lived long enough to have seen and shared the glory of his triumphs, in the quiet and quaint way he had, he said softly: "I can think of no one who has gone whom I would recall."

Henry Ford had the gift of genius. Genius, though brilliant, can be bitter at times, harsh and selfish and disinterested in the lives of others. Henry Ford never showed those traits.

His was a sensitive heart and his was an understanding mind. He had known hardship and the pangs of disappointment. He had known the agony of wanting comforts for his loved ones which he could not supply. He had known what it means to be poor of purse, and he could and did read the eyes of the unhappy. He had both sympathy and pity for the woes of others.

It was out of that feeling for his fellows the five-dollar-a-day wage came when the daily universal rate of pay for a workman was a little less than two dollars. He called it good business to have as many contented men about him as was possible. It took courage of a rare sort to lead the way to a decent living wage for the common man.

Henry Ford woke early every morning eager to greet the day and all it held for him. Nothing was too small for him to notice. He loved the earth and all it grew and all that dwells upon it. He knew the birds by name and song and habits, and found peace and happiness in their company.

He loved to escape and talk with humble men. He often said: "You can learn more from the thoughts of simple folk than you can from those of the learned and the wise. Wise minds know what can't be done, and they don't find out the things that can be done until someone not so wise comes along and tries them and does them."

Henry Ford will be missed. He will be missed in many places

where kindness is still needed; he will be missed when righting a wrong and fighting injustice is required; he will be missed by all the creatures of the woods and fields who found in him a friend; and he will be missed by many a struggling youth to whom a word of hope and encouragement would mean so much.

What an example he has set for boyhood to look up to and to follow! His life for generations to come will be a beacon of life for all ambitious youths. I can hear his voice whispering down the years to young dreamers everywhere: "It can be done! Follow your light and learn by your patient practice. Let neither sneer nor mockery daunt you. Believe in yourself; have faith in your ability and your purpose. Success will surely follow."

> *Not many come to earth so wise,*
> *So tender and so true,*
> *To show what faith and enterprise*
> *And willing hands can do.*
> *He proved how great a man can be*
> *And so much to us.*
> *Now, Lord, we give him back to Thee,*
> *A soul victorious.*

1863	Born the first of six children, in Dearborn, MI, where he grows up on the family farm.
1879	At 16, he apprentices with a machinist in Detroit.
1891	Becomes an engineer with Edison Illuminating Company and experiments with projects like internal combustion engines.
1893	Wife Clara gives birth to their only child, Edsel.
1896	Invents the Quadricycle—a carriage atop four wheels, mounted with a gasoline engine—and drives it through the streets of Detroit.

1903	Ford Motor Company is incorporated with $28,000. The new company produces only a few cars per day at its Detroit factory.
1908	Ford introduces the Model T—the first affordable, reliable, easy-to-operate car. A huge success, the Model T issues in a new era of personal transportation and urbanization.
1913	Introduces a continuous moving assembly line, resulting in cars manufactured in 93 minutes instead of 728. Ford becomes the largest automaker in the world. The following year, he increases factory wages to $5 per day (twice the industry average) and reduces the workshift to eight hours. Overnight, Ford becomes a worldwide celebrity—praised as a humanitarian or denounced as a socialist.
1914	Opposed to the war, Ford charters an ocean liner to take him and a party of pacifists to Norway, hoping to end the war through mediation.
1918	Loses his bid for the U.S. Senate.
1919	After a lengthy dispute, Ford buys out all seven minority shareholders and installs his son, Edsel, as president of the Ford Motor Company. By now, fully half the cars in America are Model T's.
1927	The company turns out a $290 Model T every 24 seconds. At its zenith, the Ford Motor Company holdings extend to factories in 33 countries, but Ford loses his strong hold on the market—most famously by refusing to offer the Model T in any color but black.
1932	A paternalistic authoritarian, Ford resists unionization efforts by employing company police and labor spies. His "Sociology Department" fires workers who gamble, have union sympathies, or have health or financial problems.
1941	Finally signs an agreement with the United Auto Workers.
1947	Dies at his Dearborn home, age 83. His stock holdings go to the Ford Foundation, instantly making it the richest private foundation in the world.

DAVID OGILVY

1911–1999

By JOCK ELLIOTT, *chairman of Ogilvy and Mather and longtime friend*

Delivered at memorial service, September 15, 1999

Lincoln Center, New York City

DAVID, YOU ALWAYS WERE THE CHAMPION AT BEING THE center of attention. But I never knew you were this good. On May 22, 1983, you wrote a memo titled "My Death." You said, in part: "No memorial service, unless Ogilvy and Mather wants to have one in New York for the staff of the agency; friends or relatives could go to that if they wished. No religious content—not even black tie. I don't want the ceremony to take place unless it is built around the following music, which would be expensive:

"The Hallelujah Chorus, with professional choir and big orchestra.

"Rule Britannia—three verses.

"The audience is to leave the auditorium to the happy strains of a high jig."

David, thy will be done. As usual. I am wearing my red Ogilvy tie. As a matter of fact, this isn't a "memorial service" anyway. It is a gathering of your clan.

My most recent memory is of your funeral. It was lovely. Your Herta had arranged everything. She was just . . . remarkable. At your beloved Touffou, of course, in the sunny gardens you planned and began to plant thirty years ago. Family, some locals—your old gardener Lami, quite feeble, was there—three or four dignitaries from nearby towns, a few of your close friends from the area, and five of your longtime partners.

Two bagpipers from Scotland, playing a lament, led your coffin, which was covered in your Mackenzie tartan. The coffin was shouldered—shouldered, mind you, none of this wheeling business—by six young hefty family members. It was placed on a stand under a Catalpa tree, alongside a rough cross that Alain had made.

Your friend, the curé from the village, Père Dhumeau, conducted the ecumenical service, after your son David had welcomed everyone. There were a few short remarks, readings, prayers, and a blessing. I think you would have approved, except perhaps for the sprinkling of holy water. Then you were off, on those shoulders again, the pipers playing happy airs, and the rest of us following behind. And we said good-bye to you, our dear David.

But my earliest memories of you go back thirty-nine years. In those days, you worked in the office until seven. Then you packed your unfinished business into a briefcase *and* an old brown leather suitcase, and headed home in the Rolls. Your house was next door to Walter Cronkite's, on Eighty-fourth Street. Walter once told me that, from his backyard, he would see you working at your desk in the window, night after night, hour after hour. In the morning, your letters had been answered, your plans outlined, your staff memos written. And we all had our marching orders. Holy smoke! You were disciplined.

The day after I joined your agency, I was invited—no, told—to come to your Magic Lantern show. "Magic Lantern"—what a beguiling label for slide presentations on how to create good advertising. At the time, nobody much taught advertising; one learned on the job, if one learned anything at all. You were a student of the business, and of advertising research. You were the greatest *teacher* of advertising ever. I learned more in my first year with you than in the previous fifteen.

Back in the early sixties, we prepared a campaign to "Clean Up New York." I was to announce it at a press conference. Ahead of time, I gave you the draft of my five-minute talk to "Please improve." You changed "the people who litter our streets" to "the barbarians who litter our streets." Only *one word* changed. Needless to say, I was full of myself. Next day, the headline on the *New York Times* story read, "Barbarians litter our streets." That took me down a peg. David, you were a genius with words. The copywriter's copywriter.

Now, I don't want to let you off scot-free. You were not always the easiest person in the world to work with. You were a perfectionist. No matter how good, everything had to be better, better. But more than that, when things weren't going to your liking, you could sink into a funk. Or blow your stack. Once you even threatened to go off and start your own agency. My goodness, your explosions were . . . well, alarming. You believed so passionately in the right course for your agency. More than once, you stalked out of a board meeting, and I had to chase you down to cajole you into coming back. Never mind. It kept us on our toes. Besides, you were usually right.

Big ideas. Some of the biggest ideas, David, had nothing to do with your famous ads. They were born of your vision. One example: You knew that you would not always be there to guide us, that you had to institutionalize your agency, and so you came up with the Big Idea of Crown Princes and Princesses. We had to identify our ablest young men and women worldwide so that they could get special training, special nurturing. Thus was our corporate culture—your culture— passed on.

These snapshots from my memory bank hardly begin to reflect your bigness, David. What made you a giant? I am rash enough to try to answer. You were born with a fine mind and a large personality. You had the curiosity and the energy to furnish your mind richly through- out your life. You had the sense—the theatrical sense—to let your per- sonality bloom and to put it to good use. More than anything, you wanted to be the best. And, unlike most of us, you unfailingly did your best.

David, you played a greater role in my adult life than anyone but my Elly. You hired me. You taught me my trade. You tugged me along on a lead rein until you made me chairman. But even as chairman, I knew the rein was still there—in case. You made me rich. Well, not really rich. Rich enough. For all these things, I thank you.

I thank you for the standards you set for all of us—standards of discipline, standards of hard work, of vision, of style, of candor, of civility.

I thank you for making us proud—proud of you and proud to be part of your agency, our agency.

Finally, I thank you for being my friend, David.

1911	Born in West Horsley, England.
1924	Attends Fettes boarding school on scholarship.
1929	Enrolls at Oxford to study history, but is—in his own words—a "dud" who cannot pass his exams. The following year, he takes a job as a chef at the Majestic Hotel, Paris.
1935	Joins the London advertising agency of Mather & Crowther, and discovers his passion. "I loved advertising. I devoured it. I studied and read and took it desperately seriously." Three years later, Ogilvy persuades his firm to send him to the U.S. to study American advertising.
1942	During the war, Ogilvy works a stint with British Intelligence at the British embassy in Washington. Subsequent jobs include Pennsylvania farmer, pollster, and director of the New York Philharmonic.
1948	Launches his own agency, Ogilvy & Mather, in New York with "no credentials, no clients, and only $6000 in the bank." He is 38. The agency goes on to become an international empire with billings of $8 billion a year. His philosophy? Find a character or symbol to communicate the brand, then turn the brand into a byword. Clients soon include Rolls-Royce, Merrill Lynch, Pepperidge Farm, Puerto Rico, Shell Oil, Dove Soap, and Sears & Roebuck.
1963	Publishes *Confessions of an Advertising Man*. The book becomes an

international best-seller translated into 14 languages. Typical advice: "Advertising should be true, credible, and pleasant. People do not buy from bad-mannered liars."

1966	Ogilvy & Mather goes public.
1973	Marries third and final wife, Herta. Retires at Chateau Touffou, a 14th-century castle in France, where he works tirelessly in his gardens.
1983	Publishes *Ogilvy on Advertising*, his second best-seller.
1999	Dies at Chateau Touffou, after a year of declining health. In a career spanning five decades, Ogilvy created not only an advertising empire but also a new ethos: Consumers are intelligent. "The consumer is not a moron. She is your wife. Try not to insult her intelligence."

JOHN D. ROCKEFELLER JR.
1874-1960

By DR. ROBERT J. MCCRACKEN, *friend*

Delivered at memorial service, June 8, 1960

The Riverside Church, New York City

WE ARE GATHERED TOGETHER TODAY IN SORROW OF heart and mind. With millions around the world we mourn the passing of a great and good man. Yet with our sorrow are mingled gratitude and thanksgiving for powers nobly employed, for a task well done, for service rendered to humanity with a rare distinction and consecration.

Mr. Rockefeller would be the last person to wish a eulogy pronounced upon him. Some men are forever courting observation, are never so happy as when basking in the sunshine of popular approval. He was not one of them. With all the weight and influence at his command, he was the most unassuming of men, innately modest and humble. For all that, he would, I think, be gratified at our assembling in such large numbers to bear witness to the indefatigable toil of the long years. He would wish above all that we would ever more zealously serve the great causes for which he labored.

Few men have so readily and consistently followed a clearly envisaged career of public service. He saw it unfolding before him like a rolled-up scroll, hiding its inner secrets till their time should come. But it unrolled without confusion because from the beginning there was no fluctuation in his life purpose. Through youth, manhood, old age he heard and responded to a call summoning him to serve his day and generation by the will of God.

What he did for the good of humanity is beyond reckoning. While time is needed to appraise in proper perspective the significance of any life, we can be certain that his name will stand out in the social history of our century. The list of his good works and benefactions is endless, and too well known to call for recital here. No province of life—religion, education, medicine, the arts, science, the social sciences—was overlooked. Not only so, he shaped the whole pattern of public giving. With his associates—how often he talked about his associates!—he worked out criteria of giving so wise and sound that he left his mark on the principles and practice of scores of foundations, large and small. Moreover, he transmitted his convictions and sense of stewardship to his sons and daughter, and to his grandchildren. Today the name Rockefeller is equated with humanitarianism and global philanthropy.

"Money," we say, "talks"—often, alas, ostentatiously, extravagantly, selfishly. Mr. Rockefeller made it talk in an altogether different fashion. He was fond of Barrie's saying that we cheat our consciences when we speak about filthy lucre, because money can be a beautiful thing, and if it is grimy, it is we who make it so. For Mr. Rockefeller money was an extension of personality, a sacramental thing, quite literally a means of grace—curing sickness, dispelling ignorance, creating beauty, making the desert places of life bloom like the rose. The question of motivation arises. With him it was more than fellow feeling, social concern, humanitarianism. It was the conviction that his vast fortune was not his own to do with as he pleased but was a sacred trust for whose rightful use he would be called to account by Almighty God. John Buchan, writing of Julius Caesar, observed, "We know the things he did, but not why he did them." With our friend it was the other way around.

We have another saying, Lord Acton's "Power corrupts." It testifies to the fact that men are continually tempted to use their power for their own selfish ends and to impose their will on others. Here, however, was a personality unspoiled by prominence and prestige, unfailingly courteous and considerate, never domineering or arrogant. We have been thinking of what he did, yet what he did is explained by what he was. Those who knew him best marveled at his industry. Bred in the Puritan tradition, he was staunchly self-disciplined and governed by a strong sense of duty to God and man. He put a vast amount of work through his hands and was attentive not only to great issues but to minor details. A hard worker himself, he respected application and efficiency wherever he encountered them and could make nothing of the dilettante and the slacker.

Especially notable was his integrity. He was the soul of honor. Nobody who knew him could conceive of him doing anything mean or small. Many, working with him in close quarters, can testify that one could always go to him and be sure that any advice he might give would be based on high principle. His moral sense was sound, his word was his bond, he could be absolutely depended upon. "A man," Kipling told the undergraduates of St. Andrew's University of Scotland, "may be festooned with all the haberdashery of success, and go to his grave a castaway." The one thing that lasts is character. It is the only thing we take with us into the other world. Mr. Rockefeller had it.

Its source and inspiration were rooted in his religion. His belief in the God and Father of our Lord Jesus Christ provides the deepest explanation alike of his sterling qualities and of his consuming concern for the public good. Always grateful for his father's influence, from his mother he absorbed the piety that was the hallmark of his life. It was the most distinctive thing about him and of the sincerest, simplest, and profoundest sort. There can be no doubt whence he derived his master motives. We know the things he did, and we know why he did them. To account for Mr. Rockefeller without reference to his Christian faith would be like accounting for Winston Churchill without reference to England. . . .

It is inconceivable that all is over for Mr. Rockefeller. There must surely be other ministries for him in other spheres.

Hail and farewell. The laurels with the dust
Are leveled, but thou hast thy surer crown,
Peace, and immortal calm, the victory won.
Somewhere serene thy watchful power inspired;
Thou are a living purpose, being dead,
A fount of nobleness in lesser lives,
A guardian and a guide; hail and farewell.

1874	Born in Cleveland, OH. His father John D. Rockefeller Sr. is founder of Standard Oil—the largest corporation in the country.
1883	The Rockefellers move to New York City.
1887	Age 13, John Jr. suffers a nervous collapse due to "overwork."
1897	Graduates from Brown University. Going to work for his father, Rockefeller comments, "From the outset he trusted me, knowing that I shared fully his high ideas of business integrity and social responsibility."
1901	Marries Abbie Aldrich, daughter of Rhode Island senator.
1903	Daughter Abby is born, dubbed "the richest of all babies" by the press. Five sons follow: John III, Nelson, Laurence, Winthrop, and David.
1910	Leaves Standard Oil to devote himself to philanthropy; the following year, the company is declared a monopoly and dismantled by the Supreme Court.
1913	With sale of Standard Oil, Rockefeller's wealth has reached an all-time high of $900 million. He establishes the Rockefeller Foundation to "promote the well-being of mankind throughout the world," endowing it with $100 million.
1914	World War I begins. The Rockefellers donate millions to relief agencies.

1922 Believing that "man is a human first and a member of industry afterward," Rockefeller leads a movement against the 12-hour workday. Complaining of exhaustion and migraines, he checks into Kellogg Battle Creek Sanitarium.

1929 The stock market crash wipes out more than half the Rockefeller fortune.

1930 Deeply interested in matters of religion, Rockefeller becomes a leader in the interfaith movement. "Only a united Christian world can stem the rising tide of materialism, of selfishness, of shaken traditions. . . ." With a $26 million grant from Rockefeller, the Riverside Church opens in Manhattan.

1939 Ceremoniously drives the last rivet into newly completed Rockefeller Center. More than 75,000 people worked on its construction during the Depression years.

1946 Rockefeller purchases land on New York City's East River for $8 million and donates it to the United Nations. "If this property can be useful to you in meeting the great responsibility entrusted to you by the people of the world, it will be a source of infinite satisfaction to me and my family."

1948 Abbie dies. Three years later he marries Martha Baird Allen, concert pianist and widow of an old friend.

1960 Dies at 86, having given more than $537 million to educational, cultural, medical, environmental, and other charitable projects.

CHARLES TIFFANY

1812–1902

By ANNABEL A. GOAN, *friend*

Delivered at memorial service, February 20, 1902

Madison Square Presbyterian Church, New York City

WHEN THE COMMUNITY LOSES A PROMINENT MAN LIKE Mr. Charles L. Tiffany, who died February 18, the world is interested in learning the causes of his success and what his influence has been upon his fellows. Few men have a strenuous business life of seventy years. Half that time is the usual length of a man's active connection with the business community, but Mr. Tiffany, from the time of the administration of President Jackson, was a potent factor in the commercial life of New York.

His great business was unique in its command of public confidence and in the harmony of its internal organization. The principle upon which he worked from the beginning to the end of his long career was "to give the public the best quality of goods and the finest service that could be secured." This was his unceasing endeavor. He established a standard in silverware that raised the quality of silver sold not only throughout the United States but in Europe also. He had an ideal for his business and he lived up to it. Absolute undeviating honesty, even in the smallest detail of the business, was the key note.

A lady traveling in Japan was questioning the Japanese Commissioner of Education about the integrity of a certain prominent Japanese merchant. "You can rely on his word," he answered, "as you can on that of the famous Mr. Tiffany of New York. You know his word is unquestioned the world over." That sort of a reputation is not made in a day or by simply having honest intentions and impulses, but by living up to one's conscientious standard every day and by having sufficient force to require others to do likewise.

Mr. Tiffany was a strict disciplinarian and, like other successful men, had a discriminating insight into human character and was an excellent judge of men and their capacity. His men were selected with care and retained for many years; they were as devoted and faithful a body of men as could be found anywhere. Their term of service ranged from fifty years down, over a hundred having been with him over a quarter of a century. This long term of service was also true of the domestics in his home.

There was a personal tie between Mr. Tiffany and his employees more binding than a merely business connection that sweetened life on both sides. They really cared for each other.

During those past months of his confinement, the tender attentions of these many men, more freely expressed than in the days of his robust health, were received by him with a lively appreciative gratitude. Among the numerous gifts sent to the sickroom was a basket of choice fruit marked "From the boys to our beloved chief." Long after the fruit was gone, he kept the basket and card where he could see them. That he had the love and esteem of the men who worked for him and with him every day and knew him better than any others could was a great comfort to him as he approached the closing days of his life.

None knew better than he how to show a delicate attention, and every little kindness extended to him received his personal acknowledgment. In these days of careless manners, Mr. Tiffany was conspicuous for the dignity of his bearing and his courtesy of the olden time, a happy reminder of that stately generation of fastidious men and women of which he was one of the few eminent examples left to us. He impressed a stranger as a man of cool reserve, but to those who were admitted to his friendship, he was a man of intense enthusiasm. To those who had his friendship, it will be a most cherished memory.

His influence over younger men was not toward luxurious living, as might be supposed, but toward a marked simplicity. He admired economy.

He had no scheme for the salvation of the human race, but his unconscious personal influence upon those who came within its range was tremendously helpful, stimulating one to do one's best.

It is a privilege to have known a man who was absolutely sincere; who failed not in fidelity to his largest and smallest duties; who had an unswerving sense of justice of man to man; who had lifted a business out of the usual sordidness until, by its successful organization, it was more like a social work of art with which men were proud to have their names identified and to which they were glad to give loving service.

Perhaps never again will this personal element so permeate a business house—the times have changed.

1812	Born Charles Lewis Tiffany to a prosperous textile manufacturer, in Killingly, CT.
1837	Opens a "stationery and fancy goods" store in Manhattan. Merchandise includes Chinese porcelains, French accessories, and bronze curiosities from India. First-week profits for Tiffany & Young: 33 cents.
1845	Publishes his first mail-order "Catalogue of Useful and Fancy Articles."
1847	As French aristocrats flee Louis Philippe's fallen regime, Tiffany buys their diamonds for cash (including Marie Antoinette's Girdle of Diamonds), accumulating the finest collection of gemstones in America. Press crowns Tiffany "King of Diamonds," and his reign as America's premier jeweler begins.

1851   Introduces the English standard of sterling silver (92.5% silver, 7.5% other base metals) into his goods. Other jewelers follow.

1853   Tiffany buys out his partner, John Young, and renames the business Tiffany & Co.

1858   As a publicity stunt, buys 20 miles of Atlantic Telegraph cable, which he then cuts and converts into paperweights, canes, umbrella handles, and watch charms. Buyers flock. Police are called in to control crowds. Tiffany garners more attention than founder Cyrus Field gets for laying the cable on the ocean floor.

1867   Takes grand prize for silver at the Paris World's Fair.

1870   Relocates store to Union Square, where he offers even more lavish displays. Never missing a day, Tiffany can be seen walking to work in his cutaway coat and high silk hat.

1877   A flawless canary diamond is discovered in South Africa. Tiffany purchases the 287-carat stone for $18,000 and cuts it into a cushion-shape gem with an unprecedented 90 facets. The gem appears lit from within, beginning a tradition of cutting for brilliance rather than size. By now, Tiffany is selling $6 million in diamonds each year.

1878   Trailing diamond dust across the globe, Tiffany is the Royal Jeweler to the European crowns, the Shah of Iran, and the Czar and Czarina of Russia. Back home, he shapes the American ideal of luxury as the Astors, Vanderbilts, Goulds, and Whitneys depend upon him for their invitations, jewels, and private silver patterns.

1885   Designs the Great Seal of the United States—still on the dollar bill.

1902   Tiffany dies after a period of declining health, at 90, leaving an estate of $35 million and a name synonymous with quality and craftsmanship.

HUMPHREY BOGART

1899–1957

By JOHN HUSTON, *director and close friend*

Delivered at funeral, January 18, 1957

All Saints' Church, Los Angeles, CA

HUMPHREY BOGART DIED EARLY MONDAY MORNING. HIS wife was at his bedside, and his children were nearby. He had been unconscious for a day. He was not in any pain. It was a peaceful death. At no time during the months of his illness did he believe he was going to die, not that he refused to consider the thought—it simply never occurred to him. He loved life. Life meant family, his friends, his work, his boat. He could not imagine leaving any of them, and so until the very last he planned what he would do when he got well. His boat was being repainted. Stephen, his son, was getting of an age when he could be taught to sail, and to learn his father's love of the sea. A few weeks sailing and Bogie would be all ready to go to work again. He was going to make fine pictures—only fine pictures from here on in.

With the years he had become increasingly aware of the dignity of his profession—actor, not star. Actor. Himself, he never took too seriously. He regarded the somewhat gaudy figure of Bogart the star with an amused cynicism; Bogart the actor he held in deep respect. Those who did not know him well, who never worked with him, were not one of the small circle of his close friends, had another completely different idea of the man than the few who were so privileged. I suppose the ones who knew him but slightly were at the greatest disadvantage, and particularly if they were the least bit solemn about their importance in the motion picture community. Bigwigs have been known to stay away from the brilliant Hollywood occasions rather than expose their swelling neck muscles to Bogart's banderillos.

In each of the fountains at Versailles there is a pike that keeps all the carps active; otherwise they would grow over-fat and die. Bogie took rare delight in performing a similar function in Hollywood. Pretensions crumpled under his attack. Yet his victims seldom bore him any malice, and when they did, not for long. His shafts were fashioned only to stick into the outer layer of complacency, and not to penetrate through to the regions of the spirit where real injuries are done.

The great houses of Beverly Hills, and for that matter, of the world, were so many shooting galleries so far as Bogie was concerned, but his own house was a sanctuary. Within those walls anyone, no matter how elevated his position, could breathe easy. Bogie's hospitality went far beyond food and drink. He fed a guest's spirit as well as his body, plied him with good will until he became drunk in the heart as well as in the legs.

This tradition of wonderful hospitality continued on to the last hour he was able to sit upright. Let me tell you at what pains it was extended through the last days. He would lie on a couch upstairs until at least five o'clock, when he would be shaved and groomed in gray flannels and scarlet smoking jacket. He was no longer able to walk, so his emaciated body would be lifted into a wheelchair and pushed to a dumbwaiter on the second-floor landing. The top of the dumbwaiter had been removed to give him headroom. His nurses would help him in and, sitting on a little stool, he would be lowered down to the kitchen, where another transfer would be made, and again by wheel-chair he'd be transported through the house into the library and his chair. And there he would be, sherry glass in one hand and cigarette in the other, at five-thirty when the guests would start to arrive. They were limited now to those who had known him best and longest; and they stayed, two and three at a time, for a half hour or so until about

eight o'clock, which was the time for him to go back upstairs by the
same means he had descended.

No one who sat in his presence during the final weeks would ever
forget his sheer display of animal courage. After the first visit—it took
that to get over the initial shock of his wasted appearance—one quick-
ened to his grandeur, expanded it, and felt strangely elated, proud to
be there, proud to be his friend, the friend of such a brave man.

As Bogart was brave, his wife was gallant. He gave no thought to
death; she knew it was there, every hour of the day and night—a
dreadful shape slowly materializing. A guest who did not leave after
half an hour. But never once did she betray her awareness. Oh, she
knew, Betty did, from the time he was operated on that at best it was
a question of a year or two. And out of the power of her love she was
able to hide her grief and to go on being her own familiar self for
Bogie. She could not even afford to let others know what she knew
because in that way the knowledge might get back to him. So she had
not only to play a role for him, but for the world. It was a flawless performance. She attended to his every single want, most often before he,
himself, knew what his want was. She never missed a trick. From the
day of her marriage to him till the hour that death parted them she was
true—truly true. It can only be put down to class—class and love.

Once years ago Bogie and a couple of others and I were shooting
the breeze, rather tipsily I'm afraid, about life and its meanings, and the
question arose as to whether there was any time of our lives we'd like
to live over again. All of us except Bogie came out with cynical an-
swers. Someone said, "God forbid." Somebody else: that he'd only like
to cancel out a couple of times. Then Bogie spoke. "Yes," he said.
"There's a time I'd like to relive—the years that I have had with Betty."

Bogie was lucky at love and he was lucky at dice. To begin with
he was endowed with the greatest gift a man can have: talent. The
whole world came to recognize it. Through it he was able to live in
comfort and to provide well for his wife and children.

His life, though not a long one measured in years, was a rich, deep life. Over all the other blessings were the two children, Stephen and Leslie, who gave a final lasting meaning to everything. Yes, Bogie wanted for nothing. He got all that he asked for out of life and more. We have no reason to feel any sorrow for him—only for ourselves for having lost him. He is quite irreplaceable. There will never be another like him.

1899	Born on Christmas to an upper-crust family in Manhattan.
1917	Expelled from Phillips Academy due to failing grades and "insolence."
1918	Joins the navy. When a war prisoner he is guarding smashes Bogart across the mouth with handcuffs, he is left with a scarred and partially paralyzed upper lip, and trademark lisp.
1920	Earns $50 a week as road manager for *The Ruined Lady*.
1922	Takes his first substantial stage role, in *Swifty*. Bogart's performance is not well received by critics, but he continues to get stage roles, playing juveniles and romantic second leads.
1926	Marries actress Helen Menken—the first of several stormy marriages—then divorces a year later.
1935	Fox scouts invite Bogart to Hollywood. Signed for $400/week, he shoots the first of several unremembered films, *Broadway's Like That*. Eventually Fox releases him from his contract.
1936	Reprises his stage role in Warner Bros.' *The Petrified Forest*. The movie is a hit, but Jack Warner has no intention of making Bogart a star, offering him a string of B movies instead. For the next six years, he makes a movie every two months, perfecting his tight-lipped, streetwise gangster.

1938   Marries Mayo Methot, an actress with a penchant for alcohol and physical violence. They become known as the "Battling Bogarts" and he begins to drink heavily.

1941   Bogart and John Huston team for *The Maltese Falcon*. The movie gives him a chance to shine romantically and entrenches him in the Warner pantheon of stars—on par with Davis, Cagney, and Flynn. The following year *Casablanca* pushes Bogart to the pinnacle of popularity. Delivers oft-imitated line "Here's looking at you, kid." For the next few years he is the highest-paid actor in Hollywood. Bogart: "The only point in making money is you can tell some big shot where to go."

1944   Meets Betty "Lauren" Bacall on the set of *To Have and Have Not*. "We'll have a lot of fun together," he tells her. The following year Bogart divorces Mayo and marries Bacall—his fourth, final, and happiest marriage.

1947   Bogart, Bacall, Huston, and fifty others fly to Washington to protest the House Un-American Activities Committee's Communist hunt.

1952   Wins an Oscar for *The African Queen*.

1957   A chain smoker, Bogart undergoes an operation for cancer of the esophagus, but the disease spreads. A veteran of 81 films, 4 marriages, countless run-ins with Jack Warner, and a record-breaking salary, Bogart dies in his sleep.

RICHARD BURTON

By EMLYN WILLIAMS, *playwright and longtime friend*

Delivered at memorial service, August 9, 1984

St. Martin's in the Fields, London

OUR DEAR RICHARD—OR, THE WAY I USED TO START A
letter to you, *ein annwyl Richard*—our dear Richard, here we all
are, joining Sally and Kate and all your family in thinking about you,
and talking a little about you. Yes, I can see the old twinkle in the eye,
as if to say, "Well, now that the smoke's clearing away, what are *you*
going to say about me? Not going to be easy, is it?"

How often, in the past three weeks, have my thoughts gone back
to the first time you and I met, forty-one years ago next month! We
spoke of that first meeting, you remember, at our last meeting, in New
York a year ago. . . .

It was one evening in Cardiff, in 1943, the Sandringham Hotel,
where I was interviewing possible young Welsh-speaking actors for a
new play. After a dismal procession of no-goods, an older man introduced himself as the schoolmaster who had written in about a pupil,
apparently a promising amateur. He beckoned, and the pupil stepped
forward: a boy of seventeen, of startling beauty and quiet intelligence.
He looked—as very special human beings tend to look at that age—
imperishable.

I asked young Jenkins what was the last part he had played
at school. The answer came clear as a bell: "Professor Higgins in
Pygmalion."

At rehearsals in London, it was interesting to watch the boy work,
for he did something very rare: He drew attention by not claiming it.

He played his part with the perfect simplicity needed, and offstage was quietly pleasant—not shy, just reserved, except for the sudden smile, which, there is no other word for it, glowed. He didn't talk much. I think he was a bit self-conscious about his accent, and the need to work on it. It's a phase actors sometimes go through. But inside there, there was humor. A twinkle in the eye, no doubt about it.

One evening, as he and I walked away from a late rehearsal, I asked what was the book he was carrying. "Dylan Thomas." Then he suddenly stopped and recited. The words resounded through the black out of the deserted street, Upper St. Martin's Lane, just up the road.

They shall have stars at elbow and foot . . .

I did *not* say to myself, in a flash, "This lad will be famous!" But it did occur to me that here was more than a well-graced adolescent who could speak lines naturally: This was a Voice. And behind the voice, a mind that, like my own, was in love with the English language.

Then I asked him, in an avuncular manner—I was thirty-seven— if his digs were all right, and was he behaving himself in London. He said he was. Even then I doubted it.

Oh, the English language—let me touch on something that had been known only by those closest to him. His devotion to spoken English has, over the years, extended to writing words on paper. Steadily, unobtrusively, he had been . . . writing.

Diaries? Autobiography? Time will tell, and may surprise us. Anyway . . .

Back to *spoken* English. After the war, five years of invaluable stage experience, and in between several films. Then in the early fifties, the young actor's life was taken over by Shakespeare, at Stratford and the Old Vic. They were salaries you couldn't save on, but grueling hard work built up to triumph.

My former schoolteacher Miss Cooke was curious about this *second* Welsh peasant who had been seduced into the theater, and I presented him to her. Richard was on his best behavior. But she did say afterward, "He's going to do well. What's more, he's got the devil in him. You haven't." I felt commonplace.

Then . . . America! The Movies, capital M, and—an even bigger capital M—the Money! The dollars poured in.

Then 1962. Which means we have to touch lightly—no names mentioned—on a certain Roman-Egyptian epic. Gossip blossomed into Sensation.

Mind you, it is my duty here to emphasize that, at the time, nobody could have guessed that what looked like an irresponsible escapade was to mature into a long, deep, important relationship. But *at the time,* all the public knew was that—as a romantic novelist might have put it—Cupid's dart had hit both targets. And set the Nile on fire. And the Tiber. Even the Thames sizzled a bit. I have an idea that the south-Wales River Tawe kept its cool.

Well, as the scandal grew and grew, *I*—oh, Richard, you and I have talked of this so often since, and it's so long ago it can come out now—I remembered that *I* had introduced you to Sybil, and that *I* was godfather to little Kate. I flew to Rome. Once again the heavy uncle, but this time on a mission. A romance puncturing mission. Sitting in the plane, I did remind myself that I was playing a very bad part, was miscast, and had paid my own fare.

I was met by our delinquent friend, and he drove me to the studios. We talked of this and that, but not of *it.* Then—bump—he stopped the car and looked at me. I was about to embark on my lecture, carefully prepared, when he said—I shall never forget it—he said, very calmly, " *'Dwi am briodi'r eneth 'ma.'* " Which is Welsh for "I am going to marry this girl." " *'Dwi am briodi'r eneth 'ma.'* "

There was, in his green eyes, the twinkle—but a mischievous, devilish twinkle; Miss Cooke had been right. And the fact that he'd said it in Welsh proved, to my Celtic instinct, that he *was* "going to marry this girl." Though even a Celtic instinct could hardly foresee that he was going to do it *twice.*

After Rome, the dollars no longer poured. They cascaded. Up to the waist, he was. Having started life as a simple child of the Valleys—the smallest luxuries out of his reach—Richard Burton Superstar found himself, like an orphan with a sweet tooth, let loose in the biggest candy store in the world. Hollywood!

He spent, lavishly. And the more he spent, the more he earned. And the media—*media,* what a useful word, plural of *medium,* however did we manage without it, covers everything—the media began to mutter. As they donned the unsuitable mantles of the old Welsh-Calvinist preachers, they hinted at Mammon, and the Mess of Pottage, and the Golden Calf . . . omitting to note that while the Superstar enjoyed getting rich (who wouldn't have?), it was a joy he shared with his beloved family, with his friends and countless acquaintances and causes in need of help. He was bountiful.

I remember, in Manhattan, a glittering party where I sat next to the elder sister who brought Richard up. He had taken his sis out shopping, and she looked stunning. She could have been a film beauty who had retired into New York society. I complimented her on the dress. She looked round—the stars were hanging from the chandeliers, Danny Kaye, Gina Lollobrigida, Sinatra, Streisand, *fabulous*. Sis looked round and said, "Well, Emlyn, I thought I'd put my Sunday best on for them all. . . ."

No need to go into the rest of an eventful saga, with its ups and downs. Many downs, because the man had a passion for life, and where there is passion, there has to be—sooner or later—trouble. Side by side with the light, the dark. Behind exaltation . . . melancholy. No, no need to go into all that, because the media were there, keeping the world up to date on every detail, true or false.

(To be fair to them, Richard, you sure did supply them with copy! You with the cheerfully cynical attitude of the quick-witted public figure trapped in limelight—"If they want something quotable, here goes, with salt *and* pepper!" And out would shoot some outrageous quip, often to your own detriment. But quotable.)

The ups and the downs . . . Permit me to administer a reproach. Concerning the recent obituaries and commentaries: They're funny things, obituaries. When something like this happens, a bolt from the blue, within a couple of hours the newspapers are swarming with meticulously detailed judgments. And we all think, "How uncannily quick. Brilliant!"

The fact is that most of the obits have, for months or even years, been lurking in cold storage along shelves ready for—I was going to say "the starting gun," but what I mean, of course, is the opposite. For any of us who have done anything public, the posthumous verdicts, signed and sealed, lie in wait. Long before the curtain is down. We can only hope the notices won't be too bad. And at least we have the comforting thought that we ourselves won't be tempted to rush out and buy all the papers.

Richard's notices have been . . . mixed. Oh, much emotional affection, some of it touching, some toppling over into the maudlin. But when it came to the career—not much emphasis on the ups, concentration on the downs. So I'd like, quickly, to set the record a bit straighter, credits versus debits.

For instance, while there has been harping on physical indulgence, has there been any mention of the crippling illness that cut short a distinguished stage appearance in *Camelot*? What of the days and nights of pain, endured with stubborn fortitude?

His mistakes. Of course he made mistakes—he has said so. We all make mistakes, unless at the age of ten we retired into a retreat, for life! Of course some of the films were trash—again, he has said so. But has there been, apart from a couple of serious articles—has there been any appreciation of such pictures as *Look Back in Anger, Alexander the Great, The Taming of the Shrew, The Night of the Iguana, Under Milk Wood, The Comedians, The Spy Who Came in from the Cold, Becket, Anne of a Thousand Days, Equus, Who's Afraid of Virginia Woolf?*, and quite recently, the immensely bold *Wagner*, with Olivier, Gielgud, and Richardson? *Trash?*

Which leaves the accusation that he turned his back on the serious theater, in order to worship that wicked old Mammon. No salute to *three* returns to the same "serious theater." First at the Playhouse Oxford, *Doctor Faustus.* No slouch Chris Marlowe.

Then two theater gambles, which he won. First his appearance in that fine play *Equus,* on Broadway, where two stars had already been successful in the same part. Second, again on Broadway, at the height of the Superstar combo, *Hamlet,* directed by Gielgud, a run that broke John Barrymore's record.

Finally, no mention of the fact that when this sadness hit us, the man was in fine shape. Richard was himself again. Which meant there was a good chance that he might, in a year or two, fulfill a dream of his and others: a return to English poetry, which he cherished with all his Welsh heart. As Prospero. As Lear.

After that, I don't much like going back to his "notices," but—two brisk quotes. Very brisk. They are one word each.

At least two journalists had the cheek to tap out on their typewriters the word *failure.* Well, if a man is a failure who on leaving this planet monopolizes the front page of every national newspaper throughout the Western world, then quite a few mortals would give *anything* to be such a failure.

And what of the other word, which has recurred so often that it has become a cliché—the word *flawed.* A "flawed" career and so on. But *this* word happens to imply a compliment. Because it takes a precious stone to be flawed. And here we have a precious stone.

We thank you, *ein annwyl Richard,* for your shining gifts, for your love of your devoted wife, of your family, of your friends, of your country, and of life. And thank you for that twinkle in the eye. I can only think at this moment of Upper St. Martin's Lane. A boy of seventeen, standing in the blackout, spouting poetry. Imperishable.

And death . . . shall have no dominion.

1925	Born Richard Walter Jenkins, son of a Welsh miner, and the 12th of 13 children. His mother dies two years later. The family borrows 10 pounds to pay for her funeral.
1935	Taught how to speak, dine, and read by teacher Philip Burton, who, perceiving his potential, eventually assumes guardianship. Richard takes his name in gratitude.
1941	At 16 wins a scholarship to Oxford, where he learns literature and how to drink a sconce of beer in 10 seconds. Three years later, he leaves Oxford to become a navigator for the British Royal Air Force. (His poor eyesight disqualifies him from becoming a pilot.)
1948	Makes screen debut in Emlyn Williams's *The Last Days of Dolwyn*. The consensus? There is something bigger-than-life about Burton. Meets first wife Sybil Williams on the set, and they eventually have two daughters—Jessica and actress Kate Burton.
1949	Stars in *The Lady's Not for Burning* with Sir John Gielgud. His smoldering looks, stage presence, and "the Burton voice" vault him to almost immediate success, upstaging the venerated Gielgud and captivating West End audiences.
1952	Burton gets his first Academy Award nomination for *My Cousin Rachel*.
1963	Cast in *Cleopatra*. After his love scene with Elizabeth Taylor, rumors spread that the couple aren't acting. "Liz and Dick" both divorce their current spouses and marry the subsequent year. The marriage lasts 10 tempestuous years. Then another year. (Burton: "Our love is so furious, we burn each other out.") The pair would team for 11 more films.
1964	Wins second Tony for *Hamlet*. It sells out for 17 consecutive weeks.
1965	Makes *Who's Afraid of Virginia Woolf?* with Taylor. Famously, their relationship develops along the same lines as warring couple George and Martha. His subsequent career choices are dazzlingly erratic, careening from classics like *Becket* to *Exorcist II: The Heretic*. Burton: "I'm so weak at saying no"—explaining bad

films, but also multiple affairs and legendary bouts with the bottle.

1977   Seventh Academy Award nomination for *Equus*—the most nominations without a single win. (In 1969, John Wayne thrust his *True Grit* Oscar at Burton. "You should have this, not me.")

1983   Takes Sally Hay as his last wife.

1984   Dies of a brain hemorrhage in Switzerland, age 58. Burton—who once professed, "The thing in life is language; not love; not anything else"—is buried with a copy of *The Collected Poems of Dylan Thomas*.

BETTE DAVIS

By JAMES WOODS, *colleague and longtime admirer*

Delivered at memorial service, November 2, 1989

Warner Bros. Soundstage 18, Hollywood, CA

A^S A CHILD, I REMEMBER READING ABOUT THE PONY Express, and it filled me with a sense of wonder—these brave young men who rode across the country, at great danger to their lives and well-being, to deliver the mail across the United States at a time when it was mostly the territories. The first thing I thought was not how could they have done that, but *why*. Why would they have risked their lives and put themselves in such enormous peril in hostile territory? For what possible personal reward could they have done such an awesome deed?

It was only twenty years later, when I was part of the Hollywood studio system, that I realized I was on familiar territory.

And it was only when I first saw *Now, Voyager* that I saw what real acting was. I was a young man, an actor in New York, with a lot of time on my hands and very little money—but I still had my student I.D. card, so I became a member of the Museum of Modern Art at a reduced rate. They were having a Hal Wallis film retrospective that day, and one of the films they showed was *Now, Voyager*. I remember sitting in the dark theater and seeing a pair of shoes come onto the staircase—and for some reason my heart broke. I sensed there was a person of deep sadness who was about to fill my consciousness. And the camera tilted up and there was Bette Davis, and she was so full of sadness and despair. Her heart was so nakedly broken that I almost had to avert my eyes.

She presented a glimpse into the human soul I thought I had no right to see. At that moment, I understood the awesome power of creative genius. I understood that even an actor could be on a par with an Albert Schweitzer or a Vincent van Gogh, that there was the same kind of hunger and yearning in this performance of naked human emotions. Or in those young men who risked their lives for some ideal or glimpse of the horizon, that I read about in a book as a child.

Another moment: Miss Davis and Paul Henreid are on the side of the stage and she tries to explain what the moment of love that they've had means to her. She talks about a banquet and how there are crumbs left on a table, and if she just had those crumbs, her life would be fulfilled.

As an actor, I think about what those words must have looked like on a printed page. I would have looked at them and retired from the profession. I would have said there's no way you can stage this kind of thing, people don't talk this way. But I watched Bette Davis do the scene and I understood the hunger of the human soul for love. What kind of courage does it take to open one's soul that deeply? She played it so ferociously, like a mother lion devouring her kill to protect and feed her young. She did it with such abandon, such need, that I knew there was some higher power at work that compelled her to rip this scene apart.

Some years after that I had the honor of working with her. We were working on a film called *The Disappearance of Aimee*—a period picture, so we were all in heavy costumes and makeup. It was easily a hundred and ten degrees every day. We were working far from home and it was a rather tense shoot. On the third day Miss Davis came on the set.

There were about a thousand extras in the big auditorium. They were working for a boxed lunch, under hot lights, for a chance to see other actors and Miss Davis. There was a moment when one of the other actors was being—I don't want to make a judgment—but a little *difficult*. And Miss Davis, for all her reputation, was being gentle as a lamb. So when one of the other actors had quarantined herself in her trailer, Miss Davis said, "I think I'll go entertain the troops." And she got up and proceeded to do a Bette Davis imitation.

God rest her soul, she wasn't very good at doing it.

She said, "I never really did this in the film, but I'll do it anyway: *Petah, Petah, Petah.*"

And there she was, the eminent trooper. They laughed, they applauded, and they stepped right into her heart in that beautiful way that she had many people do—quickly and smoothly.

Later I said to her, "Miss Davis, I don't comprehend your remarkable patience. Don't you ever get a little angered by other actors, and I wonder, how do you handle it?"

She said, "Well, first of all you have to have respect for any part, even if it's dreadful, and in any case it's really irrelevant because I'm sure she'll be dead in five years either by her own hand or somebody else's." She was eating a kosher dill pickle as she said that, and she never missed a beat.

Years later, *Life* magazine approached me and said, "You have been chosen by Miss Davis to be the actor she'd most like to be photographed with, as the great stars of 1939 pose with some new young actors." I was honored.

So we were posing for Greg Gorman, and she looked great—with the same presence she always had and a little bit more. I said, "Miss Davis, is it okay if I—"

And she said, "Oh, I think after all these years you can probably call me Bette."

I couldn't figure out what had accelerated her time process—I always had a sense that it would take at least a couple of decades to get to that point. Maybe she was softening a bit. The years wore on and somehow it had never really rolled off the tongue.

Greg Gorman said, "If you would sit there, and Miss Davis, could you just put your hand on his shoulder?"

She looks over to him and says, "I think *not*."

"Is there a problem?"

"This young man is betrothed. I don't want to cause any problems."

Greg came over to me and said, "She's kidding, right?" And I said, "No. I grew up in Rhode Island and she's from Connecticut. She knows one woman does not paw another woman's man."

Greg says, "But she is quite a bit older. I don't think she's a threat."

"Well, *she* thinks she's a threat, and I have to tell you, there's quite a bit of woman there. I think probably Miss Davis will always be a threat in that area."

A great woman has a power to move and to pain and to beguile, and she's always been aware of that. But eventually she put her hand on my shoulder and we got the shot. It was okay because she was seduced into it. She wasn't responsible.

I think the great power of Bette Davis was she always knew who she was. She had an obligation to herself and her audience. When you think of what she was compelled to do, the power she put on the screen, the fact that she took upon herself a much greater task—in a battle that took place on this very lot in Glendale, years before Gloria Steinem was in a bunny suit, and I say that with all due respect—the fact is that Bette Davis put herself on the line when she just didn't have to. She fought for women's rights when she was such a big star that she didn't need to carry that extra burden. But she planted a seed that now, decades later, sees a woman as head of a studio on this very lot.

And she lies up at Forest Lawn looking down at the studio, and she knows that we are all here and we love her.

I think of the contribution she has made to what J. D. Salinger referred to as "the fat lady in the fourth row." In *Franny and Zooey,*

Franny asks Zooey, "Why do you act?" And he says, "Because I have a secret communion. I have things in my soul that I have to do."

To communicate this makes no difference if there's not someone to listen. But out there, somewhere in the fourth row, there's the fat lady and she sits alone because she has no one in her life. She looks up at the screen and she says, "I thought only I felt like that." I don't think there's a frame of film on the face of this earth where there isn't someone, somewhere who looks up and says, "I thought only I felt that."

For all of us who will be there someday and for those who are there now, I guarantee that up in heaven somewhere they are saying, "Fasten your seat belts, it's going to be a bumpy eternity."

1908	Born Ruth Elizabeth Davis, in the middle of an electrical storm, in Lowell, MA.
1915	Her parents divorce. Defying convention, her mother raises two daughters alone at the turn of the century.
1928	Debuts on Broadway in *Broken Dishes*, age 21. Impressed, a Universal executive signs Bette and invites her to Hollywood— but thinking her too homely to be an actress, the studio gofer leaves Bette at the train station.
1932	Breakthrough film: *The Man Who Played God*. Warner Bros. signs Davis to a long-term contract, beginning her stormy 18-year relationship with a studio more accustomed to promoting its male stars. In an era of classically beautiful stars, Davis survives by sheer force of her personality, talent, and well-known mannerisms— including clipped New England diction and extravagant cigarette smoking.
1935	Wins her first Oscar for *Dangerous,* followed three years later by another Oscar for *Jezebel*. Reputedly gives Oscar its nickname, joking that it reminded her of "the derriere of my husband [Harmon Oscar Nelson]."

1939	Divorces first husband. Three more follow.
1941	First woman to become president of the Academy of Motion Picture Arts and Sciences.
1942	By now Davis is the highest-paid woman in America—frequently referred to as "the fourth Warner." Opens the Hollywood Canteen for U.S. military men, transforming an abandoned nightclub into a top-tier hospitality center. Davis: "There are few accomplishments in my life that I am sincerely proud of. The Hollywood Canteen is one of them."
1950	Bounces back from string of forgettable films with *All About Eve*, based on tempestuous star Tallulah Bankhead. Delivers unforgettable line, "Fasten your seat belts, it's going to be a bumpy night!"
1962	Her career takes an unexpected twist again with *Whatever Happened to Baby Jane?* On the set, she and Joan Crawford continue their well-documented rivalry, but the movie earns Davis her 10th Oscar nomination. Takes out a tongue-in-cheek ad in *The Hollywood Reporter*. "Situation Wanted: Mother of three, 30 years experience as an actress, more affable than rumor would have it, wants steady employment in Hollywood."
1975	Launches decade-long television career with *The Disappearance of Aimee*. Subsequently wins Emmy for *Strangers* (1979), *Little Gloria . . . Happy at Last* (1982), and *A Piano for Mrs. Cimino* (1982).
1978	First woman to receive the American Film Institute Lifetime Achievement Award.
1989	Dies at 81, in Paris, after a protracted and defiant battle with cancer. With a career spanning six decades and 100 films, 80 awards, 4 marriages, and 3 children, Davis appropriately chose the following epitaph: "She Did It the Hard Way."

JAMES DEAN

1931–1955

By REV. XEN HARVEY, *longtime friend*

Delivered at funeral, October 8, 1955

Friends Church, Fairmount, IN

I SHALL ALWAYS REMEMBER THE LIFE OF JAMES DEAN AS A drama in three acts. Act I was his boyhood and youth. Act II represents the career that gained national prominence. And Act III is the new life into which he has just entered. Here in Fairmount, it was in the very first act of this drama that we learned to love James Dean. We loved him as a small boy in and out of town; we loved him when he was fast-breaking with the basketball team; we loved him in the lean, hungry years of his career; and we loved him as he stood on the mountain peak of success.

We loved him so much, it is a bit difficult for us to be understanding with those who, in the emptiness of their lives, and littleness of their spirits, have come only out of curiosity, to look and to stare. However, in contrast to this, we appreciate deeply all of you who have come because you, too, learned to love him along the way. We know you came to share our sorrow and we humbly thank you. Also, we find it hard to be charitable with publicity-hungry amateur psychologists, who have entertained themselves psychoanalyzing our boy. Because we knew him as a normal boy, who did the things normal boys do. He was part of a good solid home in a community where understanding people live. He was loved by the members of that home, and he loved them in turn. He was not brooding, or weird, or sullen, or even odd. He was fun loving and too busy living to sulk.

Though he was a normal boy, he had an extra measure of energy

143

and talent. What energy he had! On the basketball court he didn't have the physical equipment to be a basketball star, but what he lacked in stature he made up in fighting spirit. He was one of the team's leading scorers just because of his great energy and drive.

With affection, we remember how he hustled that little English motorcycle around town in his high-school days. That motorcycle had a rough existence. When Jimmy was riding it, he was always in a hurry.

When we speak of his talent, we naturally think of the theater. But his talent was not limited to acting. He was interested in all the arts. Much has been said of his interest in bull fighting, but it is only right that you know he was a serious amateur sculptor. You know of the bongo drums, but you should know he was devoted to the best in classical music. He enjoyed also the best in fine literature and was a student of philosophy. He could intelligently discuss the great philosophers and their schools of thought.

But for all of his interest in the other arts, the theater was his first love. James Dean was an actor. He was an actor in the noblest meaning attached to the term. He lived with the characters he portrayed. He was so sensitive, he suffered when they suffered, brooded when they brooded, and rejoiced when they rejoiced. He was the master of his profession.

Like other masters of his art, he took the values of all good literature and multiplied them time upon time. To some he brought rest and relaxation and to others hope and challenge.

Just a word in regard to the worthiness of his profession. In days gone by when the Church was all-powerful politically, it would reach out with its long arm of censorship and ban the theater entirely. But the agency that always brought back the theater was the Church. It was needed, not only to dramatize that scene that happened so long ago in Galilee, but to make vivid the lessons that the best of literature has to teach.

Now the curtain has fallen on Act II of James Dean's life. We cannot help but feel that his activity here in time and space has ended far too soon. But for those of you who really loved him, will you remember you were far more fortunate to have had him as your friend and loved him for twenty-four years than to have had some other for a normal lifetime? I am sure you would not trade the twenty-four years you have had Jimmy for seventy-four years with another. It isn't how long we live that is so important, but how well. It is not how much time we have, but the use of time that really matters. And Jimmy had filled these years with accomplishment. In only a little over a score of years, he had soared to greater heights than most of us will reach in our full three score and ten. So when you think of his early departure, think not how short, but how full his life was.

We do not believe that James Dean is lying in state before us. It is only his body that was returned from California, and his body that is here before us. The real James Dean has moved on ahead of us into another world. We most certainly do not believe his life has ended! Nor do we believe that his career has ended!

In the days ahead, we will think of a new career unfolding before him. We have spoken of his tremendous energy. We will picture God as helping him harness that energy and directing it to new levels of usefulness.

A few weeks ago, Jimmy was quoted as saying this: "I've just begun searching, investigating, and trying to learn about me." In the days ahead, God will help him find his true selfhood. He will groom him for stardom in new roles, on a larger stage, before vaster audiences.

To those of you who were close to James Dean, remember that this God of whom we speak is more than trustworthy and can be trusted with your loved one. The career of James Dean has not ended, it has just begun. And remember, God Himself is directing the production.

1931   Born James Byron Dean in a farmhouse in Indiana; named after attending physician James Emmick.

1940   His mother dies from cancer. For the next decade, James lives with his aunt and uncle in their Fairmont farmhouse, busying himself with school, theater, and basketball.

1948   Plays Frankenstein in high-school production of *Goon with the Wind.*

1949   Decamps for California. Lands his first job in a Pepsi commercial: James and other teenagers dance around a jukebox, singing "Pepsi-Cola hits the spot!" Dean is paid $30.

1951   Takes acting coach's advice and moves to New York City, where he earns a living as a busboy in the theater district. Writes home: "I have made great strides in my craft. After months of auditioning, I am very proud to announce that I am a member of the Actors Studio, the greatest school of the theater."

1952   Debuts on Broadway in *See the Jaguar,* playing a boy locked in the icehouse by his demented mother. Three days later, play closes.

1954   Makes several television appearances and recognition of his talent begins to grow. He moves to Hollywood to begin filming *East of Eden.*

1955   Crescendo and crash: *East of Eden* opens to excellent reviews for Dean and is followed by lead roles in *Rebel Without a Cause* and *Giant.* Hollywood is abuzz, comparing him to Clift and Brando. But on his way to race his Porsche, "Little Bastard," Dean collides with another driver and dies instantly. He is 24. *Rebel* is released less than a month after Dean's death, cementing his status as the prototypical restless American youth, and crowning the most spectacularly brief career of any actor. *Giant* opens the following year. Testament to Dean's continued popularity, his tombstone was stolen for the third time in July 1998.

JACK LEMMON

By LARRY GELBART, *friend and poker buddy*

Delivered at memorial service, August 13, 2001

Paramount Studios, Los Angeles, CA

YOU HAD TO BE ON YOUR TOES AROUND JACK LEMMON. If only to help you get a glimpse of how high his standards were.

How the man did sparkle.

And frequently surprise us, this fellow with the agility of an Astaire and the tenaciousness of a Cagney. If it's true that in the sum of his parts he embodied the aspirations of Everyman—if there truly is so much of Jack Lemmon out there—then maybe there is yet cause for hope for this cockamamie world of ours.

But there can't be all that many Everymen who can match or boast (an activity that was completely foreign to Jack) the keenness of his mind, his articulation (in makeup—or without), the concerns he felt, and the actions he took for a saner, more sensitive society.

And guided always, in each of his choices, by an internal gyroscope—one that allowed him to remain an artist against considerable odds.

Refusing to squander his gifts, having neither the skill nor the patience for pandering, Jack was a true miracle—an orchid that blossomed amidst all of the counterproductive machinery, all of the creative land mines strewn about an industry that masquerades itself as an art form. It takes only one look at his incomparable film achievements to see that Jack thought of the situation as being completely the other way around.

In a place where sensitivity and just plain common sense are so often put on hold, his presence—his pride in being a member of the entertainment community—ennobled us all. His work, a constant reminder and encouragement to each of us to strive to fashion more than just product. To make our own values our primary audience. Whether he was performing a work by Neil or O'Neill, he would apply himself with an almost religious sense of discipline, to put himself at the service of the text. An actor who valued quality writing—just as writers value quality acting. It's highly doubtful that anyone ever found a coffee cup ring on the cover of any one of Jack Lemmon's scripts.

While talk of his admission to the pantheon of great actors is certainly fitting and proper, it is, to some degree, incomplete. It overlooks the fact that the man was his own pantheon, one memorable character standing shoulder to shoulder beside the next—characters freed from the page that Jack breathed life and fire into from the depths, and the heights, of his perceptive, so accessible, soul.

His range as an actor was, of course, stunning. From his early, eager Ensign Pulver of the navy to the more mature Morrie of so many Tuesdays, perfectly portraying the imperfect man.

Humbled or harassed.

Desperate or defiant.

In high heels or in loafers.

But if the truth be told, in his personal life Jack had almost no range at all. Throughout the whole of it, year after year, he was simply, unfailingly terrific—displaying merely various shades of marvelous.

Being predictably thoughtful.

Endlessly caring.

Instinctively kind.

In all of the medical procedures he must have had to endure in his last days among us, no matter how many scanners or tests they subjected him to, it's a certainty that they never found one mean bone in the man's body.

As it is with anyone who possesses a true sense of humor, he was a skilled practitioner of self-ridicule. We know that no dramatic role was too daunting for him to take on, but one need only think of Jack's golf game to remember how good he was at comedy. Ultimately it matters not at all how often he sliced—or shanked—or double or triple bogied. Or how many balls he sank in the ocean instead of the hole.

There are all kinds of scores to keep in life, and, in golf parlance, Jack Lemmon was a scratch human being: He was a dad totally devoted to kids, even when the press was nowhere in sight. He could never play, or listen to, enough piano. Completely self-taught, his own compositions often felt more like contemplative conversations between Jack and whatever Steinway happened to be at hand. He loved sleek, elegant cars that met his own lofty expectations of excellence and performance.

Having nothing to prove to either himself or the world at large, he had no problem with Mrs. Lemmon sitting behind the wheel. In a town rife with temptations and disposable standards, Jack and the fabulous Felicia were the rarest of couples—always seeming less a married man and his wife than two sweethearts sharing one long, perpetual date.

Perfect casting.

Without a hint of coyness.

Just two smart, complementary people, starring in a personal love story as engaging as any the big screen ever had to offer.

If the power that comes with a half-century of success and adulation, if that sort of power does indeed corrupt, if what the world saw of Jack Lemmon was his bad side . . . the mind cannot accommodate the possibility that he could have been any finer a man than the one we honor here tonight. If our hearts are heavy now, it's not because we hardly knew ye, Jack. It's because we knew ye so well.

And never with more joy than on the countless Sundays when my wife and I, along with your other buddies, would gather round a poker table—a ritual that more and more became a necessity. A way of putting the past week's bad news to bed. A nudge toward starting the next one with a smile. The stakes are low, and the volume is high, and the only real losers are those who somehow manage not to have a laugh during the evening.

It's still possible to do that.

Even now.

To remember Jack at his place among us, sitting behind his always, ever-shorter stack of chips: Studying his hand carefully before breaking up a pair of aces. Then buying four cards from the dealer so that he could try for a royal flush. We still—we temporary survivors—we still gather round the table. Draw poker is still one of our games, but we never play Jacks-or-better anymore.

For us, a better Jack is simply unimaginable.

1925	Born John Uhler Lemmon III in a hospital elevator in Newton, MA. As a child, Jack is consistently ill, requiring 13 operations before he is 13. His jaundice prompts a nurse to remark, "My, look at the little yellow lemon."
1929	First appears onstage, age 4, alongside his father—a doughnut company executive and sometime soft-shoe dancer.
1947	After a brief interruption for military service, graduates from Harvard and moves to New York City, supporting himself by playing piano in saloons. The following year, he begins a string of television appearances—400 over the next five years.
1950	Marries actress Cynthia Stone.
1954	His first film role, opposite Judy Holliday in *It Should Happen to You*, is almost his last. When director George Cukor asks him to tone down his performance, Lemmon replies, "Are you telling me not to act?" Cukor: "Oh God, yes."
1956	In a bittersweet year, wins his first Oscar for playing Ensign

Pulver in *Mister Roberts* and begins his meteoric rise, but his marriage ends in divorce.

1959   Cast in his best-known movie role, as a cross-dressing jazzman in *Some Like It Hot.*

1962   Marries Felicia Farr. After 15 straight comedies, Lemmon yearns to show his dramatic range and takes the role of an anguished alcoholic in *Days of Wine and Roses.* (Not accidentally, he admits to his own problems with alcoholism, and begins attending Alcoholics Anonymous.) Subsequently observes, "I've never had to dodge that particular bullet of having to do comedy or drama. . . . I've been able to do both, and sometimes both at once."

1968   Stars in *The Odd Couple* with Walter Matthau. Perfectly mismatched, they go on to do 10 films together. Famously, they never have an argument for the duration of their friendship. Lemmon: "It was a very unusual relationship right off the bat, the very first day, because it clicked so totally and easily and there was just nothing to it."

1973   Picks up second Oscar for *Save the Tiger.*

1985   Quits drinking altogether.

1988   Receives Lifetime Achievement Award from the American Film Institute. Accepting, Lemmon ascribes his success to fate: "My career has been full of remarkable coincidences that had nothing to do with me."

1999   Wins Emmy for his role as Morrie in TV drama *Tuesdays with Morrie.* Throughout filming Lemmon battles cancer.

2001   Dies almost exactly a year after his longtime friend Walter Matthau, at 76, with his wife and two children at his side.

WALTER MATTHAU

1920 – 2000

By CHARLIE MATTHAU, *son*

Delivered at memorial service, August 8, 2000,

Directors Guild of America, Los Angeles, CA

MY FATHER TAUGHT ME TO HAVE A SENSE OF HUMOR about everything, no matter how sad—not to take life too seriously because none of us is getting out of here alive, and little of what we do is going to matter in a few years. I remember him telling me about the funeral where everyone hated the deceased and nobody knew quite what to say, so the eulogist got up there and said, "Well . . . his brother was worse." It's the opposite of the situation we have today.

He also told me about the first-grade teacher who went around the room asking each student what his father did for a living.

Johnny said, "My father is a fireman."

"Okay, Susie, what does your father do?"

"He works at the post office."

"Burt, what does your father do?"

"My father is dead."

Teacher says, "Oh, I'm very sorry. What did he do before he died?"

He went, "Uarghhhhhhhh!"

My father was my hero and my best friend. We had our own language, which was our shorthand way of communicating. We could not only finish each other's sentences, but we could look into each other's eyes and know what the other was thinking. In his case, I could tell you within a thousand dollars how much he had bet that day and whether he had won or lost. Every morning before work I'd go over and see him, and whoever spoke first would say to the other Willy Clark's line from *The Sunshine Boys*: "What's the theme of the show?" meaning, "What's new since the last time we talked?"

In the last few weeks before my father died, our special language helped us to communicate even more. Walter was in terrible back pain from bones that were not healing properly and he was forced to take painkillers, which made him say some pretty goofy things. A week before he died, he called me over early in the morning and said, "Charlie, get in touch with Jack Seinfeld right away and tell him that I'm interested, but only if they commit to one and a half shows!"

"Are you talking about Jack Lemmon or Jerry Seinfeld?"

He said, "C'mon, Charlie, stop kidding around, will you!"

"Okay, Velvul, I'll take care of it."

After I left the room, he looked at his nurse and said, "I think something has gone wrong with Charlie's thinking!"

One night earlier this year when my father was in the hospital, he called me on the phone around midnight and said, "Charlie, I'm stuck down here in a hole two or three hundred feet underground."

"No, you're not," I said. "You're at UCLA Hospital."

"Charlie, will you listen to me? I'm stuck in a hole three hundred feet underground!"

I said, "Look in front of you, Velvul. Do you see a small brown refrigerator?"

"Oh yeah."

"And look above. Do you see the TV set?

"Oh my God, that's amazing! How the hell did they get appliances down here?"

We broke all the rules about how one is supposed to separate from a parent. We both took some criticism for it. I made my choice of where to go to college, where to buy my house, what films to direct, in order to maximize the time we could spend together. I treasured every moment. Because while we were going to Laker games and concerts and making movies and walking our dogs along the Palisades and playing *Jeopardy* against TV contestants or betting at the track, he was teaching me by example how to live with humor and compassion and love and strength, which are the only things that get me through this most difficult time of my life.

For Father's Day 1999, when my father had already survived several bouts of very serious pneumonia, emphysema, melanoma, lymphoma, congestive heart failure, emergency pacemaker operation, three angioplasties, a quadruple bypass, two heart attacks, acute respiratory distress syndrome, which had ravaged his already weakened body with an aggressive infection, and colon cancer that had metastasized into his liver (I don't know what the doctors are going to do now for business), I decided I'd better write him a very detailed Father's Day card. I wrote: "You've taught me most of what I know about what is decent and kind and worthwhile and courageous. You're a giant. One of the finest actors of the twentieth century and, because you excel at comedy, one of the most underrated. The most loyal and patient husband, and as a father a volcanic and infinite explosion of unconditional love and universal wisdom, and a supernova of everything that is right and good in this world. Apart from that, however, I'm not very happy with you."

My father broke down and cried, and then he never mentioned it again.

I always hoped that there was reincarnation, but I had trouble believing it. Now I have trouble believing that God would create a person that loving, that talented, that brilliant, then mold them by all of the experiences that my father had, from six battle stars in World War II, which he never talked about, to elevating himself from true poverty with no father and an uneducated mother into a widely respected international star for over six decades. A great husband, a perfect father, a brave fighter for his health who prevailed as an underdog at least six different times against diseases that were supposed to kill him. And then to take all of that and just return it into the ground . . .

What a waste.

My father has made me believe that there may be something after this life. And if there is, I'll look for him the first moment I cross over and I'll give him the biggest hug ever, and I'll start kissing him all over his cheeks and hugging him some more, until he says, "Stop that, Charlie, people will think we're a couple of faygeles."

And then I'll look at him and I'll say, "So, what's the theme of the show?"

1920	Born Walter Matuschanskavasky in New York City, the youngest son of Russian Jewish immigrants.
1931	Walter earns money selling soft drinks at the Second Avenue Yiddish theaters; supplements income by appearing onstage for 50¢/show.
1938	Graduating during the Depression, Walter takes a variety of jobs: Forester in Montana. Gym instructor. Boxing coach for policemen. Finally, he enlists in the army under Lt. Jimmy Stewart, as a radio cryptographer in a heavy-bomber unit. When discharged in 1945, he sports six battle stars.
1946	Taking advantage of the GI Bill, Walter enrolls in the New School drama program in New York City. Changes his name to pronounceable "Matthau."
1948	Debuts on Broadway opposite Rex Harrison in *Anne of the Thousand Days*. As understudy to a sick 83-year-old British actor, Matthau takes the stage, unrehearsed, in the role of an elderly bishop. Harrison is horrified to find a 28-year-old 6'3" youth in age makeup.

1958	His 10-year marriage to Grace Johnson ends. The following year, Matthau marries Carol Marcus—reputedly the archetype for Holly Golightly in *Breakfast at Tiffany's*.
1966	Earns a Best Supporting Oscar for *The Fortune Cookie*, his first film with Jack Lemmon. The two become lifelong friends and frequent costars, but Matthau's compulsive gambling and heavy smoking contribute to a heart attack on the set. He continues to be plagued by health problems for the rest of his life.
1967	Reprises his signature role, Oscar Madison, on film, opposite Lemmon. "Every actor looks all his life for a part that will combine his talents with his personality. *The Odd Couple* was mine. That was the plutonium I needed. It all started happening after that."
1982	Awarded a star on Hollywood's Walk of Fame.
1995	Directed by his son, Charlie, in *The Grass Harp*. Amid a busy decade, with roles in *JFK, Grumpy Old Men, Dennis the Menace,* and *Out to Sea,* Matthau recalls *Harp* as his finest performance ever.
2000	Dies after protracted illness, at 79. With more than 70 films and numerous stage roles to his credit, his trademark and best-loved character remains the cranky codger.

RIVER PHOENIX

1970-1993

By WILLIAM RICHERT, *director and confidant*

Written in commemoration

THERE ARE PEOPLE AMONG US WHO CAN TAKE OUR BREATH away with their character and style, with qualities of goodness and generosity that make us blink to be sure we are seeing correctly; they are rare, and so beautiful. River Phoenix was such a person.

Angels were not restricted to heaven until the Dark Ages. Before that, they were thought to walk among the living, ever-present benefactors and spiritual guides. River was like that; no one who ever met him can deny it, nor can anyone explain it. For me he was a bright, unexpected crack of glowing light in the universe and I mean that literally; when he died, a kind of fog and gloom settled in which I still feel now.

River was aptly named; he was a gusher of talent, of curiosity and wonder. His temperament was to go to the very edges of life, and with his humanness and the tentacles of his talent, to feel around, and to probe with that mischievous, catlike smile on his face, extending himself in empathy and generosity.

He was always asking questions. When I last saw him, he had all sorts of questions about how I was living my life, and about subjects multifarious. Nobody close to River could escape his scrutiny (or his sly, teasing wit) and I, perhaps, represented an Older Person's Point of View. We were in my funky apartment on the water side of the Pacific Coast Highway in Malibu. Still full of energy at two A.M. he asked if he could play his guitar on the deck when I said I had to sleep. I said,

"Sure," and left him looking out over the ocean and playing. I told him he could lock up after himself.

In fact, River was still there in the morning; he was sleeping on the floor with his guitar, lying on pillows he had taken off the couch. He had slept in the clothes he was wearing the night before. I woke him making coffee. Getting up sleepily, he thanked me for waking him, and drove into town to the set of the motion picture in which he was starring. From his clothes, from his very simplicity, you'd have thought he was homeless. Maybe he was.

Maybe he's home now.

Often I think about the image of River lying on the pavement toward the end of *My Own Private Idaho,* and about the image of our real-life River lying on the sidewalk in front of the Viper Room on Halloween; I wonder if the first was a prophecy and the second a destiny.

All of us who knew River miss him. For a while we decided in un-spoken agreement that we would stop speaking about him to reporters or writers because so many of us had been misquoted. That was a mis-take, I think now, because it left those who knew River less well, or almost not at all, to speak on his behalf, and misrepresentations crept into the stories that were written.

On his last night, I know River had been on a six-weeks vegan's diet of artichokes and corn, that he'd been working until late to help the film crew on the production he was starring in, and that the re-sponsibilities he'd taken on with his work, his friends, and family were bearing down on him. Among his own he was the breadwinner, and he worked tirelessly at his craft. When River started a film, he not only knew his own lines but the lines of all the other actors as well, and he could recite the stage directions to boot.

On the night he died, he had come to L.A. for R&R like any hard-working guy. He drank a fatal potion given to him by a person he trusted, and it killed him. I think his body was too pure for the common weekend-night assault that far less healthy eaters and drinkers could handle. However, I also think he wanted to touch danger, too, and that the artist he was felt he could handle death, perhaps even collaborate with it and play out a scene or two. This time, however, he opened the one door from which he could never return. He was locked out . . . or we were. The bit of heaven he brought to earth he took away with him.

1970   Born River Jude Bottom—after the "river of life" in Herman Hesse's book *Siddhartha*—to missionary parents with the radical Christian cult the Children of God. Traveling from Texas to Puerto Rico to South America, River lives his childhood on the open road.

1977   Impoverished, the 7-year-old River and sister Rain sing on the streets of Venezuela to provide food for their family.

1978   The Bottom family returns to America, stowaways aboard an ocean freighter carrying Tonka toys to Florida.

1979   River and Rain enter local talent contests. Shortly thereafter, the family receives a letter inviting them to audition at Paramount Studios. River later recalls, "I figured I'd play the guitar and sing with my sister and we would be on television the next day." Their father decides to change the family name from Bottom to Phoenix.

1980   Several television commercials later, River tires of hawking products: "Commercials were too phony for me. It was selling a product, and who owns the product? Are they supporting apartheid? I just didn't like the whole thing, even though it helped us pay the rent."

1981   Plays Guthrie McFadden in TV adaptation of *Seven Brides for Seven Brothers*. Other television roles follow.

1985   Rob Reiner casts River in *Stand by Me*. Stardom follows.

1986   Meets Martha Plimpton on the set of *The Mosquito Coast*. Despite an instant mutual dislike, their relationship would be long-lasting. Martha: "I love River's family. They brought him up to believe that he was a pure soul who had a message to deliver about the world. But in moving around all the time, changing schools, keeping to themselves, and distrusting America, they created this utopian bubble so that River was never socialized. He was never prepared for dealing with crowds and Hollywood." Gets first top-billing role in *A Night in the Life of Jimmy Reardon,* directed by (eulogizer) William Richert—his first "grown-up" role.

1987   Completes filming on *The Mosquito Coast, Little Nikita,* and *Running on Empty.* River on Hollywood: "It's got a lot of pitfalls and temptations, and [my father] doesn't want us to become materialistic and lose the values we were brought up believing in." His father moves the family to Gainesville, FL.

1989   Nominated for Best Supporting Actor for *Running on Empty,* River attends his first Oscar ceremony with his mother and Martha Plimpton. By summer, his relationship with Plimpton has ended.

1990   River flies to Portland to research gay hustling for *My Own Private Idaho.* The role helps him shed his teen-idol image once and for all.

1993   Presciently, he prepares his will. October 31: In a well-publicized incident at Hollywood's Viper Room, in the company of brother Joaquin and friends, River overdoses on a combination of heroin and cocaine. Arrives at hospital in full cardiac arrest. He is 23.

MAE WEST

1893-1980

By KEVIN THOMAS, *longtime friend and*
L.A. Times *film critic*

Delivered at funeral, November 25, 1980

Forest Lawn Cemetery, Hollywood Hills, CA

NOT LONG AGO, IN FRONT OF A CHINESE RESTAURANT IN downtown Los Angeles's produce district, one of the resident loiterers stared at the diminutive blonde in evening dress as she stepped out of her long black limousine and yelled, "Hey Mae, you're still lookin' good!"

Mae West, at eighty-plus, repaid him with a dazzling smile. You could believe for the world that it was Diamond Lil arriving at Gus Jordan's Bowery saloon. And, in a sense, it was, for the woman and the image had long since become one. She was hard to know in the conventional sense of the phrase. You could dine with Mae West three times in the same week and realize that she remained essentially an enigma to all but a handful of people. She had an absorption of self that bordered on totality, yet the more she concentrated on being Mae West the more she gave of herself to others. To spend an evening with her was to be entertained by her always vivid and often outrageous reminiscences and her favorite songs. Wherever she was was a place that was filled with fun and laughter. It's hard to believe that she's gone, dead at eighty-seven.

While Mae West candidly spoke of the importance of maintaining a starry aura of mystery, she allowed that handful of people to see behind that shady lady, pleasure-seeking Diamond Lil image to discover a woman who could be thoughtful of others, for someone so seemingly self-occupied. She could be concerned that Greta Garbo might be standing in a draft, but could also respond to a priest's request that she visit his ailing mother—and then keep his heartfelt letter of thanks for the rest of her life. Whenever she played a town where she enjoyed a profitable run, the rule rather than the exception throughout her career, she made it a practice to make a donation to the local church (the denomination was of no matter) before she departed.

Her most touching gesture may well have been toward her younger sister, Beverly. In later years, withered and alcoholic, Beverly found that she could no longer trim her own toenails, due to a childhood accident that had left one leg markedly shorter than the other. Not wanting anyone to see her deformity, she turned to the one person she knew she could trust. Mae West didn't hesitate, and thereafter did her sister's pedicures herself.

In recent years, an aura of campiness surrounded Mae West's pictures and famous quips, threatening to obscure her significance as a beloved national institution embodying twentieth-century American show business. But in her liberating impact upon sexual attitudes and the role of women, she was without equal. Mae West was a mistress of paradox and ambiguity, and a social commentator more complex than she (who saw herself as an entertainer) realized.

She loved the stimulus of a question-and-answer session. Once when a reporter asked what she thought about the Black Panthers, she shot back, with characteristic innuendo, "Depends what angle you're lookin' at them from." When UCLA named her Woman of the Century in 1971, she was asked if she would consider running for office. She said no and quipped, "I don't know much about politics, but I do know a good party man when I see one."

She was unfailingly gracious to her fans, asking them about themselves and tireless about signing autographs—unless the fan made the mistake of submitting a photo she considered unflattering or, more frequently, a picture that predated the glamorous studio shots of her Paramount years. Faced with a decidedly dated pose, Miss West would often sweetly say, "Oh, I don't have that one! If you would give me that, I will give you one of mine and autograph it for you."

It was unforgettable fun to accompany her on these public occasions, where she was always greeted with affection and respect. The event that amused her the most—and for which she looked her most agelessly glamorous—was a banquet at the University of Southern California chapter of the Sigma Chi fraternity, which had named her its Sweetheart. At a ceremony following the dinner, the chapter president pinned a fraternity pin on the neckline of Miss West's form-fitting white evening gown. On the way home in her Cadillac limousine, she was in high spirits and spoke of what a good time she had had—but was then genuinely dismayed to realize that her pin was missing. We looked everywhere but it was not to be found.

Back at her apartment, she excused herself to change while I sat on the sofa in the living room going through the yards of her pink feather boa in search of that Sigma Chi pin. Soon Mae reappeared in one of her exquisite lace-trimmed satin negligees. She flashed a smile of triumph and exclaimed, "I found the pin. It had slipped inside my bra." She then added, in that trademark sultry voice, after a perfectly timed pause that could only come from coming of age in vaudeville, "I wouldn't have minded if that guy had reached in and pinned it on right."

In both her professional and private life, Mae West liked us to believe that she belonged to no one man, yet she was actually caught up in a singularly tender love story. For more than a quarter of a century, Paul Novak—who had been in the chorus line of her nightclub act in the fifties—had been her devoted companion. She returned his love and when he wasn't around would say, "Paul is the greatest," yet mischievously couldn't resist adding, "Of course, there are forty other guys who'd love his job!" They were a touching couple: the broad-shouldered genial giant and the tiny, curvaceous blonde invariably in white and sparkling with diamonds.

Mae West always said that no one was ever to feel sorry for her, and she would not want anyone to start now. She was a serenely contented woman who accomplished all that she had set out to do. She wanted for nothing and was grateful in return. Even contemplating death, her fabled alter ego served her well. Surely, she thought, a lifetime of self-creation would not end with mere death but continue on another plane. Mae West figured that in one way or another she would live forever. And she probably will.

1893	Born in Brooklyn to John Patrick West, sometime boxer, and corset model Matilda Doelger-Delker.
1900	Wins gold medal in amateur talent contest, age 7. Youth is spent on the vaudeville and burlesque circuits, and by 13 she is billed as the "Baby Vamp."
1911	Debuts on Broadway in the revue *A La Broadway*. Allegedly marries song-and-dance man Frank Wallace. At the height of her Hollywood career her marriage certificate surfaces, leading to an eventual divorce and considerable settlement. She never remarries.
1926	Encouraged by her mother to write her own plays, she pens *Sex*—earning her headlines and jail time on obscenity charges. Undeterred, she writes *The Drag, The Wicked Age, Pleasure Man,* and *Diamond Lil,* which earns her a small fortune in receipts and an invitation to Hollywood.
1932	Films *Night After Night*. In just four scenes, she all but walks away with the picture, her racy dialogue accounting for much of the film's success and voluminous fan mail. When *Diamond Lil* is filmed as *She Done Him Wrong*, Mae West insists on casting Cary Grant over studio objections. Grant hits stardom. The film receives a Best Picture nod. And box-office sales pull Paramount back from the brink of bankruptcy.
1933	Re-teams with Grant for *I'm No Angel*. Thwarting the

Production Code, she loads her scripts with double entendres, gleefully maneuvering them past the censors. "It isn't what I do, but how I do it. It isn't what I say, but how I say it, and how I look when I do it and say it."

1935   Mae West is the highest-earning woman in America.

1943   Inspired by her 43-inch assets, the British Royal Air Force names an inflatable life jacket after her. No longer interested in close-ups, she passes on *Sunset Boulevard* and returns to the stage—staying for 25 years.

1954   Launches Las Vegas nightclub act featuring a chorus line of toga-clad bodybuilders, touring with it for six years.

1959   Publishes her autobiography, *Goodness Had Nothing to Do with It.* Characteristic advice: "I learned early that two and two make four, and five will always get you ten if you know how to work it."

1978   Appears in her final motion picture, *Sextette,* with Timothy Dalton.

1980   Dies of complications from a stroke, at 87, in Los Angeles. Survived by her sister, Beverly West, and legions of admirers, she bequeaths an immortal image and a clutch of one-liners that have become part of the language.

CHALLENGER ASTRONAUTS

FRANCIS R. SCOBEE, *Commander (1939–1986)*

MICHAEL J. SMITH, *Pilot (1945–1986)*

JUDITH A. RESNIK, *Mission Specialist 1 (1949–1986)*

ELLISON S. ONIZUKA, *Mission Specialist 2 (1946–1986)*

RONALD E. MCNAIR, *Mission Specialist 3 (1950–1986)*

GREGORY B. JARVIS, *Payload Specialist 1 (1944–1986)*

SHARON CHRISTA MCAULIFFE, *Payload Specialist 2 (1948–1986)*

By PRESIDENT RONALD REAGAN

Delivered at memorial service, January 31, 1986

Johnson Space Center, Houston, TX

WE COME TOGETHER TODAY TO MOURN THE LOSS OF seven brave Americans, to share the grief we all feel and, perhaps in that sharing, to find the strength to bear our sorrow and the courage to look for the seeds of hope.

Our nation's loss is first a profound personal loss to the families and the friends and loved ones of our shuttle astronauts. To those they have left behind—the mothers, the fathers, the husbands and wives, brothers, sisters, and yes, especially the children—all of America stands beside you in your time of sorrow.

What we say today is only an inadequate expression of what we carry in our hearts. Words pale in the shadow of grief; they seem insufficient even to measure the brave sacrifice of those you loved and we so admired. Their truest testimony will not be in the words we speak, but in the way they led their lives and in the way they lost those lives—with dedication, honor, and an unquenchable desire to explore this mysterious and beautiful universe.

The best we can do is remember our seven astronauts—our

Challenger Seven—remember them as they lived, bringing life and love and joy to those who knew them and pride to a nation.

They came from all parts of this great country—from South Carolina to Washington State; Ohio to Mohawk, New York; Hawaii to North Carolina to Concord, New Hampshire. They were so different, yet in their mission, their quest, they held so much in common.

We remember Dick Scobee, the commander, who spoke the last words we heard from the space shuttle *Challenger*. He served as a fighter pilot in Vietnam, earning many medals for bravery, and later as a test pilot of advanced aircraft before joining the space program. Danger was a familiar companion to Commander Scobee.

We remember Michael Smith, who earned enough medals as a combat pilot to cover his chest, including the Navy Distinguished Flying Cross, three Air Medals, and the Vietnamese Cross of Gallantry with Silver Star, in gratitude from a nation that he fought to keep free.

We remember Judith Resnik, known as J.R. to her friends, always smiling, always eager to make a contribution, finding beauty in the music she played on her piano in her off-hours.

We remember Ellison Onizuka, who, as a child running barefoot through the coffee fields and macadamia groves of Hawaii, dreamed of someday traveling to the moon. Being an Eagle Scout, he said, had helped him soar to the impressive achievement of his career.

We remember Ronald McNair, who said that he learned perseverance in the cotton fields of South Carolina. His dream was to live aboard the space station, performing experiments and playing his saxophone in the weightlessness of space; Ron, we will miss your saxophone and we will build your space station.

We remember Gregory Jarvis. On that ill-fated flight he was carrying with him a flag of his university in Buffalo, New York—a small token, he said, to the people who unlocked his future.

We remember Christa McAuliffe, who captured the imagination of the entire nation, inspiring us with her pluck, her restless spirit of discovery; a teacher, not just to her students, but to an entire people, instilling us all with the excitement of this journey we ride into the future.

We will always remember them, these skilled professionals, scientists and adventurers, these artists and teachers and family men and women, and we will cherish each of their stories—stories of triumph and bravery, stories of true American heroes.

On the day of the disaster, our nation held a vigil by our television sets. In one cruel moment, our exhilaration turned to horror; we waited and watched and tried to make sense of what we had seen. That night, I listened to a call-in program on the radio: People of every age spoke of their sadness and the pride they felt in "our astronauts." Across America, we are reaching out, holding hands, finding comfort in one another.

The sacrifice of your loved ones has stirred the soul of our nation and, through the pain, our hearts have been opened to a profound truth—the future is not free, the story of all human progress is one of a struggle against all odds. We learned again that this America, which Abraham Lincoln called the last best hope of man on earth, was built on heroism and noble sacrifice. It was built by men and women like our seven star voyagers, who answered a call beyond duty, who gave more than was expected or required, and who gave it with little thought to worldly reward.

We think back to the pioneers of an earlier century, and the sturdy souls who took their families and their belongings and set out into the frontier of the American West. Often, they met with terrible hardship. Along the Oregon Trail you can still see the grave markers of those who fell on the way. But grief only steeled them to the journey ahead.

Today the frontier is space and the boundaries of human knowledge. Sometimes, when we reach for the stars, we fall short. But we must pick ourselves up again and press on despite the pain. Our nation is indeed fortunate that we can still draw on immense reservoirs of courage, character, and fortitude—that we are still blessed with heroes like those of the space shuttle *Challenger*.

Dick Scobee knew that every launching of a space shuttle is a technological miracle. And he said, "If something ever does go wrong, I hope that doesn't mean the end to the space shuttle program." Every family member I talked to asked specifically that we continue the program, that that is what their departed loved one would want above all else. We will not disappoint them.

Today we promise Dick Scobee and his crew that their dream lives on; that the future they worked so hard to build will become reality. The dedicated men and women of NASA have lost seven members of their family. Still, they, too, must forge ahead, with a space program that is effective, safe, and efficient, but bold and committed.

Man will continue his conquest of space. To reach out for new goals and ever greater achievements—that is the way we shall commemorate our seven *Challenger* heroes.

Dick, Mike, Judy, El, Ron, Greg, and Christa—your families and your country mourn your passing. We bid you good-bye. We will never forget you. For those who knew you well and loved you, the pain will be deep and enduring. A nation, too, will long feel the loss of her seven sons and daughters, her seven good friends. We can find consolation only in faith, for we know in our hearts that you who flew so high and so proud now make your home beyond the stars, safe in God's promise of eternal life.

May God bless you all and give you comfort in this difficult time.

The space shuttle Challenger flew nine successful Space Shuttle Missions before exploding before a stunned nation on January 28, 1986. Here is a record of what happened at the Kennedy Space Center that day.

T=0.000   Ignition command is sent. Astronaut Judy Resnik: "Aaal riiight!"

T+0.008	*Challenger* is freed from launchpad.
T+0.678	Film later shows first evidence of abnormal black smoke near a rocket booster.
T+5.000	Flight director Jay Greene, Houston: "Liftoff."
T+11.000	Shuttle pilot Michael Smith: "Go, you mother."
T+21.124	Roll maneuver completed. *Challenger* is on the proper trajectory.
T+45.217	A flash is observed downstream of the shuttle's right wing.
T+48.118	A second flash is seen trailing the right wing.
T+48.418	A third, unexplained flash is seen downstream of the right wing.
T+58.788	Tracking cameras show the first evidence of an abnormal plume of smoke on the right rocket booster.
T+59.00	*Challenger* passes through maximum aerodynamic pressure, experiencing 720 pounds per square foot.
T+60.000	Smith: "Feel that mother go!"
T+66.764	Pressure in liquid hydrogen tank begins to drop, indicating massive leak.
T+71.10	Commander Dick Scobee: "Roger, go at throttle up."
T+72.624	*Challenger* beams back its last navigational reading.
T+73.000	Smith: "Uh-oh . . ."
T+73.191	A sudden brilliant flash is seen. Fireball engulfs *Challenger*.
T+4 minutes	*Challenger* crew cabin smashes into Atlantic at 200 mph. Still strapped to their seats, the astronauts experience a breaking force of 200 times normal gravity. The crew cabin disintegrates and settles at the bottom of the ocean.

AMELIA EARHART

1897–1937

By MURIEL MORRISSEY, *sister*

Written in commemoration

To A.E.

Earthbound, we watched, enthralled,
As unafraid you climbed the cloud strewn sky
Your flight a symbol of that great heart
That dared apathy and prejudice defy
"Own your soul!" your voice rings clear
So gaily began your last long flight
Circling the globe Electra's *gallant crew*
Through wind and fog missed finding Howland's light
For me, A.E., you'll never die
The world, fleetingly, became less sad and drear
For the courage and concern we saw
In your brief, joyous sojourn here.

1897	Born in Atchinson, KS.
1907	Seeing her first airplane at the state fair, Amelia confesses, "It was a thing of rusty wire and wood and not at all interesting."
1920	Takes her first flight: 10 minutes over Los Angeles, in open cockpit. The following year, she purchases her first airplane—a Kinner Airster—with help from her sister, Muriel.

1921   Fascinated with testing the limits of her flying machine, she sets the women's flying record of 14,000 feet.

1928   Amelia becomes the first woman to fly across the Atlantic Ocean as a passenger. The event is orchestrated by publisher George Palmer Putnam. Upon landing, she becomes an instant celebrity. Writes *20 Hours, 40 Minutes* about the crossing, and Putnam sends her on the lecture circuit. Amelia: "I was interested in aviation, so was he. . . . We came to depend on each other, yet it was only friendship between us, or so I thought at first."

1929   Continuing on the lecture circuit, Amelia is given writing assignments for *Cosmopolitan* and others. Putnam's wife divorces him.

1930   Sets women's flying speed record of 181 mph.

1931   Becomes the first president of the Ninety-Nines, a women pilots club. Amelia marries Putnam, who organizes her flights and public appearances. Continuing to fly under her maiden name, Amelia refers to their marriage as a "partnership with dual controls."

1932   Five years after Charles Lindbergh's flight, Amelia sets another record: first solo transatlantic flight by a woman. After flying through a lightning storm, nearly crashing into the ocean, and being forced to make an emergency landing in an Irish cow pasture, Amelia returns to a ticker-tape parade. That same year, she designs a line of clothes for "the woman who lives actively," carried by Macy's and Marshall Field's. Awarded the Army Air Corps Distinguished Flying Cross.

1937   Embarks on the first around-the-world flight on the *Electra*, with Fred Noonan as navigator. After a month, they miss a refueling stop at Howland Island in the Pacific. Despite an exhaustive search—authorized at a cost of $4 million by President Hoover—no trace of Amelia has ever been found. Her disappearance remains a mystery.

THOMAS EDISON

1847–1931

By J. F. OWENS, *friend and president of*
National Electric Light Association

Written on the occasion of his death

BEWITCHED AND AWED, WE APPROACH THAT ALTAR OF simple greatness exemplified by Thomas A. Edison during his entire long and useful life. How futile seem our efforts to appraise his real worth. Ours is not a requiem but a glorification of a life filled to completeness with service to mankind.

Embellishments are inappropriate to fittingly pay tribute to one so human, considerate, tolerant; so moderate, plain, and retiring. His example of modesty and simplicity in the acceptance of international honors and tributes in life is a monument in itself. But his greatest monument is the blessings left for us.

Passionately fond of work, a genius in applying organized knowledge, infinitely patient, undaunted by failures, he brought inventions that have broadened the lives of all mankind.

He knew no class distinction, no national boundaries, no allegiance to any definite group, either political, religious, or fraternal. His was the vision of the masses.

Through him the masses heard again, "Let there be light." He brought amusement, joy, and romance to man, woman, and child. He lessened their labor. He widened their education for a fuller enjoyment of their daily lives. Great industries with employment for millions followed in the wake of his discoveries. From his laboratory we can truthfully say there came a supreme gift—a higher standard of life and living for the world.

To him material gain was not an end but merely incidental and a means for further accomplishments and service. His unselfishness, coupled with his devotion to the millions whose ability to repay him is limited to affection and respect, has endeared him to the world.

Without Edison, civilization would be rolled back many years.

On his deathbed he said, "It is very beautiful over there." And how true that must be with his coming, and how equally true it is that he made it very beautiful over here.

For us in the electric light and power industry there is left the challenge contained in his message of five months ago: "Be as brave as your fathers before you. *Have faith. Go forward.*"

1847	Born Thomas Alva Edison in Milan, OH.
1857	Believed by his teachers to possess below-average intelligence, Al is kept home for his schooling. Sets up his first chemistry lab in the cellar.
1859	Loses most of his hearing due to unknown causes. Thirty years later he writes, "I haven't heard a bird sing since I was 12 years old."
1862	Al saves a boy from being hit by a train. In gratitude, the boy's father, a stationmaster, shows him how to use the telegraph. Edison soon begins working as a telegraph operator, sending messages for the Union army.
1867	Invents an electric vote recorder, which doesn't sell. The upshot? Edison vows to create useful, popular products here on out, going on to patent more than 1000 inventions.
1873	Marries Mary Stillwell. Four children follow.
1877	Creates the world's first phonograph by wrapping a cylinder in tinfoil, reciting "Mary Had a Little Lamb," then listening as it plays his words back. On the phonograph: "This is my baby and

I expect it to grow up and be a big feller and support me in my old age." It does.

| 1878 | Invents the electric light. Four years later he opens first electric power station, at 255 Pearl Street, New York City. |

| 1882 | Wife Mary dies at the age of 29. |

| 1886 | Marries Mina Miller, moves to West Orange, NJ, and opens a new laboratory. Over the next years, Edison invents the motion picture camera while losing millions in an iron mine. Success of his phonograph keeps him afloat. |

| 1894 | The first "peephole parlor" opens in New York City. Patrons pay a nickel to look at a short movie through tiny pegs. A few years later, thousands of Americans are watching movies on large screens. |

| 1914 | Fire destroys the factories surrounding his lab. Returning to work, Edison states: "I am 67, but I'm not too old to make a fresh start." With World War I in full swing, Edison lends his talents to the navy, going to work on inventing weapons. |

| 1916 | Goes on first of several camping trips with famous friends, including Henry Ford and Harvey Firestone. |

| 1925 | Half of all U.S. households have electric power. |

| 1928 | Receives a Congressional gold medal "for the development and application of inventions that have revolutionized civilization." |

| 1931 | Dies at home, age 84. By the time of his death most Americans live in cities lit by Edison's lights. |

ALBERT EINSTEIN
1879–1955

By ERNST STRAUS, *assistant to Professor Einstein*

Delivered at memorial service, May 22, 1955

Royce Hall, University of California, Los Angeles

WHEN I WAS TOLD OF THIS MEMORIAL, I WAS INFORMED that we were to divide his memory into that of Einstein the man, the scientist, the humanitarian, and the Jew. This is in a sense an impossible task, for he was a man of a single mold and there was no dividing line between his various aspects. I shall try therefore to tell you of the Einstein in his daily association rather than the public figure manifest in his discoveries, his thoughts and actions. It is fortunate that over the years I jotted down some of his remarks that seemed significant or characteristic, so that where my words would be feeble I'll be able to speak with his.

Einstein often referred to himself as a lonely man—he would call it that loneliness that is so hard on the young, but so sweet to the old—and in a sense that is true. He always preserved a certain emotional detachment, yet even if he was not deeply involved, he had a genuine liking and respect for people. Often on our way to work someone would waylay him, tell him how much he had looked forward to meeting the great Einstein. Einstein would pose with the waylayer's wife, children, or grandchildren as desired and exchange a few good-natured words. Then he would go on shaking his head, saying, "Well, the old elephant has gone through his tricks again."

He was very fond of small children and animals. With children he would go through various tricks, making funny noises with his hands and wiggling his ears. In fact, his ability to wiggle his ears was the only accomplishment of which he would boast shamelessly and which he was quite eager to show off.

Tiger, his old tomcat, was mainly the pet of the ladies of the house, but in an emergency he would come to the master. Whenever it rained he would complain bitterly. Einstein would be quite apologetic; he'd say, "I know what's wrong, my dear, but I really don't know how to turn it off."

Our own cat would make it a habit to walk over to the institute and cry under our office window until we let her in. Or if we proved hard-hearted, she would wait at the front door, slip in with the first comer, and then scratch at our office door for admission. Then she would sit perfectly quietly on the chalk tray or the bookcase and watch us work. Einstein grew quite fond of her, and later most of his letters to us in California would end with "regards to your dear cat." When the cat had kittens, he was quite eager to see them and came home with us in a detour on his walk home. He was dismayed when he saw that our neighbors were all people from the institute and said, "Let's walk quickly. There are so many people here whose invitations I've declined. I hope they don't find out that I came to visit your kittens."

While he hated all competitive games, he loved little puzzles of all kinds and was very fond of gadgets—not the kind that reduce the labor in some chore by thirty seconds but the kind that are based on some clever design. Once we were at his house for dinner when he had just received a little mechanical bird that would dip into a glass of water and keep this up as long as its head stayed moist. He watched it delightedly all through dinner and stroked its head gently to start it off again. When we saw him last, another bird—one that walked up walls on suction-cup feet—had just become popular, and my wife said, "I'll bet Einstein has one." Sure enough, after dinner he said, "I have a treat for you." First he brought a big umbrella, then he wound up the bird and started it up the wall. Then he opened the umbrella upside down "so it won't fall so hard," and caught it gently as the suction gave out.

Let us now speak of Einstein the enthusiastic, indefatigable seeker, thinker, and worker. Among my notes I find the following quotes:

"Two things are needed for our kind of work: One is indefatigable persistence; the other is the ability to discard something in which one has invested great labor and many ideas."

"God is inexorable in the way in which he has distributed his gifts. To me he has given the stubbornness of a mule and nothing else—on second thought he has also given me intuition."

"When we think for ourselves but not for publication, we dismount from our logical steed and sniff the ground. Afterward we cover our tracks in order to enhance our godlike stature."

I might mention here a good anecdote he told about himself. We were looking for a paper clip for a manuscript and finally found one too badly bent to be usable, so we looked for a tool to straighten it. In doing so we found a drawer full of perfectly good paper clips, and Einstein was just about to bend one out of shape when I asked him what he was doing. "If you hadn't been here, I should certainly have ruined this clip in order to straighten the bent one. This always happens to me when I get stuck on a problem."

I cannot recall a single moment that Einstein was not thinking about some great problem that he had posed for himself; even when he was talking with people or engaged in another activity, part of his mind would always stay on the task.

The first theory on which we worked when I came to be his assistant he had worked on alone for over a year, and we continued working on it for about nine months more. Then one evening I found a class of solutions to the field equations which in the light of the next morning seemed to show that the theory could not have physical significance. We turned it over and over all morning but the conclusion was inevitable. So we left for home one half hour early. I must say that I was quite dejected. If the pick-and-shovel man feels so badly about the collapse of his edifice, how badly must the architect feel! But when I came to work the next morning, Einstein was eager and excited: "You know, I've been thinking last night, and the proper approach seems to be . . ." This was the start of an entirely new theory, also relegated to the trash heap after half a year's work and mourned no longer than its predecessor.

He would allow himself some wry remarks on the failure of a theory, such as: "It is already a success if you can force nature to stick out its tongue at you." "In this nature is truly satanic—that she makes one think one is on the way to the greatest triumph when one has gone completely astray." "Mathematics is the only perfect method to lead yourself around by the nose."

The last theory on which we worked was his last. He knew this, saying, "If nothing comes of this theory, then I will not find the right one, for I am too old for a fundamentally new idea." However, he had great and growing confidence in his theory. Often when he noted a satisfactory feature he would exult: "This is so simple God could not have passed it up." The fact that the mathematical difficulties were tremendous did not surprise him. "The further we advance, the simpler logically and the more complicated mathematically things become. We are like children who have found a giant hammer. They can't even lift it." His greatest sorrow was that, as he would say, "I'll have to bite the dust before finding out whether this theory is the right one." I do not believe that he ever seriously entertained the thought that there might be no such perfect theory as the one he was seeking. . . .

It may be appropriate here to say a few words about Einstein the political figure. He had been described as naive, a babe in the woods of politics, by those who disagree with his views, and as a social and political thinker of a stature that rivals his stature as a scientist by those who agree. Neither of these extremes would be his own appraisal. He kept himself very well informed on political issues and brought the same lucid and dispassionate mind, the same courage and forthrightness to bear on them. Yet he did not have the same sense of involvement and feeling of destiny that he had in his scientific thinking. He would speak out courageously to prevent a wrong or to promote a right, but he did not often express himself publicly on the laws that govern social and political life.

Once after a meeting of his Committee of Atomic Scientists, he said, "Thus one is forced to divide one's time between politics and our equations, but these equations are ever so much more important. Political problems are problems of the moment but such an equation is a matter for eternity." He would often express his regret about his role in bringing the atomic bomb to the world. That is, he regretted the fact that an overestimate of Germany's atomic research had prompted his letter to President Roosevelt. I never heard him express regret about the role his scientific discoveries had played.

Einstein did not like to shock people. On many occasions when he did, he did so unintentionally because he simply did not expect their emotions. He told me that when he was a little boy in Munich he was taken to see a parade of the Royal Guards in their splendid uniforms. He cried bitterly because he felt so sorry for those poor people who were made to strut about in this ridiculous fashion and in those silly outfits. He had since learned that some people like to march, but in his heart he never believed it. As he would put it: "Often evidence convicts you of the validity of a statement but it doesn't convince you." In a similar vein he would never be convinced that Americans really enjoy the ownership of all those shiny cars and household appliances. He felt that they were foisted on people in order to keep the economy going, diverting them from what they would really like to do—such as play music or hike in the woods.

He liked to stand alone on his own two feet and never lean on anyone or anything, nor did he have much sympathy for the feelings of those who needed something to lean on. "Nothing is so hateful to me as to belong in any group, be it a nation or a party, an academy or an institute. One always has the responsibility for actions on which one has no influence. My only refuge is not to take it too seriously."

This same feeling of independence made any plea of a personal god or an immortal soul quite unacceptable to him. When he was invited to speak on his faith at an anniversary of the Jewish Theological Seminary of New York, he said this, and was quite bewildered by the result: "Never did I get so much mail, and such vituperations! What concern is it of theirs what I believe?" After this he would reply to public questions concerning his faith that his god was the god of Spinoza, who manifests himself in the order of his universe only.

As a matter of fact, this did not give a completely accurate picture of his faith, for he judged the order of the universe to be a matter of logical simplicity alone and not a creation of any being, personal or otherwise. This is the way he put it: "What really interests me is whether God had any choice in the creation of the world; that is to say, whether the demand of logical simplicity leaves any alternative. One must admit after all that this logical simplicity determines the universe far more precisely than one would have thought fifty years ago." I think that in this remark he expressed both the fundamental goal of his scientific work and his estimate of his success.

Let me close with this thought and challenge that was so typical of him: "Greatness in the world of ideas is basically a question of character. The main thing is never compromise."

1879	Born in Ulm, Germany.
1884	Albert is given a magnetic compass, triggering his lifelong quest to investigate the natural world.
1898	Falls in love with classmate Mileva Maric.
1902	Mileva gives birth to their daughter, Lieserl, but puts her up for adoption. All records of her disappear. Albert and Mileva marry. The following year, Albert Jr. is born, and Einstein is frequently seen wheeling a baby carriage along the streets—occasionally stopping to scribble down mathematical ideas.

1905   The "Miracle Year": Einstein postulates that e = mc² and the
       Special Theory of Relativity is born, offering a four-dimensional
       universe. At 26, Einstein establishes a pillar of 20th-century
       physics. At the time, he works in the Patent Office in Geneva,
       earning $600/year.

1914   Mileva and Albert divorce. Einstein is appointed Professor at
       University of Berlin, without teaching responsibilities. In August,
       World War I begins.

1915   Einstein completes the General Theory of Relativity.

1916   After serious illness, and near death, he is nursed back to health
       by his cousin Elsa.

1919   A solar eclipse in May offers physical evidence for the General
       Theory of Relativity. Einstein marries his cousin Elsa.

1922   Awarded the Nobel Prize in physics.

1932   Adolf Hitler rises to power. As a Jew at the height of his fame,
       Einstein begins to feel the heat. The following year, he and Elsa
       sail for America and settle in Princeton, NJ, where Einstein as-
       sumes a post at the Institute for Advanced Study. Princetonians
       quickly get used to long-haired figure wandering the campus
       with unpressed pants and a pullover sweater.

1936   Elsa dies after a long illness.

1939   Reversing his pacifist idealogies, Einstein writes famous letter to
       President Roosevelt warning of the possibility that Germany is
       building an atomic bomb, urging that the U.S. develop one.

1940   Becomes an American citizen.

1944   Shocked by the nuclear bombing of Hiroshima and Nagasaki,
       Einstein rallies for formation of a world government and disar-
       mament. Becomes chairman of the Emergency Committee of
       Atomic Scientists, spreading awareness about the horrors of
       atomic warfare.

1955   Einstein dies in his sleep, age 76. His body is cremated and his
       ashes are scattered at an undisclosed place.

CARL JUNG

1875–1961

By SIR LAURENS VAN DER POST, *friend*

Delivered at memorial evening, October 20, 1961

The Analytical Psychology Club of New York, New York City

THOSE PEOPLE IN THIS WORLD WHO HAVE GONE THROUGH the fire of analysis have no difficulty in acknowledging their debt to Dr. Jung. I have not had that experience but I am aware of the debt in another dimension. I would like to acknowledge that debt today on behalf of the artist, of the writer, of the soldier, of the statesman, because they, too, owe an immense debt. Many of them have taken from Dr. Jung and are not yet prepared to acknowledge it. But I would like to acknowledge it among you here tonight. And I do it all the more readily because for years I was one of the people who rejected what Dr. Jung stood for. Not rejected it so much, but wouldn't look at it. I was so horrified by what I had found in the latter Freud that I wouldn't have anything more to do with psychology. I believed when people said Jung's psychology was just vague, mystical nonsense.

But I met Dr. Jung one day, in Zurich, and somehow I knew at once that I was walking in the presence of somebody who was truly great. We ignore the signs of greatness when it stares us in the face. They are very simple. In a look in the eye, I knew it. He asked me to come and see him, and we talked on that first day for five hours without a stop.

It was a very cold winter's day. It was snowing and dark, and I had the most extraordinary sensation as he talked to me. He was a wonderful listener as well as a great talker. I had an extraordinary feeling I had, in the dark jungle in Africa, come across somebody who had found fire. I realized I was in the presence of an explorer—a true explorer in the twentieth-century way. I knew enough then to know how the journey had begun.

From that day, I had a feeling for him which grew stronger. We had a very rare relationship: He truly loved Africa but couldn't go back, and I could bring him something of Africa. Now, this was what happened not only to me but to people all over the world. All my life I had carried a certain loneliness with me in regard to Africa because I saw it in a way I couldn't share with anyone. Suddenly I was talking to a Swiss who was deeply immersed in the European tradition, and what I said somehow made sense to him. My loneliness vanished from that moment, and I found through this a way to share what I had to share of Africa with a new kind of community.

This to me was one of the immense achievements of Carl Gustav Jung—he was open to every culture, every religion, every urge, every facet of the reality of his age. And he wasn't pushed out of shape by it. He gathered it into his own cultural tradition, and he enriched the spirit of European man by it. He didn't do what so many people do— throw their own culture out of the window—but truly integrated and enriched this very great European tradition. He did what only the great can do; he truly renewed it. And what was even more wonderful, having this very deep insight into reality, he never lost the way of talking about it to people in their common language.

When he appeared on television in England it was absolutely amazing how his exceedingly rational interviewer was suddenly overcome: Even he felt that he was in the presence of great new meaning. Jung spoke to the common people of England about meaningful things in a way they could understand. The next morning, a char lady asked me if I'd seen the wonderful television show the night before. The ordinary people understood him. This was, I think, perhaps the greatest manifestation of his greatness: that he maintained the lines of communication with people in all walks and shapes of life.

When he wrote *Answer to Job,* one of the most meaningful correspondences he had was with a nun in the Black Forest in Bavaria. She worked her way with the other nuns through that storm-battered book, and she said at the end of it: "For the first time now is the reality of the Father, the Son, and the Virgin Mary clear and meaningful to us."

I truly believe with him a tide in the history of man was turned, and is turning now for the good. It begins like that: One person who has the courage and the dedication to live the improbable vision that is communicated to him, and C. G. Jung lived it fully. When he died, his death was not an end but a fulfillment and perhaps a rebeginning of that vision.

I would also like you never to forget that he was a child of life. He had the love of life. I've never known anybody who made me laugh so much. Don't let us always think of him in terms of solemnity. Let us always remember this divine laughter that was in him. Only this year in February when I saw him last, I said, "You are really an honorary Bushman because you are the only European I've ever met who laughed like the first man of life." He had an immense and wonderful laugh, which is a sign of real grace. Let us remember that.

And let us remember what a good advertisement he was for his vision. There is an extraordinary association between greatness and longevity, and he was nearly eighty-six years old when he died, as though life recognized this in him and wanted him to live until what was in him was fulfilled.

I shall never forget my visit in February. When I arrived the last day to have dinner with him, I found him reading. "Dr. Bennett has come from London and he wants to know where I got this quotation which is over the door of my house." Translated into English, it means "Called or not called, God is here." "Of course it comes from Erasmus." He had a copy of Erasmus that he had bought as a young man of twenty-one, a first edition in Latin, and he was reading it as easily as I would drink a glass of water. He found the quotation and gave it to Bennett, and was so happy over it that he ate a full-course meal. He carved the joint himself. He and Bennett drank two bottles of wine and each smoked an enormous cigar. That was in February. I couldn't even smoke half a cigar, but he did. And let us please remember it.

I have here quotations from two letters he wrote to me that I want to read to you. I wrote to him from Africa and he replied, "Your letter revived all my old longing to see once again Africa, God's unspoiled wilderness and its wonderful animals and human children. Alas, although I've seen and faced it once at least, so many things cannot be repeated and so many happy things cannot be called back. No wonder the thoughts of old people dwell so much in the past as if they were listening for a living echo that never comes. Time and again I have to make a vigorous effort to tear myself away from the things that have been, in order to pay attention to things present and even more important, to pay attention to the future, as if I too was meant to be in it."

Now, thank God, he never shirked this challenge. Right to the end, he lived not only for the present but the future, as if he were meant to be in it. Let us remember this.

The other occasion: I wrote to him after Mrs. Jung died, and he wrote me a very moving letter, but I only want to quote one thing from it. He said, "I'm glad at least that I've been able, though not through any merit of my own, to spare my wife what follows on the loss of a lifelong partner, the silence that has no answer."

But the silence had an answer. Three months later he told me that he had had a dream, and in this dream he was going into a dark theater—immensely dark—and in the distance there was a brilliantly lit stage. He walked down toward it until he came to the orchestra pit, which he knew he couldn't cross yet. But there on the stage was Mrs. Jung looking more lovely than ever, and his agony was resolved. The silence had an answer. With your permission—I wouldn't do it anywhere else but here—I would like to tell you what I believe is an answer to the silence that we must all feel now that he is gone: When Dr.

Jung died, I was at sea. My mind was occupied with Africa and I wasn't thinking about Europe at all. I was feeling very devastated and rather disintegrated, and I went to bed one night and I had a dream in which I was in a dark valley where avalanches were mounting up on the side, and at the end of the valley I saw a lovely mountain in the snow. On top of this Dr. Jung was standing, and as I saw him he saw me, and he waved his hand at me, and in that funny schoolboy English he used from time to time (he loved phrases like *hellish* and *devilish* and so on), he said, "I'll be seeing you."

And I had a very good sleep and early the next morning, my steward brought me a cup of tea and a transcript of the radio news. I opened it and read that Dr. Jung had died in Zurich last night.

Now, I'm aware of the subjective implications of this dream. I cannot ignore the timing, and I cannot ignore the fact that the last time I saw Dr. Jung, we talked a great deal about mountains. He loved mountains.

There's one last thing. His family wrote to me from Zurich saying that about the time he was dying, there was a violent thunderstorm, so violent it was as if the whole of nature were taking part. Lighting struck a tree in Dr. Jung's garden, a tree of which he was particularly fond and under which he often sat. When I heard this, I just felt, well, this can't be ignored because in this natural world he loved so much, lightning is an image of the imperative awareness just as thunder is the image of the coming of the word. In the beginning, when the first people burned the body of the person who died in fire, they did so to help the soul on its way, to release it from its perishable elements and set the imperishable ones free. Then they heaped everything that was costly and valuable—all the horses, everything that the person had valued—they heaped that on the fire and burned them, too—*not* to destroy them, but to remove the perishables from those elements as well, so that the imperishable would accompany the imperishable soul on its way.

It is as if this tree, too, was sent to accompany Dr. Jung on his way. You know, the first people I knew in Africa said to me, "The wood burns out but the fire goes on forever."

Here we are in the presence of somebody who had brought us a fire that will never again die on earth.

1875	Born in Kesswil, Switzerland, the son of an evangelical priest.
1884	Sent to boarding school, Carl is a loner. He develops an embarrassing tendency to faint under pressure.
1895	Studies at the University of Basel. Attending seances with his cousin Helly, a medium, Carl is fascinated with spiritualism, setting the stage for his study of an ancient unconscious.
1903	Marries Emma Rauschenbach—heiress to a Swiss watch fortune.
1906	Begins famous correspondence with Sigmund Freud after reading *The Interpretation of Dreams*. The following year in Vienna, Jung and Freud meet for the first time, talking for thirteen hours straight.
1909	Relationship with Freud begins to cool, then completely breaks down over disagreement about psychic phenomena, psychosexual theory, and Freud's "unwillingness to give up his personal authority to advance the truth."
1911	Jung's colleagues also abandon him. Newly published *Transformations of Libido* is declared rubbish, and Jung is relegated to the status of "mystic." His interest in occultism, witchcraft, Buddhism, yoga, alchemy, flying saucers, and obscure tribal rites only fuels his ostracism.
1912	Jung has visions of a monstrous flood engulfing Europe. Thousands drown and civilizations crumble. The waters turn to blood. Weeks later, World War I begins.
1916	Feeling "haunted," Jung writes *Seven Sermons of the Dead*, outlin-

ing his most essential ideas, including the conflict of opposites and the concept of individuation.

1920   Jung begins his study of primitive cultures. Builds a stone tower next to his home, using it as a place to read, meditate, and write. The following year he publishes *Psychological Types,* introducing the concepts of extroversion and introversion into everyday language.

1933   The Nazis incorporate Jungian philosophies into their own works, but Jung hastens to discredit their interpretations.

1948   C. G. Jung Institute is founded—a haven for scholars interested in researching analytic psychology and learning Jungian theory.

1955   Emma Jung dies, and Jung begins to retreat from public life.

1961   Jung dies peacefully at home on Lake Lucerne, surrounded by family. He is 85.

TIMOTHY LEARY

1920-1996

By WINONA RYDER, *goddaughter*

Delivered at memorial service, June 9, 1996

Santa Monica Airport hangar, Santa Monica, CA

THREE MONTHS AFTER I WAS BORN, MY DAD, WHO WAS Tim's archivist, went to see him in Switzerland, where Tim was living in exile after escaping prison and being called "the most dangerous man in the world" by Nixon, who was furiously trying to hunt him down.

My dad and Tim took acid and went skiing, and my dad pulled out a picture of me—the first one ever taken (I was a day old)—and showed it to Tim and asked if he would be my godfather. Tim said, "Sure."

We didn't meet until seven years later, after Tim was released from prison and came to visit us on our commune in Mendocino County. We were walking along a dusty road on a remote mountain ridge. It was sunset and we were holding hands. I looked up at him and said, "They say you're a mad scientist."

Tim smiled and said, "I know." I think he liked the sound of that.

Around the time I became a teenager I wanted to be a writer. This, of course, thrilled Tim and we constantly talked about books. My favorite literary character was Holden Caulfield; his was Huck Finn. We talked about the similarities between the two characters—especially their feelings of alienation from polite society. I wanted to catch all the kids falling off the cliff and Tim wanted to light out for the territory. It was a time when I was in my first throes of adolescence and experiencing that kind of alienation. And talking to Tim was the light at the end of the tunnel.

He really understood my generation. He called us "free agents in the Age of Information."

What I learned from Tim didn't have anything to do with drugs, but it had everything to do with getting high. His die-hard fascination with the human brain was not all about altering it, but about using it to its fullest. And he showed us that that process—that journey—was our most important one. However we did it, as long as we did it. "You are the owner and operator of your brain," he reminded us.

Tim was a huge influence on me—not just with his revolutionary ideas about human potential, but as someone who read me stories, encouraged me, took me to baseball games—you know, godfather stuff. He was the first person outside my family—who you never tend to believe while growing up—to make me believe I could do anything. He had an incredible way of making you feel special and completely supported.

F. Scott Fitzgerald wrote a letter to his daughter in which he said that he hoped his life had achieved some sort of "epic grandeur." Tim's life wasn't "some sort of" epic grandeur. It was flat-out epic grandeur.

It's easy sometimes to get lost in all the drug stuff that Tim's famous for—all the "Turn on, tune in, drop out" stuff, especially in a society that loves a sound bite. But it wasn't Tim's only legacy. It was his vitality, enthusiasm, curiosity, humor, and humanity that made Tim great—and those are the real ingredients of a mad scientist.

1920   Born in Springfield, MA, the only child of a dentist and a schoolteacher.

1941   Attends West Point but eventually resigns, disenchanted with the white authoritarian archetype. Proceeds to graduate school at U.C. Berkeley, where he gets his Ph.D. in clinical psychology.

1955	First wife Marianne commits suicide, leaving Leary to raise their school-age son and daughter.
1959	Joins Harvard's faculty.
1960	Tries magic mushrooms in Mexico and has life-transforming experience, "without question the deepest religious experience of my life."
1961	At Harvard, he and Ram Dass begin experimenting with LSD, giving the drug to prison inmates, researchers—and students. "Turn on, tune in, drop out," he encourages. Pied piper of consciousness or corrupter of youth? Younger and older generations are intensely polarized.
1963	Fired from Harvard.
1967	Marries Rosemary Woodruff—his third wife.
1969	Busted on marijuana charge, Leary is sentenced to prison for 10 years. "Consider my situation. . . . The American government was being run by Richard Nixon, Spiro Agnew, G. Gordon Liddy, John Mitchell, and J. Edgar Hoover. Would you have let men like this keep you in prison for life for your ideas?"
1970	Leary escapes. Flees to Algiers, then on to Switzerland and the Middle East.
1973	Caught in Afghanistan, Leary is returned to prison in California—where he is Charles Manson's cellmate. Paroled after testifying against other drug icons, Leary finds himself denounced by Allen Ginsberg, Ram Dass, and his own son.
1977	Guru becomes dilettante: Over the next 2 decades, Leary tries to make a legal living as a stand-up comic, actor, author, software developer, director of a psychological research foundation, and manager of a rock band.
1982	Goes on lecture tour with Watergate villain G. Gordon Liddy.
1993	Well into his 70s, still clad in white sneakers, Leary continues to

address youth, rallying them toward the electronic exchange of information. His new motto: "Just say know."

1995   Dying of inoperable prostate cancer, Leary sets up website where fans can take a tour of his house, learn what drugs he takes to counter pain, and possibly watch him commit suicide in real time and be cryogenically frozen. Eventually he discards this as an option.

1996   Dies just after midnight, quietly, surrounded by friends. His last words: "Why not?" Afterward, a spaceship company launches seven grams of his ashes into space. His legacy? An astounding 27 books, 250 articles, more than 100 interviews, and an inner-pointed moral compass: "Don't ask me anything. Think for yourself and question authority."

MARSHALL McLUHAN

1911–1980

by JOHN CULKIN, *longtime friend and colleague, founder of the Center for Understanding Media*

Delivered at memorial service, January 3, 1981

Holy Rosary Church, Toronto, Canada

WE HAVE BEEN FRIENDS TOGETHER. BUT IT IS A NEW year and a new time and we are to be together in a new way. Marshall no longer walks among us as a friend, nor beside us as a member of a family, nor before us as a guide. But even his leaving was all in harmony with his great and gracious ways, because it included all that was most important to him in his life—his family, his work, his God.

He saw his children's children. The family was together giving each other the strength and love that it has always done and has always been generous enough to share with those of us whose lives have been touched by it. It was a special family because Marshall was a special man and because Corrine was a special woman.

His work was complicated. He had worked in company with his son to finish a major book. And through the warm and life-giving presence of Father Frank Stroud through the final days, he was close to his God, to his beliefs.

As we sit here today, we all have our own personal memories of Marshall as we are touched by his mortality and reminded of our own. Some of them are so private as to be protected with that same kind of fierce energy that he protected many of his most private feelings. Some are to be shared because we need them for ourselves and for each other. I remember coming back from a conference, and Marshall asked his regular two questions: "John, did you hear any new jokes?" and

194

"John, did you learn anything?" And the jokes were always important, as you know, because Marshall knew that we spell manslaughter and man's laughter the same way and that it depends on where we choose to put the emphasis. His humor was not icing added to his thoughts: His humor was integral to it. It was a special form of courtesy to allow those who wanted to maintain their seriousness to stay there and those who would easily be distracted to have an easy way not to pay attention.

But I think often of his question, "Did you learn anything?" I know myself that you tend as you go along to get your box and you want things within that box tidy. You want to get them all in order and you make small changes, large changes, but always within that box. Marshall was one who questioned whether the box itself was adequate to life. He always said, "Nothing is inevitable if we are willing to understand." And so the comfortable way of rearranging small things in small boxes was not given to him. He chose a more dangerous way and, in an incredibly artistic performance, in a world that would have been more comfortable with scientists dealing with these truths, he teased and cajoled, and tempted and invited, and tried to persuade us to join him in the pursuit. And it was a pursuit that mattered. He was in the company of those who did work that made a difference. The work is not finished, and there are many in our number today who will be part of bringing it to completion. But the years teach what the days could never know. In many ways his work has not been read for the first time. It is still remaining to be read, to be understood, to be incorporated.

We have been friends together. But it is a new year and a new time, and we are together in a new way. The family goes on; the friends go on; the ideas go on; the work goes on; Marshall goes on. For such as him, there is no death.

1911	Born in Alberta, Canada.
1920	Begins tinkering with radios and thinks of becoming an engineer. Influenced by his mother's interest in oration, develops a fascination with poetry, memorizing substantial passages of English poetry.
1928	Enters University of Manitoba. Graduates in 1935 with a Master's in Arts. He quips, "I read my way out of engineering and into English literature." Later receives a Ph.D. from Cambridge University.
1936	Teaching Elizabethan philosophies at University of Wisconsin, McLuhan complains, "I was confronted with young Americans I was incapable of understanding. I felt an urgent need to study their popular culture in order to get through."
1939	Marries Texan Corinne Lewis.
1946	Accepts teaching position at University of Toronto, where he remains for the rest of his teaching career.
1963	Establishes the Center for Culture and Technology, devoting himself to the study of electronic media. Enjoys popular success in the 1960s and becomes a media "guru," although he rarely goes to movies or watches TV.
1964	Publishes *Understanding Media*. Core idea: The way we acquire information affects us as much as the information itself. Tells students, "The public has yet to see TV as TV. Broadcasters have no awareness of its potential. The movie people are just beginning to get a grasp on film." Believes that electronic media can create a "global village," unifying and retribalizing the human race.
1967	Accepts the Albert Schweitzer Chair at Fordham University for one year.
1977	Makes a cameo appearance as himself in Woody Allen's *Annie Hall*.
1980	Dies in his sleep on New Year's Eve. With the advent of the Internet two decades later, his ideas enjoy a resurgence, gaining greater significance than they enjoyed in his own lifetime.

CHET ATKINS

By GARRISON KEILLOR, *friend*

Delivered at memorial service, July 3, 2001

Ryman Auditorium, Nashville, TN

IT'S FITTING TO MEET HERE AT THE RYMAN BECAUSE IT WAS here, on a Saturday night in the summer of 1946, Red Foley came on *The Grand Ole Opry* and sang "Old Shep" and then, before the commercial break for Prince Albert in a can, nodded to his guitarist and said, "Ladies and gentlemen, Mr. Chester Atkins will now play 'Maggie' on the acoustic guitar," and Mr. Atkins did, and afterward Minnie Pearl came up and kissed him and said, "You're a wonderful musician, you're just what we've been needing around here."

He played guitar in a style that hadn't been seen before, with a thumb pick for the bass note and two fingers to play the contrapuntal melody, and at a time when guitarists were expected to be flashy and play "Under the Double Eagle" with the guitar up behind their head, this one hunched down over the guitar and made it sing, made a melody line that was beautiful and legato. A woman wrote, who saw him play in a roadhouse in Cincinnati in 1946, "He sat hunched in the spotlight and played and the whole room suddenly got quiet. It was a drinking and dancing crowd, but there was something about Chet Atkins that could take your breath away."

Chester Burton Atkins was born June 20, 1924, the son of Ida Sharp and James Arley Atkins, a music teacher and piano tuner and singer, near Luttrell, Tennessee, on the farm of his grandfather who fought on the Union side in the Civil War.

Chet was born into a mess of trouble: His people were poor, his folks split up when he was six, he suffered from asthma, he grew up lonely and scared, tongue-tied and shy. His older brothers played music and he listened, and when he was six, he got a ukulele. When he broke a string, he pulled a wire off the screen door and tuned it up. He took up the guitar when he was nine, a Sears Silvertone with the action about a half-inch high at the twelfth fret, torture to play. He'd tune it up to a major chord and play it with a kitchen knife for a slide, Hawaiian-style "Steel Guitar Rag." When he was eleven, he went to live with his daddy in Columbus, Georgia, where on a summer day you could see the snake tracks in the dust on a dirt road, but at night the radio brought in Cincinnati and Atlanta and Knoxville and even New York City.

That was the music that spoke to his heart.

Chet got a lot of music from his dad, who was a trained singer—the old hymns and sentimental ballads, which Chet remembered all his life. He could sing you several verses of "In the Gloaming" or "Seeing Nellie Home," whether you asked for them or not—and he knew the fiddle tunes and mountain music that he picked up trying to play the fiddle—but on the radio he heard music that really entranced him, that was freer and looser and more jangly and elegant and attitudinous. His brother Jim played rhythm guitar with Les Paul when Les was with Fred Waring and His Pennsylvanians and Chet paid close attention to that, and to George Barnes and the Sons of the Pioneers and the Hoosier Hot Shots, and Merle Travis, who he heard on a crystal set from WLW in Cincinnati. (Merle was a big hero of his and he named his daughter Merle; luckily for her, Chet didn't feel so strongly about Riley Puckett or Low Stokes or Gid Tanner.) Chet tried to get the Merle Travis sound, and in the process, he came up with his own, and then he discovered Django Reinhardt and that set something loose in him. You might be shy and homely and puny and from the sticks and feel looked down upon, but if you could play the guitar like that, you would be aristocracy and never have to point it out—anybody with sense would know it and the others don't matter, anyway.

He met Django backstage once in Chicago when Django was touring with Duke Ellington and got his autograph. Chet said, "I wanted to play for him but I didn't get the chance." But in Knoxville, doing the *Midday Merry-Go-Round,* he met Homer and Jethro, Henry Haynes, and Kenneth Burns, who were hip to Django, too, and on Chet's wavelength, and in 1949 they made an instrumental album called *Galloping Guitar*—sort of the Hot Club of Nashville. It got some airplay and that was his first big success and he was on his way.

Chet had dropped out of high school to go into radio and the music business—first with Jumping Bill Carlisle and Archie Campbell in Knoxville, and Johnnie and Jack in Raleigh, then Red Foley in Chicago and Springfield, Missouri, and Mother Maybelle and the Carter Sisters. In Cincinnati he met Leona Johnson, who was singing on WLW with her twin sister, Lois, and after a year of courtship they married in 1946. He wrote in 1984: "Our percolator went out the other day and we counted up . . . she has stayed with me through four of them. If I were her, I wouldn't have stayed around through the first one, which was a non-electric. After drinking coffee, there would be a residue on the cup and folks would read it and tell your fortune. Anyway, she is mine and she is a winner."

Chet got himself fired plenty of times along the way, a badge of honor for a musician with a mind of his own, and he kept getting fired in an upward direction and wound up coming to Nashville and WSM and the Opry and RCA, under the patronage of Fred Rose and Steve Sholes. He got to see the end of the era of the medicine show and the hillbilly band with the comedian with the blacked-out teeth and the beginnings of rock and roll—Chet had a front-row seat, as the guitarist, and he remembered everything he saw and he knew stories about a lot of people in this room who are not in your official press packets. In his recollections, he was kind but he was honest, like the bartender in *Frankie and Johnny*: "I don't want to cause you no trouble but I ain't gonna tell you no lies." This was a man who knew the icons close-up—he could talk about Hank Williams and Elvis and Patsy

Cline and Mother Maybelle Carter and who they really were and what was on their minds and what they ate for breakfast. He knew so many giants.

This man was a giant himself. He was the guitar player of the twentieth century. He was the model of who you should be and what you should look like. You could tell it whenever he picked up a guitar, the way it fit him. His upper body was shaped to it, from a lifetime of playing: His back was slightly hunched, his shoulders rounded, and the guitar was the missing piece. He was an artist and there was no pretense in him; he never waved the flag or held up the cross or traded on his own sorrows. He was the guitarist. His humor was self-deprecating; he was his own best critic. He inspired all sorts of players who never played anything like him. He was generous and admired other players' work and he told them so. He had a natural reserve to him, but when he admired people, he went all out to tell them about it. And because there was no deception in him, his praise meant more than just about anything else. If Chet was a fan of yours, you never needed another one.

He was not a saint. He was a restless man. He'd be in a room and then he'd need to be somewhere else. He had deep moods that came and went and that he couldn't enunciate. He had a certain harmless vanity to him. There was an album cover late in his career with a picture airbrushed to make him look about twenty-three that we had to kid him about. He liked synthesizers more than he maybe ought to have. He sometimes kicked his golf ball to improve his lie.

When he was almost fifty, he had a stroke of good luck when he got colon cancer and thought he was going to die, and when he didn't die, he found a whole new love of life. He walked away from the corporate music world and fell in love with the guitar again and went all over performing with Paul Yandell, playing with all the great orchestras, notably the Boston Pops, and started living by his own clock, so he had time to sit and talk with people and pick music with them and enjoy the social side of music and have more fun. "I haven't learned to exercise the right of privacy," he said. "Folks are always calling and I drop everything and entertain them." He had a gift for friendship. He was so generous with stories. Some of us are able to impersonate storytellers, but Chet was the real thing, and if you drove around Nashville with him, he remembered one after another—it was a documentary movie about country music. Chet loved so many people. He especially loved the ones who seemed a little wild to him and who made him laugh. He loved his grandkids, Jonathan and Amanda, and talked them up every chance he got, though I don't know how wild they were. Dolly Parton always made him laugh, the way she flirted with him. A few months ago, she came to see him—he was in bed, dying—and she made him laugh for about an hour, telling him things I'm not about to repeat here. He loved Waylon Jennings. He loved Lenny Breaux. Jerry Reed. Ray Stevens. Vince Gill. Steve Wariner. And Brother Dave Gardner, the hipster revivalist comedian who Chet discovered doing stand-up in a Nashville club between sets as a drummer and who said, "Dear hearts, gathered here to rejoice in the glorious Southland. Joy to the world! The South has always been the South. And I believe the only reason that folks live in the North is because they have jobs up there."

He loved doing shows. He never had a bad night. He played some notes he didn't mean to play, but they never were bad notes. They simply were other notes. He was such a professional it was hard to bug him, but I succeeded when we did a show together and at the end I took his hand and we took a bow together. The next night, he said to me before the show, "Don't take my hand onstage that way, you know what people will think, you being a Northern liberal and all." I found that during the bow I could make him flinch just by gesturing toward him.

He liked to be alone backstage. He liked it quiet and calm in the dressing room and he counted on George Lunn to make it that way. I remember him backstage, alone, walking around in the cavernous dark of some opera house out west, holding the guitar, playing, singing to himself; he needed to be alone with himself and get squared away, because the Chet people saw onstage was the same Chet you hung around with in his office, joking with Paul about having a swimming pool shaped like a guitar amp, the joke about "By the time I learned I couldn't tune very well, I was too rich to care," and singing "Would Jesus Wear a Rolex" and "I just Can't Say Goodbye" and ending the show with his ravishing beautiful solo, "Vincent," the audience sitting in rapt silence. It was all the same Chet who sat at home with Leona, watching a golf tournament with the sound off, and playing his guitar, a long stream-of-consciousness medley in which twenty or thirty tunes came together perfectly, as in a dream, his daddy's songs and "Banks of the Ohio" and "Recuerdos de la Alhambra" and "Smile" and Stephen Foster and Boudleaux Bryant and the Beatles and Freight Train, one long sparkling stream of music, as men in plaid pants hit their long, high approach shots in a green paradise.

He said, "I enjoy the fruits of my efforts but I have never felt comfortable promoting myself. The condition is worsening now that I am on the back nine. My passion for the guitar and for fame is slowly dying and it makes me sad. I never thought my love for the guitar would fade. There are a lot of reasons; as we get older the high frequencies go, music doesn't sound so good. And for some damn reason after hearing so many great players, I lose the competitive desire. Here I am baring my soul. That's good, though, isn't it. I'm not a Catholic but I love that facet of their religion."

Chet was curious and thoughtful about religion, though he was dubious about shysters and TV evangelists. He said, "I am seventy and still don't know anything about life, what universal entity designed the body I live in or what will come after I am gone. I figure there will be eternity and nothing much else. Like pulling a finger out of water. If it is as the Baptists claim, I think I would tire of streets of gold and would want to see brick houses. I believe that when I die I'll probably go to Minnesota. The last time I was up there, it was freezing and I remember smiling and my upper lip went up and didn't come back down."

God looks on the heart and is a God of mercy and loving-kindness beyond our comprehension, and in that faith let us commend his spirit to the Everlasting, may the angels bear him up, and may eternal light shine upon him, and may he run into a lot of his old friends, and if he should wind up in Minnesota, we will do our best to take care of him until the rest of you come along.

1924	Born Chester Burton Atkins in Luttrell, TN, into a musical family: His father is a music teacher; his mother plays the piano.
1933	At six, Chet is a resourceful musician: He repairs his ukulele with wire from a screen door. ("We were so poor," he recalls afterward, "that it was the forties before any of us knew there had been a depression.")
1941	Drops out of high school.
1942	Auditions at Knoxville's WNOX, earning a solo instrumental spot on the station's *Midday Merry-Go-Round*.
1946	Marries country singer Leona Johnson. Atkins's musical style is a hindrance to his career—the local radio stations want simple, twangy "hillbilly" guitar, not the sophisticated, arty guitar playing Atkins has developed. The couple moves to Cincinnati.
1948	Performs at the Grand Ole Opry in Nashville for the first time. Releases his first hit single, "The Galloping Guitars," for RCA the following year.
1952	Begins a second career as a talent scout when RCA asks him to build up the label's roster. By the mid-fifties he is recording his own albums and producing 30 artists a year for RCA—including Elvis Presley, Waylon Jennings, and Perry Como. He later recalls, humbly, "All I was trying to do was keep my job. And the way to keep your job is to surprise the friends and neighbors with each new record."

1954   RCA issues his debut LP, *Gallopin' Guitar,* and sends him on tour.

1957   Taking notice of Atkins's gift for finding distinctive voices and ear-catching hit songs, RCA promotes him to Manager of Operations. Amid a declining market for country music, Atkins plays a pivotal part in moving the genre toward a harder, honky-tonk style—then later a pop style with lush choruses and vocals. Dubbed "the Nashville Sound," this softer approach saves country from the rock and roll juggernaut.

1961   Performs for President Kennedy at the White House.

1967   Wins first of 11 Grammy Awards—Best Instrumental Performance for *Chet Atkins Picks the Best.*

1973   Atkins becomes youngest inductee into the Country Music Hall of Fame.

1981   Hungering to prove himself a talented jazz musician, Atkins leaves RCA for Columbia Records.

1997   Undergoes surgery to remove a brain tumor. Spends his last years in his office on Nashville's Music Row. Offered honorary degrees by various universities, he never accepts one, preferring the designation he bestows on himself: Certified Guitar Picker.

2001   Dies of cancer at 77, in the city whose sound he helped define.

IRVING BERLIN
1888 - 1989

By SAMUEL GOLDWYN JR., *family friend*

Delivered at memorial service, February 6, 1990

The Music Box Theater, New York City

I'M PROBABLY THE ONLY PERSON HERE WHO BEGAN A relationship with Mr. Berlin without having the slightest idea what he did for a living. In fact, my first impression of what he did was play cards and backgammon. Mary Ellin's mother and mine were not only close friends but fellow card widows. The game was either at Joseph Schenck's—lovingly called Uncle Joe by Mary Ellin—or above Grauman's Chinese Theater in Uncle Sid's office. I thought it was nice that Mr. Berlin spent so much time with his relatives.

But there was a difference between Mr. Berlin and the other card-players—including, at times, my own father. Whenever I came into the room, he would summon me to his side, drop his cards, peer over his glasses, comment on my growth, inquire into my general well-being, and bring me news of Mary Ellin and the family. And he made me feel special. That's important when you're five or six.

I knew that Mr. Berlin worked very hard, but he always seemed to have time to play with Mary Ellin and me. I remember asking Mary Ellin what her father did for a living. Her comment was, nonchalantly: "He writes some songs for a Miss Merman to sing. But sometimes she doesn't sing them the way he wants, and Daddy gets very angry."

The summer of 1937, he turned from a card game and asked me to join the family on a yachting trip through the Alaskan inland water-ways. Together with Mrs. Berlin, Mary Ellin, and baby Linda, we took a yacht north to Juno, stopping along the way to fish, camp, look for brown bears, or whatever activities he had planned: He took a great deal of pleasure in making each day's project a production and a surprise. He also spent a great deal of time in checking out the restaurants in each small Alaskan town, and allowed no one to enter until he conducted a full kitchen inspection. One day he was absolutely ecstatic because he had found that the head cook at a restaurant in Ketchikan had once worked at Dinty Moore's—his favorite eating place in New York.

Our boat had a salon where Mary Ellin, Linda, and I played, but there was one problem: The room had a piano, and each morning Mr. Berlin would come in and bang on it while we were trying to play. It was very distracting for us. When he would finally finish, Mary Ellin asked, "What's that, Daddy?"

His only reply was, "New song," and he came over to join us in our games.

Years later, I realized that during that trip, he had composed the songs for the movie *Carefree*, and that the incessant banging had produced "I Used to Be Colorblind."

By now I knew that Mr. Berlin also wrote songs for Mr. Astaire—which was nice, because I knew them both and was sure that Mr. Astaire would be nice to him even if Ethel Merman wasn't. But oddly enough, it wasn't until I saw the movie *Alexander's Ragtime Band* that I fully grasped who Irving Berlin was, and how privileged I was to know him. Still, I've never been able to separate that musical genius from the loving husband, devoted father, and friend who has been so much a part of my life.

As the years passed, I've only snapshot memories: Him with Elizabeth as a baby. A Christmas vacation during the war. A train trip across the country with him. A runthrough of *Annie Get Your Gun*—and his great delight as he listened to Ethel Merman sing "You Can't Get a Man with a Gun."

As Mr. Berlin became more reclusive, our relationship became a telephonic one. I would speak to him on his birthday, or some other occasion. After asking about me, he always had news of something special to impart—like his great joy over Mary Ellin's first novel. The arrival of a grandchild. Or his concern over a friend like Irving Hoffman or Oscar Levant. Sometimes he would call asking for information or a small favor. One never knew what was on his mind, but he would begin with the assumption that the task—no matter how small—was a great imposition on me, which he would only presume on because of my closeness to Mary Ellin.

He never realized how flattered I was to be asked.

Shortly after the release of a comedy I'd made about two Harlem cops, I received a call from him: He loved the film and wanted to talk about Harlem—the Harlem he knew, the Harlem that had inspired his song "Harlem on My Mind." This segued into his thoughts about an unfinished project he'd toyed with for many years—a musical about the life of Josephine Baker. He began to outline scenes and incidents, and how the songs would both evoke her life and the background of Harlem. When I asked him if he wanted to do it, he said, "Yes, but I'm afraid it's for someone else." But the more he insisted on this, the more the ideas seemed to energetically pour forth from him.

We got cheated of that Berlin musical. Still, I like to think that that lovely man is still somewhere interrupting his card games, banging on his piano, and bursting with ideas for making heavenly music.

1888 Born Israel Baline in Siberia. The family immigrates to America and settles in a New York City tenement—eight children, three rooms, no windows.

1902 At 14, Israel leaves home to sing for pennies in Bowery saloons.

1907 As a singing waiter in Chinatown, he discovers his talent for creating lyrics to other people's music. His first published song, "Marie from Sunny Italy," is mistakenly ascribed to I. Berlin. He keeps the name and expands the I to "Irving."

1911   Al Jolson sings Berlin's "Alexander's Ragtime Band," catapulting sales of the sheet music to over a million copies in three weeks. Berlin follows with a string of popular songs, netting him royalties of $100,000 a year and a nickname: the Hitmaker.

1912   Marries Dorothy Goetz, who dies of typhoid five months later. Devastated, Berlin pens "When I Lost You," later claiming it was the only time he injected his personal life into a song.

1919   Forms his own music publishing company, Irving Berlin Music.

1926   Elopes with WASPy socialite Ellin Mackay. Her father disinherits her, but the couple remains together until her death in 1988. Mary Ellin is born and Berlin pens the hit "Blue Skies" in celebration.

1929   Stock market crash wipes out Berlin's fortune.

1935   Feeling that the automobile has changed the rhythm of life, Berlin uses a new syncopated tempo in Fred Astaire's *Top Hat*. Begins a new phase of writing for screen and stage.

1939   With America on the brink of war, Berlin writes "God Bless America," donating his royalties to the Boy Scouts.

1954   *Annie Get Your Gun* opens to raves. The razzle-dazzle anthem "There's No Business Like Show Business" becomes a standard.

1962   His last musical, *Mr. President,* flops. As his influence wanes, Berlin stops writing and refuses requests for interviews.

1977   President Ford honors him with the highest civilian honor, the Medal of Freedom.

1988   At 100th birthday celebration at Carnegie Hall, Leonard Bernstein serenades Berlin with his original composition "My Twelve-Tone Melody."

1989   Dies at 101, in his sleep, in his townhouse in New York City, having penned over 1500 songs, 30 Broadway shows, and 17 Hollywood musicals. Jerome Kern: "Irving Berlin has no place in American music—he *is* American music."

SAMMY DAVIS JR.

1925–1990

By GREGORY HINES, *friend and admirer*

Delivered at memorial service, May 18, 1990

Forest Lawn Memorial Park, Los Angeles, CA

THE FAMILY HAS ASKED ME TO SPEAK TODAY. I HAVE A hard time with death, and "grieving in a good way"—for me it's just not possible because I miss him so much already. It's going to take me a little time.

I idolize Sammy Davis Jr.

The first time I saw Sammy was in 1956 at the Apollo Theater in Harlem. I was ten years old—I'd been tap-dancing for seven years. I'd seen a lot of great tap dancers at the Apollo, but there was something about going to see Sammy Davis there. I'd seen him on television on the *Colgate Comedy Hour,* and it seemed like black people connected with tap dancers in a way that in my young life I'd never connected with any other black artist. He just had *something*.

The Apollo had four shows a day. It was our custom to get a seat wherever we could, and at the end of each show we'd move down closer to the front. By the third show we were in the front row. . . .

It was indescribable. He could do everything. He just looked so *good* up there. He was wearing those short jackets—an Eaton suit—and his hair was beautiful. And he sang. Then he did impersonations—and they were of white stars. It was amazing that he could do that: In 1956 black people were really struggling, and there were things as a young boy that I shouldn't do. I had to be careful, but Sammy Davis did whatever he wanted. He couldn't be denied on the stage.

He played instruments. He played the bass. He played the trumpet. He played the drums. And he wasn't jack-of-all-trades. . . . No, he could really *play* those instruments. To the point where trumpet players wanted to see Sammy Davis. And bass players? He wasn't just playing the bass—*boom boom*. He would . . . *doodja-da-dum-boom*. He would get into it. And he was so relaxed; I'd seen performers and I knew people had an act. But Sammy Davis? In the middle of the act, he did different things. At one point he began telling a joke, and he couldn't finish the joke—he was laughing so hard. And I couldn't believe that he was so relaxed on the stage.

And then he tapped.

I knew good tap dancing. And I knew the really great tap dancers. And he was a really great tap dancer, *too*. He could do all those things and he could tap also.

I could only *tap*.

That was the beginning of my relationship with him. I was in the front row, and he was singing "Hey There" and he saw me. I guess he'd seen me for three shows just moving down. There was a spot in the song where he was singing ". . . better forget her . . . ," and he looked at me. You know, I'd been performing onstage and saw the audience as just a big black hole. I never looked at anybody, but he was so relaxed that he actually looked at me and *winked*.

Afterward we went backstage. I wanted to see him and touch him. We went up to the floor of his dressing room, and there were a lot of people there. He was sitting in his dressing room and he had no shirt on, leaning back in his chair. He looked through the door and saw me and reached out his hand—just like I'm doing now—and I just walked toward him. And he held his hand out. And I reached out and touched his hand and he went like that:

[Squeezes my hand.]

It was a moment of my life that affected me in every aspect: How I felt. What I did. How I carried myself. For about six years after that, I *was* Sammy Davis Jr. I put a lot of pressure on my parents to get me one of those Eaton jacket suits. Slicked my hair back.

I walked exactly how Sammy Davis walked.

The last time I saw Sammy Davis Jr. was about four weeks ago. He was sitting home watching TV—and he looked so good to me. When I was leaving I kissed him and told him I loved him. I walked a few steps, then turned around, because it felt like that was going to be the last time I would see him. He looked at me. And he reached down for an imaginary ball and threw it.

I caught it.

I take that very seriously. I'm going to carry that ball, then give it to somebody else. From this day on, I charge myself and everyone here with the responsibility to let people know who Sammy Davis was. We have to make the documentaries, write the books, sing the songs, tell people who he was and what he did. We have to transform Sammy Davis into the folk hero that people become who are like Sammy Davis in life.

It's our responsibility.

1925	Born in a Harlem tenement. His vaudevillian parents leave him in care of his grandmother.
1928	Age 3, Sammy joins his father in vaudeville after his mother leaves the act. When authorities are sent to investigate the working minor, Sammy is given a cigar to hold and billed as "Silent Sam, the Dancing Midget."
1941	Opens for Frank Sinatra in Detroit, beginning their 50-year friendship.
1943	Drafted into the army, Davis learns how to read from a black sergeant who supplies him with comic books. Battling Nazis, he finds a more insidious foe in army racism; he takes to the stage to "neutralize the [GI] bigots and get them to acknowledge me."
1954	Signs with Decca and releases the first of 40 records. Later that year, loses left eye in near-fatal auto crash. Declaring an affinity

between Jews and blacks, who have both "been oppressed for centuries," Davis converts to Judaism—catching both Jews and blacks off guard.

1956	Debuts on Broadway in *Mr. Wonderful*. The show runs for more than four hundred performances.
1959	Sporting a broken nose, gold jewelry, and a trim tux, Davis rides a crest of popularity—singing, tapping, and generally charming audiences on both sides of the color barrier. Joins Sinatra's Rat Pack. Starring in his best-known movie role, Sportin' Life in *Porgy and Bess*, Davis becomes one of the first black performers to gain mainstream acclaim.
1960	Marries white actress May Britt. Their union invites slurs from both whites and blacks, and the following year JFK asks Davis and wife not to participate in the presidential election, lest the sight of an interracial couple provoke Southerners. Shoots first Rat Pack movie, *Ocean's Eleven*.
1970	His marriage to Britt over, Davis marries dancer Altovise Gore.
1972	Releases his number one hit, "The Candy Man." For the next two decades, Davis continues entertaining onstage, on television, and in books. A bon vivant, he smokes, drinks, and spends extravagantly—going through $50 million with ease and generosity.
1989	Final bow: Davis shoots *Tap* with Gregory Hines. Completes world tour with Frank Sinatra and Liza Minnelli. Pens last of three autobiographies, *Why Me?* And finally conquers alcohol and cocaine addiction. "The hardest thing is waking up in the morning and realizing that's as good as you're going to feel all day."
1990	A lifelong smoker, Davis dies of throat cancer at age 64.

DUKE ELLINGTON

1899–1974

By STANLEY DANCE, *close friend and jazz journalist*

Delivered at funeral, May 27, 1974

Church of St. John the Divine, New York City

IT IS HARD TO DO JUSTICE IN WORDS TO A BELOVED FRIEND, especially when the friend was a genius of the rarest kind.

So, first the basic facts of his temporal existence: Edward Kennedy Ellington, "Duke" Ellington, born in Washington, D.C., 1899, died in New York, 1974.

Now, some might claim him as a citizen of one or the other of these cities, but he was not. In the truest sense of the phrase, he was a citizen of the world. That is a cliché perhaps, but how few are those who deserve it as he did. He was loved throughout the whole world, at all levels of society, by Frenchmen and Germans, by English and Irish, by Arabs and Jews, by Indians and Pakistanis, by atheists and devout Catholics, and by communists and fascists alike.

So, no, not even this city in which, as he said, he paid rent and had his mailbox—not even New York can claim him exclusively for its own.

Of all the cities he conquered—more than Napoleon, and by much better methods—I remember particularly Buenos Aires when he went there the first time. He had played his final concert and sat in the car outside the theater before going to the airport. People clutched at him through the opened windows, people who were crying, who thrust gifts on him, gifts on which they hadn't even written their names. It was one of the few times I saw him moved to tears.

As a musician, he hated categories. He didn't want to be restricted,

213

and although he mistrusted the word *jazz*, his definition of it was "freedom of expression." If he wished to write an opera, or music for a ballet, or for the symphony, or for a Broadway musical, or for a movie, he didn't want to feel confined to the idiom in which he was the unchallenged, acknowledged master.

As with musical categories, so with people categories. Categories of class, race, color, creed, and money were obnoxious to him. He made his subtle, telling contributions to the civil rights struggle in musical statements—in "Jump for Joy" in 1941, in "The Deep South Suite" in 1946, and in "My People" in 1963. Long before black was officially beautiful—in 1928, to be precise—he had written "Black Beauty" and dedicated it to a great artist, Florence Mills. And with "Black, Brown, and Beige" in 1943, he proudly delineated the black contribution to American history.

His scope constantly widened, and right up to the end he remained a creative force, his imagination stimulated by experience. There was much more he had to write, and would undoubtedly have written, but a miraculous aspect of his work is not merely the quality, but the quantity of it. Music was indeed his mistress. He worked hard, did not spare himself, and virtually died in harness. Only last fall, he set out on one of the most exhausting tours of his career. He premiered his third Sacred Concert in Westminster Abbey for the United Nations, did one-nighters in all the European capitals, went to Abyssinia and Zambia for the State Department, and returned to London for a command performance before Queen Elizabeth. When people asked if he would ever retire, he used to reply scornfully, "Retire to what?"

His career cannot be described in a few minutes. Where would one start? With the composer, the bandleader, the pianist, the arranger, the author, the playwright, the painter? He was a jack-of-all-trades, and master of all he turned his hand to. Or should one start with the complex human being—at once sophisticated, primitive, humorous, tolerant, positive, ironic, childlike (not childish), lionlike, shepherdlike, Christian? He was a natural aristocrat who never lost the common touch. He was the greatest innovator in the field, and yet paradoxically a conservative, one who built new things on the best of the old and disdained ephemeral fashion.

I certainly would never pretend that I wholly knew this wonderful man, although I spent much time in his company and enjoyed his trust. The two people who knew him best were his son, Mercer, and his sister, Ruth, and their loss is greatest of all. Otherwise, his various associates and friends knew different aspects of him, but never, as they readily admit, the whole man.

Song titles say a great deal. "Mood Indigo," "Sophisticated Lady," "Caravan," "Solitude," "Don't Get Around Much Anymore," "I'm Beginning to See the Light," and "Satin Doll" are part of the fabric of twentieth-century life. But the popular-song hits are only a small part of Duke Ellington's priceless legacy to mankind. His music will be interpreted by others, but never with the significance and tonal character given it by his own band and soloists, for whom it was written. In that respect, his records are the greatest of gifts to us. Here one can enter a unique world, filled with his dreams, emotions, fantasies, and fascinating harmonies. He brought out qualities in his musicians they did not always know they possessed. He had the knack of making good musicians sound great, and great musicians sound the greatest. As the best arranger in the business, he was able to furnish them with superb backgrounds, and as one of the most inventive—and underrated—of pianists, he gave them inspiring accompaniment. He was, in fact, more of an inspiration than an influence, and though he made no claim to being a disciplinarian, he ruled his realm with wisdom.

The importance of this realm did not go unrecognized, and he was by no means a prophet without honor in his native land. He celebrated his seventieth birthday in the White House, where President Nixon bestowed the highest civilian honor upon him, appropriately the Medal of Freedom. Presidents Johnson, Eisenhower, and Truman had all recognized his achievements in different ways. No less than seventeen colleges conferred honorary degrees upon him. Other high honors came to him from the Emperor Haile Selassie, from France, and from Sweden. His likeness appeared on the postage stamps of Togoland and Chad.

Duke Ellington knew what some called genius was really the exercise of gifts that stemmed from God. These gifts were those his Maker favored. The Son of God said, "Fear not. Go out and teach all nations. Proclaim the good news to all men." And Duke knew the good news was an opportunity to acknowledge something of which he stood in awe, a power he considered above his human limitations. He firmly believed what the mother he worshiped also believed, that he had been blessed at birth. He reached out to people with his music and drew them to himself.

There must be many here who can testify to his assumption—conscious or unconscious—of a father's role. Those he befriended are legion. His sense of family embraced not only the members of his band throughout the years, but people from all walks of life whose paths crossed his. Wherever or whenever he could, he personally resolved for those about him problems involving doubts, anxieties, illness, or grief. Loyalty was the quality he greatly esteemed in others, and it was generously reciprocated by him.

It is Memorial Day, when those who died for the free world are properly remembered. Duke Ellington never lost faith in his country, and he served it well. His music will go on serving it for years to come.

1899   Born Edward Kennedy Ellington in Washington, D.C. His father, James Ellington, works as a White House butler.

1913   In high school, earns the name Duke for his impeccable taste in dress, food, and lifestyle—even insists his female cousins bow to him in respect. To earn money, Ellington washes dishes at a hotel and works as soda jerk. The latter job inspires his first composition, "Soda Fountain Rag."

1915   Leaves school at age 16 to pursue music full-time. Forms The Duke Serenaders and acts as booking agent for the increasingly successful band.

1918   Marries childhood sweetheart Edna Thompson. Son Mercer follows a year later.

1922   Moves to Harlem and joins the Washingtonians. By now he is clearing a highly respectable $10,000/year.

1927   Begins a five-year stint at famed Cotton Club. Entertaining whites-only audiences in the gangster-owned establishment, Ellington survives with dignity intact: Crowds flock to soak up Ellington's music and Prohibition liquor. Over the next five years, he records more than 180 songs and begins to tour, playing everywhere from New York to New Delhi, Chicago to Cairo.

1929   "Mood Indigo" catapults Duke to international fame. Follows up with songs like "It Don't Mean a Thing If It Ain't Got That Swing" and "Sophisticated Lady." Inflecting jazz with African and Latin elements, Ellington prefers to call his style "music of freedom of expression."

1939   The Ellington Orchestra tours Europe amid World War II mayhem with its strongest collection of players ever, including new addition Billy Strayhorn, who becomes Ellington's chief collaborator.

1943   The King of Swing debuts at Carnegie Hall. Performs his monumental work "Black, Brown, and Beige."

1961   Begins an 81-day tour around the world as part of a relentless schedule of composing, performing, recording, and traveling.

1965   Tries something completely new: begins composing religious music for a series of Sacred Concerts.

1968   Awarded the Presidential Medal of Freedom, the highest honor bestowed on a civilian.

1974   A year after completing his autobiography, *Music Is My Mistress,*
Ellington dies of lung cancer in New York City, age 75.
Encompassing 2000 songs and 20,000 performances, Ellington's
music is more than mistress. Jazz critic Ralph Gleason: "The man
is the music, the music is the man, and never have the two things
been more true than they are for Ellington."

GEORGE HARRISON

1943–2001

By ERIC IDLE, *longtime friend*

Delivered at memorial evening, June 28, 2002

The Hollywood Bowl, Hollywood, CA

WHEN THEY TOLD ME THEY WERE GOING TO INDUCT MY friend George Harrison into the Hollywood Bowl Hall of Fame posthumously, my first thought was: I bet he won't show up. Because, unlike some others one might mention—but won't—he really wasn't into honors. He was one of those odd people who believe that life is somehow more important than show business. Which I know is a heresy here in Hollywood, and I'm sorry to bring it up here in the very Bowel of Hollywood, but I can hear his voice saying, "Oh, very nice, very useful, a posthumous award—where am I supposed to put it?" What's next, then? A posthumous Grammy? An ex-Knighthood? An After-Lifetime Achievement Award? He's going to need a whole new shelf up there.

So, "posthumously inducted"—sounds rather unpleasant. Sounds like some kind of afterlife enema. But "induct," in case you are wondering, comes from the word *induce*, meaning to bring on labor by the use of drugs. And "posthumous" is actually from the Latin *post*, meaning after, and *hummus*, meaning Greek food. So I like to think that George is still out there somewhere—pregnant and breaking plates at a Greek restaurant.

I think he would prefer to be inducted *posthumorously* because he loved comedians—poor, sick, sad, deranged, lovable puppies that we are—because they, like him, had the ability to say the wrong thing at the right time, which is what we call humor. He put Monty Python on here at the Hollywood Bowl, and he paid for the movie *The Life of Brian,* because he wanted to see it. (Still the most anybody has ever paid for a cinema ticket.)

His life was filled with laughter; even his death was filled with laughter. In the hospital he asked the nurses to put fish and chips in his IV. The doctor, thinking he was delusional, said to his son, "Don't worry, we have a medical name for this condition."

"Yes," said Dahni, "humor."

I'm particularly sorry Dahni isn't here tonight, because I wanted to introduce him by saying "Here comes the son"—but sadly that opportunity for a truly bad joke has gone.

George once said to me, "If we'd known we were going to be *the Beatles,* we'd have tried harder." What made George special, apart from his being the best guitarist in the Beatles, was what he did with his life after they achieved everything. He realized that this fame business was, and I'll use the technical philosophical term here, complete bullshit. And he turned to find beauty and truth and meaning in life—and, more extraordinarily, found it.

This is from his book *I Me Mine*:

> *The things that most people are struggling for [are] fame or fortune or wealth or position—and really none of that is important because in the end death will take it all away. So you spend your life struggling for something, which is in effect a waste of time . . . I mean I don't want to be lying there as I'm dying thinking, "Oh shit, I forgot to put the cat out."*

And he wasn't. He passed away here in L.A. with beauty and dignity surrounded by people he loved; he had an extraordinary capacity for friendship. People loved him all over the planet.

George was in fact a moral philosopher: His life was all about a search for truth, and preparing himself for death. Which is a bit weird for someone in rock and roll. They're not supposed to be that smart. They're supposed to be out there looking for Sharon. Not the meaning of life. Mike Palin said George's passing was really sad, but it does make the afterlife seem much more attractive.

He was a gardener: He grew beauty in everything he did—in his life, in his music, in his marriage, and as a father. I was on an island somewhere when a man came up to him and said, "George Harrison, oh my God, what are *you* doing here?" And he said, "Well, everyone's got to be somewhere."

Well, alas, he isn't here. But we are. And that's the point. This isn't for him. This is for us, because we want to honor him. We want to remember him, we want to say, "Thanks, George, for being. And we really miss you."

So this is the big drag about posthumous awards: There's no one to give 'em to. So I'm gonna keep this and put it next to the one I got last year.

No, I'm going to give it to the love of his life, his dark, sweet lady, dear, wonderful Olivia Harrison, who is with us here tonight. Liv, you truly know what it is to be without him.

Thank you, Hollywood Bowl. You do good to honor him. Good night.

1943   Born in Liverpool, England, to a working-class family.

1956   Attending Liverpool Institute, George meets school chum Paul McCartney. Spends his free time practicing chords on his guitar; subsequently becomes lead guitarist for the Quarrymen, a group that includes McCartney and John Lennon.

1960   Renamed the Beatles, the band goes to Germany, where they quickly become a popular local act. On the early days: "It was fun . . . but then we got famous and it spoiled all that, because we'd just go round and round the world singing the same 10 dopey tunes."

1963	"I Want to Hold Your Hand" is the band's first U.S. release.
1964	Appearing on *The Ed Sullivan Show*, the Beatles vault to immediate fame. Due to brooding demeanor, Harrison becomes known as "the quiet Beatle"—a title that belies his contributions. Overshadowed by McCartney and Lennon, he goes on to pen classics like "Something," "Here Comes the Sun," and "If I Needed Someone."
1966	Marries model Patti Boyd, who introduces him to Indian culture, a lifelong obsession. Amid Beatlemania frenzy, he travels to India to study sitar and Eastern philosophy. "Everything else can wait but the search for God."
1970	A year of trials and triumphs: The Beatles break up. Harrison's mother dies of cancer. Releases solo album *All Things Must Pass,* which goes to No. 1.
1971	Organizes the Concert for Bangladesh for the famine-ravaged nation. Recorded live at Madison Square Garden, the event earns Harrison a Grammy for Album of the Year and sets the stage for subsequent all-star benefits like Live Aid and Farm Aid.
1974	Becomes the first Beatle to mount a solo world tour.
1976	Accused of using the Chiffons' hit song "He's So Fine" as the basis for his "My Sweet Lord," Harrison is found guilty of "unconscious plagiarism."
1978	Divorced from Patti, Harrison marries Olivia Arias—who gave birth to their son, Dhani, a month earlier. (Patti goes on to marry Harrison's friend Eric Clapton, but the three remain close.)
1979	Founds Handmade Films to produce Monty Python's *Life of Brian.*
1980	Publishes autobiography *I Me Mine.*
1999	Harrison and his wife are attacked in their London home by a

deranged intruder. Stabbed four times in the chest, Harrison recovers.

2001   Dies of cancer, age 58, in Los Angeles with wife Olivia and son
        Dhani by his side. As required by his spiritual beliefs, he is cre-
        mated within hours of his death, and his ashes are scattered in the
        Ganges River.

JANIS JOPLIN

1943 – 1970

By RALPH GLEASON, *friend and music journalist*

Written on the occasion of her death

GOD KNOWS, THAT LOVELY BLAZING CANDLE DID CAST A lovely light, even though from time to time when it flickered and the light dimmed, the looming face of tragedy appeared.

For Janis, gamin-faced, husky-voiced little girl lost, seemed to me from the moment I first saw her to have that fatal streak of tragedy present. And what's more, to know it.

Laughin' just to keep from crying.

It was just paralyzing to hear the radio bulletin that she was dead. Inevitable but paralyzing still when it happened. How could it be? Why?

And it makes no sense, really, what any inquest finds. She's dead and that's it, and the truth, which is sometimes much more difficult to see than the facts, is that she was driven to self-destruction by some demon deep within her from the moment she left that Texas high school where they had laughed at her.

She showed them, all right, she showed them plenty, and the dues she paid to show them proved too much in the end.

Janis's effect on the San Francisco scene was like a time bomb or a depth charge. There was a long lag before it went off. She came up from Texas, a beatnik folksinger, and sang in the Coffee Gallery and the other crummy joints that were available at the end of the Beat era and just before the Haight blossomed so briefly, only, like Janis, to self-destruct.

It wasn't until she came back from Texas with Chet and joined the band that she really hit, and what a hit it was. It took me a while to absorb it, but once that group got to you, they were a turn-on of magnificent proportions—much, much heavier than anything else she ever got on record. That's why her own group, when she went out with it, was such a disappointment. Janis with Big Brother was magic, never mind that they played out of tune, never mind any of the criticisms; over in the corner on the stage at the Avalon when she screamed, our hearts screamed with her. And when she stomped on that stage at Winterland (and *stomped* is the word) and shook her head and hollered, it was just simply unbelievable.

For all the notoriety (what feature writer could overlook a girl who insisted on drinking like an F. Scott Fitzgerald legend?), Janis's greatest moments came at Monterey, really, which were perhaps the finest moments that movement of which she was so integral a part has ever seen.

There she was, this freaky-looking white kid from Texas onstage with all the hierarchy of the traditional blues world, facing an audience that was steeped in blues tradition, which was older than her ordinary audience and which had a built-in tendency to regard electric music as the enemy.

The first thing she did was to say "shit," and that endeared her right away. Then she stomped her foot and shook her hair and started to scream. They held still for a couple of seconds, but here and there in the great sunlit arena, longhairs started getting up and out into the aisles and stomping along with the band. By the end of the first number, the Monterey County Fairgrounds arena was packed with people writhing and twisting and snaking along in huge chains. It was an incredible sight. Nothing like it had ever happened before in the festival's ten years and nothing like it has happened since.

It was Janis's day, no doubt about it. She turned them on like they had not been turned on in years. Old and young, long hair or short, black or white, they reacted like somebody had stuck a hot wire in their ass.

Janis had been scared silly before going onstage (I think she was scared silly every time she went onstage), and when she came off, she knew she had done it even though she was out of her mind with excitement. We had been filming for Educational Television that weekend and Janis's manager at the time, in a burst of paranoia still to be equaled, had refused to okay our filming Janis's performance. "Did you film it?" she asked, quivering, when she got off the stage and I had to tell her, "No." She was disappointed. She knew what it had been. And God knows, the world has less than it might because we couldn't film that incredible performance.

There were so many, though. Everywhere, but especially in the city she had adopted. At Winterland and California Hall and the Old Fillmore and Fillmore West and the Avalon and all around Robin Hood's barn. But then Janis was really a part of the city when she was home. You'd see her anywhere, likely to pop up at a flick, in the park, at Enrico's. Anywhere. She dug it, and the city, with its tradition of eccentricities back to Emperor Norton, dug her.

Janis was a phenomenon, no question about it. Nobody else ever came close to doing what she did. The whole stance of American popular music has been to sound black, and generations of white girl singers, from Sophie Tucker to Dusty Springfield, have tried to do it. Some of them have been driven to as tragic an end as Janis in the attempt. But none of them, Peggy Lee, nobody, has ever made it in their own terms as a white girl singing black music to the degree Janis did.

It was only partly the voice and only partly the phrasing. It was, I am convinced, the concept. Janis was the very first white singer I ever saw who moved onstage with the music in a totally unself-conscious manner. She did not seem to *care* about anything but the music. And she conceived of it in different terms than did her predecessors, all of whom were trying to be blues singers of the forties or thirties or earlier. Janis was a blues singer of right now. And she took the blues, even the blues of ten or fifteen years ago, and made it immediate in its sound, by the way she propelled the words out of her mouth, by the way she shaped the sounds, and by the volume she poured into it.

When she recorded that first time with Big Brother for Mainstream, she won my heart. I had said something about what an artistic crime it had been for Mainstream to make such a bad representation of what the band did. I met her a bit later in the dressing room at the Avalon. "Hey, man, thanks for what you said about our shitty record," she said.

And her own albums on Columbia had their good and bad points, too. When I first heard "Little Girl Blue," I didn't dig it at all because I felt Janis lacked something that was necessary for that jazz-bent number. But it haunts me now as a symbol of her loneliness, her despair, little girl lost in the big wicked world.

She was impulsive, generous, softhearted, shy, and determined. She had style and class and in a way she didn't believe it. What did she want? It was all there for her but something that she knew wasn't fated to happen. Many people loved her a very great deal, like many people loved Billie Holiday, but somehow that was not enough.

We'll never know and it doesn't matter, in a sense, because that brightly burning candle made an incredibly strong light in its brief life.

They heard Janis Joplin round the world, loud and clear, and they will continue to hear her. I am only sorry for those who never had the flash of seeing her perform.

Janis and Big Brother sang hymns at Monterey. It never seemed to me to be just music. I hope now that she's freed herself of that ball and chain, that she is at rest. She gave us a little piece of her heart and all of her soul every time she went onstage.

Monterey, 1967. Otis, Jimi, Brian, Janis. Isn't that enough?

Little girl blue, with the floppy hats and the brave attempt to be one of the guys. She took a little piece of all of us with her when she went. She was beautiful. That's not corny. It's true.

1943	Born Janis Lyn Joplin into a comfortable middle-class family in Port Arthur, TX.
1958	A loner by her early teens, Janis retreats into art, literature, and music, studying—and later emulating—the sounds of legends like Bessie Smith, "Leadbelly" Ledbetter, and Odetta.
1960	Enrolls in Lamar College. While there, she discovers the beatnik scene in Houston; records a jingle—"This Bank Is Your Bank"—for a local bank; deals marijuana on campus and starts experimenting with drugs.
1963	Drops out of college. Hitches a ride with friend Chet Helms to San Francisco, where she sings on the local coffeehouse circuit and lives off passing the hat and unemployment checks. Begins drinking and drugging heavily.
1965	Burnt out and drug weary, she returns home to dry out. Re-enrolls in a sociology program at Lamar. But the claustrophobia of small-town life overwhelms Joplin and she takes up singing the blues again in Austin.
1966	Helms invites Joplin back to the Bay Area to front a blues/folk band called Big Brother and the Holding Company.
1967	One of the star attractions at the Monterey Pop Festival, Joplin gives a mesmerizing performance of the blues classic "Ball and Chain," thrusting Big Brother into the spotlight.
1968	Her first New York City appearance at the Anderson Theater receives rave reviews. Signs with Columbia Records. Big Brother's first album, *Cheap Thrills*, holds at No. 1 for 8 consecutive weeks and "Piece of My Heart" is a hit single. Nevertheless, Joplin's talent has come to overshadow the band and she walks out on Big Brother, forming a new group—the Kozmic Blues Band.
1969	Returns to her blues roots with second album, *I Got Dem Ol' Kozmic Blues Again Mama*. The album is not as well received as her first. Joplin behaves erratically at performances as she becomes increasingly dependent on drugs and alcohol, often performing with a bottle of Southern Comfort in hand. Tries to go clean.

1970   Dies of a heroin overdose at the Hollywood Landmark Hotel, age 27. Joplin is cremated and her ashes are scattered over Stinson Beach, CA. Released posthumously, her album *Pearl* yields the "Me and Bobby McGee" single which tops the charts for weeks—thrusting Janis into the spotlight yet again, making her one of music's youngest legends, and closing a chapter on sixties music and life.

LAWRENCE WELK

1903–1992

By SHIRLEY WELK FREDRICKS, *daughter*

Delivered at funeral, May 21, 1992

Holy Cross Cemetery, Culver City, CA

SUNDAY NIGHT I WAS DRIVING HOME ON A PEACEFUL, clear evening. There was little traffic and I was musing about the life of my dad, who had slipped from our arms just a few hours before. My first thought was of him young, tanned, vibrant, whizzing along that same road in his Dodge convertible, shouting with pleasure over the wind and sun. He would often say, "See that car up ahead? I bet I can beat that fellow by the next corner. Watch this . . ."

Wasn't that what we all loved about him, that rakish air of boyishness, that joie de vivre, that sense of competition? He could be careful and conservative, but lurking just below the surface was the daredevil, the risk taker—always looking for the golden ring. And wasn't it this man, still and always a child at heart, whose giant imagination and the fantasies it spun, made us believe that we, too, could recapture that playful and creative child within each of us? The best part of us. That was what the world responded to.

The word *irrepressible* was coined for him. My mother often said, "Your father is like a cork. If you push him down in one part of the water, he soon pops up in another part and keeps floating along." He had many failures in his life—businesses he started that didn't work out, useless designs he patented, great ideas that collapsed. He would come home about once a week and announce enthusiastically at dinner, "Kids, I've just had a brilliant idea." Or, "Kids, I think I've just invented something wonderful." These phrases struck terror in our hearts. Forks paused midair. Spoons clattered to the floor. Someone ran to turn off the radio. All eyes were on him as he outlined, with gusto, yet another impractical scheme while we searched for a response that would strike a balance of encouraging but cautionary.

Anyone remember the Squeezburger with Accordion fries, Vibrant vegetables, and Piccolo pickles? He wanted to launch a nationwide restaurant chain, based on his prototype in Chicago. If you're still hungry, you might want to consider Lawrence Welk's Chicken restaurant, for which he wrote the song "Let's Start Pickin' on a Chicken." Or how about his design for an automobile with recessed wings that you could unfold and fly? Sometimes I thought that this man, who found screwing in a lightbulb fulfilling, fancied himself a minor Thomas Edison.

The rigors of travel on the road were an accepted and often relished part of life. We learned very quickly that personal comfort was a low priority—any old roach motel was fine. Give him hot and cold running water and he felt like a prince. We learned to keep a wary eye out for decent accommodations, urging him to drive on rather than turn into the first available lodging in town.

We learned the euphemisms of the road. "Rustic" meant unpainted rathole. "Cabin" meant spider's playground. "All the comforts of home" meant uninhabitable. My favorite was "Mom's cooking," which meant that the chef is a drunk. Dad wasn't the least concerned about status. He was living a life rich in ideas and emotional experiences; as long as his surroundings sustained life, what more could you ask?

A deeply ingrained respect for every person made him the confidant of factory workers and financiers, of peasants and presidents. He saw beyond race, creed, and gender to the essential humanity of people. Playing the macho male was hard for him—he gave my mother so much credit for being a wonderful mom and superb manager. When he punished us, this amounted to a mild admonition— usually a time-out in our rooms. He'd slip us some candy about an hour later.

His was one of the first programs to showcase the talents of all races, to play the music of many religions, and show the joyous contributions they made to America's culture. He was the first entertainer to institute a profit-sharing policy with his orchestra—a policy that continues today.

His life was shadowed by the harsh realities of his early years: He had only a fourth-grade education, poor health as a boy, grindingly hard farm work to perform, and an eighteenth-century peasant life in which success equaled surviving another winter. No one would have expected any artistic or psychological sensitivity to flourish there. Yet his family was musical, brave in the face of adversity, and with a great faith in God.

These hardships provided a major strength when he struck out on his own as a self-taught musician. No matter that he had to sleep in cornfields or in cars. A life of music, which found its expression in his accordion, seemed like a miracle. Into that music he poured his immense sense of wonder, joy, and zest for life. And people listened—and are still listening.

He could be stubborn. Some of his early emotional deprivation made him vulnerable and therefore defensive. But if he was wrong, he asked forgiveness. He had a remarkable generosity of spirit—surrounding himself with performers better than himself. To those of you he may have hurt, I know he would offer an apology and ask for your forgiveness. To those he loved, he would now want you to turn toward the living and, in his name, nurture the talents of young people, and validate and comfort the elderly.

Now, Dad, we say our last farewell—our hearts brimming with love and thanksgiving for your life.

We thank you for teaching us to be tender and generous with one another. We thank you for giving us an example of tolerance. We thank you for teaching us to dance, with our feet and our hearts. We thank you for sharing your faults with us, which challenged us and helped us grow. We thank you for your lifelong dedication to your principles and steadfast integrity. We thank you for infusing our lives with a love of music that enriches us forever. We thank you for setting standards of excellence for us.

Today your grandchildren are carrying forward your legacy into a future that will need your reach and vision. Last night your granddaughter slipped a tiny silver angel into your pocket. That angel will be buried with you today. May choirs of angels lead you into paradise. Beyond grief is our gratitude for your remarkable life. Your memory will live on—not only in our minds but in our hearts. Your life was a benediction. Your legacy is our affirmation and celebration of life. In your honor we intone the sublime words of an Irish poet:

"Earth, receive an honored guest."

1903	Born to German immigrant parents in a sod farmhouse in Strasburg, ND.
1914	Recuperating from a ruptured appendix, Lawrence spends the year in bed practicing on the family accordion.
1920	Borrows $400 from his father to buy his own accordion. In return, Lawrence promises to work on the farm for four years and turn over all his musical earnings. His work at weddings and parties nets Mr. Welk up to $100/night.
1924	Agreement fulfilled, Welk leaves the farm on his 21st birthday. Joins the Lincoln Boulds Orchestra in Aberdeen, ND, where he receives his first lesson in how not to manage a band: They frequently "forget" to pay their band members.
1927	Welk's newly formed band, the Hotsy Totsy Boys, signs with WNAX Radio and releases their first recording, "Spiked Beer." Cost: $400. Sales: virtually none.
1931	Marries nursing student Fern Renner.
1933	When daughter Shirley is born, Welk buys a hotel in Dallas, TX,

to provide a stable location for the family, but feeling the pull of the road, sells it for a $1700 profit, buys a sleeper bus, and resumes touring.

1938	Dubs his style Champagne Music after a fan tells him his music is "effervescent."
1940	Signs on for a two-week stint at Chicago's Trianon Ballroom. Stays for 10 years.
1951	The Lawrence Welk Orchestra debuts on local television station KTLA in Los Angeles. Spiked by Welk's good-natured jokes, the show enjoys a 4-year run. Typical Welkisms: "How do you spell conductor after C-U-N?" Or "You go over there and play the accordion. I'll stay here and beat off the band."
1955	*The Lawrence Welk Show* debuts on ABC, quickly climbing to the top 20. Sporting a heavy Germanic accent undiluted from his years of touring, Welk soon becomes America's most successful bandleader, dominating the airwaves for 25 years. With his new-found platform, Welk sells more than 1 million records annually.
1961	Signs contract to play the Hollywood Palladium for "the rest of his life, so long as he elects to do so."
1971	Publishes his best-selling autobiography, *Wunnerful, Wunnerful.*
1992	Dies of pneumonia, age 89. Attended by 200 mourners, his funeral is a simple affair worthy of his farmboy roots. It concludes with a spontaneous rendition of "Adios, Au Revoir, Auf Wiedersehn"—Welk's closing song.

STANLEY KUBRICK

By JAN HARLAN, *brother-in-law and colleague*

Delivered at memorial service, April 12, 1999

Stanley Kubrick's garden, Hertfordshire, England

STANLEY LOATHED FUNERALS. IN THE PAST FEW DAYS I WAS arguing with him in my mind about this and could hear his voice: "Funeral? You must be kidding—I hate this sort of thing. Just forget it."

We can't forget it. This gathering, this saying good-bye is part of our culture and of our need to deal with our great loss. And though I am worried of taking advantage of the fact that Stanley can't interfere, we have made this day a day for us: his family and friends. We tried to shape it in such a way as to honor and celebrate him to our fullest abilities and to do right by him.

Who was Stanley?

Today would be the day to find out. We have here the largest number of Kubrick experts ever assembled under one roof. They will have all sorts of experiences and will tell different stories. But they will all have come across this one characteristic that he brought to everything he did: an intensity that found no match in more ordinary beings, who were often inspired by him and found being with him an exhilarating and sometimes exhausting experience. He could make you soar high. He could wear you out.

I would like to concentrate on two aspects of Stanley: SK my boss, for whom I have worked for thirty years, and Stanley my brother-in-law, my sister's husband, the patriarch of a family of three generations, protector of dogs and cats in need. I leave it to others to talk about the unique filmmaker.

Stanley loved work. Not only did he live here, he also worked at home in this house. All preproduction and postproduction was done here, and he only left this place when he had to go to locations, the studio, the dentist—and every two months or so to do some shopping in St. Albans.

His bliss was to work in his top-floor office, far away from the everyday interruptions, while watching Christiane paint in the garden—surrounded by her dogs. Not being able to spot *all* the dogs could cause an interruption; not being able to see Christiane—or, more truthfully, not knowing where she was at any given moment—caused loss of concentration and eventual abandonment of work to go in search of her.

All those he loved he wanted to be around him, including his animals. He had endless suggestions for improving their lot. He could be extremely generous with time and money, but he found it difficult to accept that those close to him, particularly his daughters, could wish to do things differently—or worse, want to move away and lead their own lives. It was one of the few things he could not prevent. I am not sure whether he ever reconciled himself totally to the fact that children become grown-ups. I think he did.

As a boss, SK was a challenge. He was demanding, argumentative, difficult. Nothing was ever done the easy, obvious way. He was quick to anger and quick to forgive or make up. But not everybody was able to write off bad-hair days as he was and keep pace with him—those who did not want to submit to his benevolent dictatorship left, which often puzzled him. He felt justified in his way since, as he often said, no committee has ever written a great novel or symphony or made a great film.

He did not understand ordinary mortals' need to have weekends, holidays, or simply time to do something else. He was focused on his lifestyle and work, and the idea of voluntary travel to other places just for enjoyment was very alien to him. All form of travel was unwelcome: Emilio driving him to wherever he had to go—book, papers, or telephone in hand—was the exception to the rule.

He was also kind, forgiving, and very funny—full of irony and black humor and always overflowing with ideas and enthusiasm. He appreciated it enormously if anything any of us had ever done turned out right, since he naturally anticipated that nothing ever would. One of his favorite sayings was, "Paranoia is when you figured out what's going on."

I will not describe Stanley's huge range of interests outside his profession and the energy with which he pursued them. I will only touch briefly on his obsession with health—other people's health. He came completely into his own when presented with a medical problem. A cat or dog or child in distress really got him going. His solutions were often highly unconventional. Once he suggested my wife install a thermometer with a remote read-out in our baby's bed so that she could check on the temperature under the blanket at all times. It took some persuading to stop him from going into action on this. Most of the time, however, his concerns and suggestions were justified and helpful.

He was a shy man. He had to push himself when meeting new people. Chistiane's hope of turning him into a lion of society did not come true—and I suspect she always knew this. But last year was bursting with social activity—he attended the two weddings of his nephews and spent three evenings in London. Stanley loathed to be identified outside his domain, and did not like to use his name on the rare occasions when he had to appear in person—consulting an optician for his glasses, for instance. He would typically use my name and address, often without telling me. (As you can imagine, this led to some confusion and alarm—especially when I had just ordered new glasses for myself.)

I will miss him badly. I will so miss the permanent challenge, the man on the other line of the telephone. I calculated that we had around fifty thousand telephone calls between us. Half of these were one-line questions like "Do you know where Christiane is?" The other half was real work. Not being reachable, regardless of when or where or in which country, was a severe faux pas.

I will also miss our weekly meetings, where we wrestled with paperwork and tried to reduce, not always successfully, the vast amount of topics and decisions—"shoveling shit," as he typically called it. And I will miss him, this complex man I really loved.

He was particularly happy about his work during the few days before his death. The last conversation with him was last Saturday. He called me in Los Angeles and told me how glad he was to have found a piano piece by Ligeti. We discussed tempi, acoustics, the sound recordist. Very precise and typical SK style.

Eighteen hours later I had Christiane's message about his death, and my life was upside down. As I was thinking of Christiane and struggling to overcome my inner turmoil, I came across the following text. It is by Thich Nhat Hanh. He called it an exercise.

I want to leave you with this text.

Knowing I will get old,
I breathe in.
Knowing I can't escape old age,
I breathe out.

Knowing I will get sick,
I breathe in.
Knowing I can't escape sickness,
I breathe out.

Knowing I will die,
I breathe in.
Knowing I can't escape death,
I breathe out.

Knowing that one day I will have to abandon all that I cherish today,
I breathe in.
Knowing I can't escape having to abandon all that I cherish today,
I breathe out.

Knowing that my actions are my only belongings,
I breathe in.
Knowing that I cannot escape the consequences of my actions,
I breathe out.

Vowing to offer joy each day to my beloved,
I breathe in.
Vowing to ease the pain of my beloved,
I breathe out.

1928	Born in the Bronx, NY.
1934	In school, Stanley receives an Unsatisfactory in "Works and Plays Well with Others," "Completes Work," "Is Generally Careful," and "Speaks Clearly."
1943	Repeatedly absent from school, Stanley never fails to catch movies at the local theater. Later remarks, "Seeing run-of-the-mill Hollywood films eight times a week . . . I felt I could do them a lot better." Develops a passion for chess and photography at age 15.
1944	When President Roosevelt dies, Stanley photographs a distraught news vendor and sells the photos to *Look* magazine for $25. Impressed, the photo editor gives Stanley a job. He finishes high school with a D average, then travels America snapping pictures.
1948	Marries first wife, Toba Metz.

1950   Shoots *Day of the Fight*, a 16-minute documentary about a boxer. Two other shorts follow. Kubrick underwrites costs by playing chess at Washington Square Park.

1953   His first feature film, *Fear and Desire*, is released. A budding auteur, Kubrick writes, directs, photographs, and edits on a limited budget. (Shooting a fog scene, Kubrick uses crop spray and nearly asphyxiates the cast and crew.)

1958   Meets third wife, Christiane Harlan, on the set of *Paths of Glory*.

1964   Releases *Dr. Strangelove*—earning great praise and contempt at the same time. From now on, reaction to Kubrick films is split.

1968   Has a premonition that his film *2001: A Space Odyssey* will do well. Buys $20,000 of MGM stock. The movie breaks box-office records on opening day, going on to become Kubrick's defining masterpiece, and joins *Dr. Zhivago* and *Gone with the Wind* as one of MGM's top moneymakers.

1971   *A Clockwork Orange* sparks episodes of copycat violence in England. Disturbed by allegations that he is personally responsible, Kubrick asks Warner Bros. to remove his film from distribution for 20 years.

1974   Establishes residence in England, where he becomes one of the few American directors to command big-budget respect while working outside the Hollywood mainstream. His stamp? Cold, brilliant films exploring humanity's baser instincts with visual flair. Known for extreme perfectionism, Kubrick often does up to 100 takes for a scene, resulting in an emotionally exhausted cast and crew, and a diversity of choices in the editing room.

1980   Releases his contribution to the horror genre, *The Shining*.

1996   Begins shooting *Eyes Wide Shut* after a 10-year absence. Starring Tom Cruise and Nicole Kidman, the film is shot under conditions of almost military secrecy for 15 months. His longest shoot. And also "the best film of my life."

1999   Dies in his sleep, age 70. A renowned recluse, Kubrick is buried in his garden.

IRVING "SWIFTY" LAZAR
1907–1993

By LARRY MC MURTRY, *longtime client and close friend*

Delivered at memorial service, January 6, 1994

Westwood Memorial Park Chapel, Los Angeles, CA

THE FIRST REFERENCE I CAN REMEMBER SEEING TO IRVING Paul Lazar was in S. J. Perelman's *Paris Review* interview. Mr. Perelman, himself a notably stylish and fastidious traveler, mentioned in passing that the only man he knew who could step off an airplane anywhere in the world with his hands in his pockets was Irving Lazar.

I was a youth when I read that passage, and did not understand what a resonant tribute it was: a compliment paid by one great stylist to another. As a wordsmith, S. J. Perelman was impeccable. As a traveler, like most of us but unlike Irving, he tended to get frazzled.

Irving Lazar's style, at home or abroad, did not tolerate frazzlement. He stepped off the plane with his hands in his pockets—excellently turned pockets, too—minus such impediments as the suit bags, claim checks, diaper bags, crumpled tickets, and lost composure that burden most mortals when they travel.

A mere six weeks before Irving's death I dined with him at Chasen's. He was in a wheelchair then. When we returned home he wheeled himself around his house for a while, looking for some object or other to give me; while he wondered and considered, remembering the nice shop off Bond Street where he picked up his bone china, or the gallery in Nice where he secured the little Matisse, I happened to open a silver cigarette box given to him by Walter and Carol Matthau. It was engraved with the following tribute: "You have that rarest of things, an evolved heart."

Well, so he did—and he had an evolved style, too. But there is a catch-22 to great styles: the higher you wind them, the tighter they catch. Our styles tend to make us; then, if we last long enough and nothing beats them to it, they break us. Irving's devotion to find European footwear rotted his feet and contributed its jot to his demise; but then, we are all going to demise in some way. Who's to say that too-tight English shoes shouldn't introduce the finale?

When I read the Perelman interview, I had no suspicion that the man named Irving Lazar, who stepped off planes on the preferable continents with hands in his pockets, would someday be my agent. At the time, and for many years afterward, I had an agent, Dorothea Oppenheimer, a wonderful if eccentric woman who got through life on an intricate balance of beauty and bravura. Dorothea was born in a castle on the Danube and died in a one-room apartment on York Avenue, in New York City. In the three painful years that it took her to die, Irving, with uncustomary discretion, quietly did the work of agenting me. He treated Dorothea with the distinguished courtesy he bestowed on those who possessed what he called "quality."

Dorothea Oppenheimer had "quality," even in the dusty apartment on York Avenue, and unto the hour of her death. Irving deferred to it, and behaved impeccably. A dying, impoverished European woman got the credit—then minimal—for selling *Lonesome Dove.*

A few years later, Irving's eye for quality instantly spotted this elusive element in the appearance and demeanor of a much younger woman—my goddaughter Sara Ossana, then twelve. Irving and Mary were in London, ensconced in their accustomed suite at Claridge's, a suite the King of Spain was allowed to use when Irving didn't happen to be in town. Sara and her mother, Diana Ossana, now my screenwriting partner, happened to pass through on short notice; on even shorter notice (an hour, approximately), I called Irving and suggested dinner. The Lazars had planned to go to a birthday party to which numerous Windsors were coming, including the Queen and the glamorous young Princess of Wales.

Irving instantly changed his plans. "I see those people all the time," he said, and an hour later Sara and Diana and I were dining with Irving and Mary in the grand ballroom of Claridge's. Irving spent the evening admiring Sara's haircut—a world-class haircut she had given herself, only the day before—and harassing the captain to rush ever more delicacies to Sara's plate. On the basis of an excellent haircut and a few minutes' conversation, Irving took Sara up and was unfailingly generous to her from then on. She was one of the few young women of her generation allowed to bring her boyfriend to the Oscar party; to the end, Sara loved Irving and Irving, Sara.

T. S. Eliot once made a famous remark about Henry James, who, Eliot said, had a mind so fine that no idea could penetrate it. Irving's mind was not unlike Henry James's. The texts that he agented rarely, if ever, penetrated it, except by osmosis. For years, once he became my agent, I waited for some chance statement that would indicate that he had read at least a page or two of the many books he agented for me; the statement never came.

Life, in the Scott Fitzgerald sense, was always glimmering out there somewhere; drinks, fine women, dancing, French food, exciting talk, and the endless parade of the great and famous, the beautiful and bold, were Irving's texts. Not for him the contemplative hour with Homer or Virgil; despite which he was, in his bones, a literary man. He honored writers and never, to my knowledge, allowed himself to confuse the work of literature with the subliterary best-seller. He reaped millions off best-sellers—in the way of the street—but his first and fiercest loyalties were to those who attempted literature, and, Truman Capote excepted, he didn't expect to find them at Spago or Le Cirque.

As a man of the café and the boulevard, Irving lavished his energies on not a few people who were spoiled well past the point of putrification; he was sometimes careless when it came to separating the wheat from the chaff. But manners—what he called "the correct thing"—mattered to him in the end. If Irving really cared about you, as he cared, for example, for Dorothea and Sara, it was necessary that you do the correct thing. With Dorothea this meant dying with her courage intact. With Sara it meant exacting discipline in the matter of haircuts. When people abandoned their standards, and proved unable, in the difficult situation that life is sure to bring us, to do the correct thing, Irving's judgment was immediate and, frequently, final.

In the year of bereavement, after Mary's death, Diana and Sara and I saw Irving often. On our last visit a few weeks ago, he rose out of sedation and talked lucidly and lovingly, for almost an hour, about Bogart and Hemingway. He spoke about Bogart's death and Hemingway's torment. But then he began to reminisce about their good times—he ceased to talk about them as if they were dead and spoke as he might speak of people who were traveling, people whom he would probably see again when he was passing through Paris, or lunching at '21.'

In humans the grace that lasts is probably always moral, and always tragic. Irving and Mary are gone, and the community of the arts is diminished. Irving was a larger-than-life figure in a town that, but for the great magnifying glass of the screen, would be in most ways smaller than life. His intelligence and his taste brought an element of refinement to a culture in most ways crude. His taste reached back to the Europe of the great West Coast émigrés: Mann, Stravinsky, Renoir.

There are few links to that time left, and none who sustained the range of contact and reference that Irving Lazar commanded. With his passing, in the words of Thomas Nashe, the Renaissance poet, a brightness has fallen from the air. Irving himself, at his eighty-fifth birthday party, lamented the devaluation of glamour in a town where movie stars seldom take the trouble to be movie stars anymore.

Once, speaking of President Reagan, whose memoirs he didn't get to agent, Irving consoled himself with this reflection: "That's all right—pretty soon he'll be where Franco is."

As it happened, Irving took ship first. The prince of agents, the man who could step ashore, or out of a plane, or off a train with his hands in his pockets, is traveling now. We can be sure that a car will be waiting at the dock, or the airport, or the station. The best suite will be his, and the best hotel; the clothes will have been unpacked; the captain will be waiting deferentially at the best table in the restaurant, where the best company will soon gather to dine and drink till eternity cracks.

He won't be sitting with Franco, though. Irving will be traveling in that greatly peopled bourne where Mr. Kafka dines with Ms. Woolf and Papa breaks bread with Baudelaire. And should it be that either the Lord of Light or (better yet) Prince of Darkness is ready to sell his memoirs, Irving Paul Lazar will get right on the phone.

1907	Born in a tenement on Manhattan's Lower East Side to Jewish Russian immigrants.
1920	As a teenager, Irving idolizes vaudevillians. Begins to emulate their dress at age 13—jacket, tie, freshly ironed shirt, immaculate haircut—developing the signature style that earns him a reputation as a dandy.
1925	While attending Fordham University, Lazar earns money as a stenographer at a prestigious Manhattan law firm—with enough left over to attend Broadway shows. An idea percolates: He will become involved in show business.
1929	Enrolls in Brooklyn Law School.
1935	Does legal work for the very vaudeville performers he idolized as a child.
1941	By now Irving Lazar, Esq., represents jazz musicians like Benny Goodman and Tommy Dorsey, but with the country on the verge of war, he walks out on his job at MCA.
1942	Enlists in army at age 35. Surrounded by younger men, Lazar finds the army difficult but perseveres. (His sartorial fixations are

exposed when, as a low-ranking officer, Lazar chooses to wear the flashier uniform of a captain—leading to unpleasant encounters with higher-ups.)

1945	Discharged after developing an ulcer, Lazar catches the next plane to New York. Returns to work for MCA.
1947	East Coast talent is in high demand in Hollywood. Seizing the opportunity, the Irving Paul Lazar Agency opens its doors in Beverly Hills. His clients are playwrights, choreographers, composers. With his innate sense of what will sell and how to sell it, Lazar earns a reputation as "the agent who doesn't read." His knack for wooing clients from other agents becomes legendary.
1949	Humphrey Bogart bets he can't make him 3 deals in one day— Lazar proves him wrong, earning himself the nickname Swifty.
1960	Negotiates the most difficult deal of his career, selling *The Sound of Music* screenplay for $1.25 million plus an unheard-of 10% gross.
1963	Marries model Mary Van Nuys. The bon vivant couple become famous for their star-studded Oscar galas.
1974	When Nixon resigns, Lazar sells his memoirs for $2 million. By now, Lazar is an undisputed superagent, brokering high-profile deals for top-tier actors, producers, musicians, authors, and now politicians. "Sometimes I wake up in the morning and there's nothing doing, so I decide to make something happen by lunch."
1993	Mary, his "guiding light," dies of bone cancer. Lazar suffers a stroke later the same year and his health declines rapidly. In December he consciously decides to discontinue his medication and dies at the age of 86. Lazar is buried alongside his wife.

DAVID O. SELZNICK

1902-1965

By TRUMAN CAPOTE, *friend*

Delivered at memorial service, June 25, 1965

Church of the Recessional, Glendale, CA

DAVID'S FRIENDS AND COLLEAGUES WILL NOT BE SURPRISED to learn that the occasion that gathers us here today was, consistent to his attention to detail, the subject of a memo. With his characteristic humor, he noted, however, that a critical follow-up would not be possible. But I think his generosity would have permitted us to stretch a point, which instructed brevity—impossible brevity to honor an excitingly energetic, enchanting man.

Enchanting was his word, his presence, and his life. His achievements are legion and legend, but the true measure of his stature lies in his individual impact as a human being, on his wife, his children, his friends, his coworkers, this industry, and the world at large. Therein is the enormity of the loss that we mourn, for which we are perceptibly poorer.

We have lost an irreplaceable individualist who was as tender as he was tenacious, as courageous as competitive, as inventive as ingenious, as sensitive as stalwart. His fantastic vitality was matched only by the profoundness of his sense of integrity, responsibility, honor, and loyalty; his good taste by his originality. These are the throbbing tenets of his existence, the landmarks of his being, and the monuments of his passage on earth.

He was a son, a brother, a husband, and a father who gave unstintingly of himself, and who found myriad ways to do even more—to

247

whom the word *family* spelled undying devotion—another quality in which he was rich.

To his friends, his ear and shoulder were always available, for comfort or for counsel; his interest, infallible and unshakeable.

It is tempting not to mention David's professional achievements at all for they are public facts and a part of our cultural history. Still it must be said that among filmmakers, David Oliver Selznick was unique. He was at once genuinely creative and deeply cultured. He combined down-to-earth acumen and virile ambition with daring and showmanship, guided by his sensibility, refinement, and taste, orchestrated by his bedrock principles of quality. And of this, he created a new image of the filmmaker for the world—an image that did us all honor—and one that cannot be replaced.

In short, David was a big man. That is the truth and the heart of the matter. He was a big man and he took up a lot of space. He leaves as big a void in the world.

1902	Born into a wealthy Pennsylvania family, David is immersed in movies from the beginning: His father is a successful silent-film producer.
1920	Enrolls at Columbia University, but his education is cut short when his father goes bankrupt. The Selznicks move from a 22-room apartment on Park Avenue to three furnished rooms where Mrs. Selznick does the cooking.
1926	Moves to Hollywood. Working as a script reader at MGM, David persuades the studio to pay him an extravagant $100/week. ("I'll do more for you than read scripts. I'll help you fix them. I'll write titles.")
1930	Marries Irene Mayer, daughter of MGM czar Louis B. Mayer, despite his employment at rival studio Paramount.

1933   Produces *King Kong*. With its dazzling special effects, the film pulls RKO Studio back from the brink of bankruptcy, and earns Selznick an invitation to work for his father-in-law. Heading his own production division, Selznick enjoys creative autonomy and access to the best MGM resources. (Jealous executives quip, "The son-in-law also rises.")

1936   Founds Selznick International. While filming *The Garden of Allah,* he receives a telegram urging him to buy film rights to a new Civil War epic.

1938   Shoots *Gone with the Wind.* At $4 million, it is the most expensive movie ever made. Selznick's work habits become legend on the set: works three-day stretches without sleep; subsists on Benzadrine; dictates hundreds of memos to two exhausted stenographers. (Once he sends a memo to Vivien Leigh that weighs half a pound and takes the actress ten days to reply to.)

1939   *Gone with the Wind* grosses $10 million and sweeps the Oscars. Selznick uses the profits to fuel a massive expansion of his company. Brings Alfred Hitchcock to Hollywood.

1940   Signs Hitchcock to film *Rebecca.* They quarrel throughout.

1945   They team again on *Spellbound.* Again they quarrel, but the film goes on to earn them both Oscars—and signals the rise of Hollywood directors: From now on, the director helms the artistic vision.

1946   *Duel in the Sun* flops, nearly bankrupting Selznick.

1948   Divorces Irene, who remains a close friend. Selznick goes on to marry Jennifer Jones, hiring her for most of his films.

1957   Releases his last movie, *A Farewell to Arms.*

1965   Dies of a heart attack, after years of declining health. On movies: "Nothing in Hollywood is permanent. Once photographed, life here is ended." Best remembered for *Gone with the Wind,* Selznick leaves behind 80 films featuring three trademarks: top writers, top stars, and no expense spared.

BILLY WILDER

1906 – 2002

By LARRY GELBART, *longtime friend and fan*

Delivered at memorial service, May 1, 2002

Academy of Motion Picture Arts and Sciences, Los Angeles, CA

ALMOST THE WHOLE OF THE COVER OF CAMERON CROWE'S book *Conversations with Wilder* is taken up by a photograph of a massive motion-picture camera adorned with a stunning assortment of knobs, dials, and focusing gizmos. The mysteries and capabilities of the Rube Goldbergian contraption pale, however, in comparison to the intricate, wondrous mind of the man seen peering through its viewfinder. There, almost physically willing the camera to absorb his vision, and sporting the obligatory dangling cigarette, is the maestro.

There is Billy Wilder, the director, wearing a rakish, soft-brimmed hat—a fedora that also functions as a helmet for the protection of the writer's side of Billy Wilder's brain.

In the blink of a lens, the book's cover traps for all time: Billy's sense of command; Billy making certain of his shot—waiting for the approval of his imagination; the hat that he continually wore; and there, on the third finger of his left hand . . . we see his wedding ring.

A reminder of a personal constancy that was every bit as strong as his professional one.

Perpetuating his mentor's, Ernst Lubitsch's, ever-present cigar as some sort of eternal flame, it's a rare picture in which Billy Wilder is ever seen without a cigarette between his lips—or between his fingers—or between his fingers and his lips. In truth, this book bears the distinct danger of exposure to secondary smoke.

My candidate for the book's best snapshot is not among the countless ones showing Billy in the company of the stars that were to form his constellation; it's one of a simple bookshelf—one that sports a collection of his leatherbound screenplays, the works of literature that informed each and every one of his films. Considering that a great percentage of them were, indeed, written in stone, it's a wonder the shelves that held them never cracked in half.

If in those works Billy could glide so smoothly between belly laugh–filled comedy and gut-wrenching drama, it was because he was as attuned to the world beyond the soundstage as he was to the one within. He understood that laughter and tears are, at most, just a broken heartbeat away from one another.

These are the indelible creations that have influenced anyone who ever tried to follow in Billy's tasseled footsteps. More than an influence, they are a foundation. For whatever it's worth, here's what I get from that row of masterworks, and from what I know of the master who assembled them:

- Throw away any rules that you don't write for yourself. And you might want to do another draft of those every once in a while as well.

- Remember what worked before. Then forget it.

- If what you're writing isn't likely to offend or annoy anyone at all, go back and start again.

- Once you've told your characters who they are, let them speak for themselves.

- If an audience has the intelligence to buy a ticket to your work, return that intelligence with the very best of your own.

- Have a healthy disregard for conventional wisdom, which never has a clue about the value of unconventional whimsy.

- Never give advice. Let others interpret your opinion as such, if they are so inclined.

- A synonym for *oracle* is *weatherman*—and we know how accurate they can be.

- Be proud of your work. But only the best of it.

- To defend whatever of yours is indefensible will only make people wonder if you really did write whatever they thought of yours was so great in the first place.

- Keep thinking of ways that might improve a screenplay long after it's been filmed, perhaps even forgotten. It's no help for what you've done in the past, but it's great practice for what you might do in the future.

- Treat your failures the same way you treat your successes. Either one is a natural outcome of your efforts. Either way, just mush on.

- Be generous in acknowledging the contributions of your collaborators. Sharing credit with someone enhances rather than reduces your own.

- Another word to consider using in place of *cynic* is *realist*.

- One final thought: There is nothing in this world as overrated as having the last laugh.

We could have used hundreds more from Billy Wilder.

1906	Born Samuel Wilder in Susha, Austria–Hungary (now Poland). Nicknamed Billy, after Buffalo Bill, by his Americana-loving mother.
1924	Graduates from a high school for problem children. In accordance with his mother's wishes, he attends law school—lasting three months. Taking a job reporting for a Vienna tabloid, Wilder entertains himself with billiards, sports, and jazz.
1926	Leaves Vienna for Berlin. Begins writing movie scripts while working as a professional dance partner for rich women.
1930	Hired by UFA, the top movie studio in Germany.
1933	After penning a dozen scripts, the 26-year-old Wilder flees Nazi Germany—starting an exodus of 1500 German filmmakers. The

following year he arrives in Hollywood. Knowing only titles of pop songs, Wilder listens to the radio ceaselessly, learning 20 words a day.

1936   Paramount teams him with Charles Beckett, a Harvard-educated writer. They go on to pen 13 screenplays, including hits like *Ninotchka* and *Hold Back the Dawn,* but have a stormy partnership; Wilder ducks a continual stream of objects hurled in exasperation.

1942   Persuades Paramount to let him direct his first film, *The Major and the Minor,* starring Ginger Rogers.

1944   Receives the first of eight Best Director nominations, for *Double Indemnity*—a classic film noir. He goes on to explore other genres, slipping seamlessly into each: *Sunset Boulevard* (old-fashioned melodrama); *Some Like It Hot* (American farce); *Sabrina* (romantic comedy); *Witness for the Prosecution* (courtroom thriller); and *The Lost Weekend* (drama). Making every type of film except a Western, he quips, "I'm afraid of horses."

1949   Marries singer and actress Audrey Young.

1960   With *The Apartment,* Wilder becomes the first person to win three Oscars in one night—Director, Producer, and Co-Screenwriter.

1964   Turning point: Wilder's sex farce *Kiss Me, Stupid* is condemned by the Catholic Church. United Artists removes its logo, theaters cancel bookings, and a rush of bad reviews follows. The consensus: Wilder is out of touch with audiences.

1981   Makes his last film, *Buddy, Buddy*—a failure at the box office. Spends the rest of his years accepting tributes he calls "Quick, before they croak!" awards—including the American Film Institute Life Achievement award (1986) and the Irving Thalberg award (1987). Often remarks that he would trade all the awards for the chance to make another film.

2002   Dies of pneumonia, age 95, leaving behind a diverse array of films united by sardonic wit, and ending an era of above-the-title directors.

DARRYL F. ZANUCK
1902–1979

By ORSON WELLES, *friend and colleague*

Delivered at funeral, December 27, 1979

Westwood United Methodist Church, Los Angeles, CA

AT WINSTON CHURCHILL'S FUNERAL, THERE WAS A MOMENT when the coffin was to be carried out of Westminster Abbey and onto a barge for a trip up the Thames River. A special group of pallbearers from the various military services in Great Britain was selected for this. One, a sailor, broke his ankle carrying the coffin down the stone steps of the Abbey. For a moment it seemed that the coffin would drop to the ground, but it was safely carried onto the barge.

Afterward officials said to the sailor, "How did you manage to go on?"

And the sailor said, "I would have carried him all over London."

That's the way I feel about my friend Darryl Zanuck.

Churchill wrote the script for his own funeral. Lord Mountbatten recently did the same thing in England—in England, if you're going to have a state funeral, they let you do that. They give you what amounts to a final cut. We don't have state funerals in our movie community, but if we did, Darryl would certainly have been given one—and he would have produced it. And what a show that would have been. Virginia and Dick have reminded me that Darryl himself would not wish this occasion to be too lugubrious. That's true. I'm pretty sure that if he was the producer in charge of this occasion, Darryl would have wished for us all to leave this gathering with lightened spirits. The trouble is that I'm the wrong man for that job—I can't find anything cheerful to say about the loss of my friend.

To understand the special nature of his contribution, we must understand the full meaning of the word *producer* in Darryl's day. In the Golden Age of Hollywood, it meant something quite different than it does now. There were producers assigned to each movie, and then there was the man in charge of all the movies. In Darryl's day that was a lot of movies—forty, fifty, sixty, seventy feature pictures a year. He was one of the legendary tycoons presiding over production.

The whole point about Darryl was that he did not just preside. He did so very much more than preside. Of all the big-boss producers, Darryl was unquestionably the man with the greatest gifts—true personal, professional, and artistic gifts for the filmmaking process itself. He began as a writer and in a sense he never stopped functioning as a writer. Others may have matched him as a star-maker, but with all of Darryl's flair for the magic personalities, his first commitment was always to the story. For Darryl that was what it was to make a film: to tell a story.

God bless him for that. With half a hundred and more stories to tell every dozen months, this great storyteller was, of necessity, an editor and a great editor. There never was an editor in our business to touch him.

Every great career is a roller coaster and Darryl had his disasters. He knew eclipse. He knew comebacks and triumphs. It was a giant roller coaster. And then there were studio politics, and that's the roughest game there is. But has anybody—anybody—ever claimed that Darryl Zanuck advanced himself by dirty tricks? Or by leaving behind him the usual trail of bloody corpses? Of course, there were some aching egos and some bruised temperaments. If you're in charge of a regiment of artists, some of your commands are going to hurt. Some of your decisions are bound to seem arbitrary, but Darryl didn't sign on to be the recreation director of a summer camp. Of course he was tough. That was his job. But unlike many of the others, he was never cruel. Never vindictive. He wasn't—and what a rare thing it is to say in the competitive game of ours, he was a man totally devoid of malice. But he was great with irony. Great sense of humor, even about himself; of which of the others can we say that?

I always knew that if I did something really outrageous, that if I committed some abominable crime, and if all the police in the world were after me, there was one man and only one man I could come to, and that was Darryl. He would not have made a speech about the good of the industry or the good of his studio. He would not have been mealymouthed or put me aside. He would have hid me under the bed. Very simply he was a friend. I don't mean just my friend. I mean that friendship was something he was very good at.

And that is why it is so very hard to say good-bye to him.

1902	Born in Wahoo, NE.
1916	Falsifying his age to enlist, the 14-year-old Darryl joins the Nebraska National Guard. For his service, he is later awarded the Victory Medal.
1923	Fade in: Zanuck moves to Hollywood and joins Warner Bros. as a staff writer. Adept at crafting unusual plots, Zanuck quickly climbs the ranks—then hits pay dirt with *Rin Tin Tin*.
1924	Marries Virginia Fox, after meeting on a blind date.
1929	Promoted to chief of production, Zanuck produces the talkie *The Jazz Singer*. With the changeover to sound, Warner Bros. becomes a major studio, and Zanuck introduces a lineup of gangster films, social melodramas, and musicals that become Warner Bros.' calling card, becoming Hollywood's eccentric boy wonder in the process. (He frequently acts out scenes during story conferences in his office.)
1933	At 31, launches new studio Twentieth Century Pictures with Joseph Shenck. On their dynamic partnership: "If two men on the job agree all the time, then one is useless. If they disagree all the time, then both are useless."

1934   Merges with Fox Pictures. As chief of production, Zanuck shows a sixth sense for surprising the public with its own unanticipated wants. From sentimental Shirley Temple flicks to John Ford's Americana to postwar "problem" movies like *No Way Out,* he turns out a cycle of movies that deliver on two fronts: entertainment and profit.

1944   During World War II, Zanuck serves in the U.S. Signal Corps in Algiers.

1947   Wins Best Picture Oscar for *Gentleman's Agreement.*

1950   . . . and another for *All About Eve.*

1956   In the grip of a middle-age crisis, Zanuck walks out on Hollywood—and Virginia—and moves to Europe, producing the occasional movie. He suffers a long line of flops.

1962   Bounces back with his most celebrated film, *The Longest Day,* a dramatization of the Normandy invasion. Returning to Fox to tend to the budgetary overruns of *Cleopatra,* he saves the studio from fiscal ruin. Names his son Richard as vice president.

1970   Fade out: With the advent of indies, only a few movie tycoons cling to power. Zanuck fires his son for financial mismanagement. Then, amid declining studio fortunes and rampant philandering, is himself forced from power. Moves to Palm Springs and spends retirement in physical decline.

1979   Newly reconciled with Virginia, Zanuck dies of pneumonia, age 77. At his funeral there are no chorales or hymns, only the theme song from *The Longest Day,* played over and over. Credits: close to 1000 films to his name, plus an equal inventory of colorful Hollywood lore.

ERMA BOMBECK

1927–1996

By PHIL DONAHUE, *neighbor and friend*

Delivered at memorial service, April 28, 1996

St. Thomas the Apostle Church, Phoenix, AZ

IN 1961 IN CENTERVILLE, OHIO, ON CUSHWA DRIVE, I lived diagonally across the street from the Bombecks. We were all thirtysomething and were making about fifteen thousand dollars a year, and after you paid the pediatrician, you still had a little walking-around money. We all had stairstep kids, and most of us were Catholic. And the most fun that was to be had on Cushwa Drive in Centerville—where, incidentally, there are some places where the grass is greener than at other places—the most fun you could have was at the Bombecks'. Erma would not let you fail. No matter what the joke may have been, she was the most generous audience—then and now and forever.

She was working at the *Kettering-Oakwood Times*—if you call an occasional column working. We would entertain each other in our homes. We all had the same house. It was a plat house—fifteen thousand dollars—three bedrooms, two bathrooms, and the fireplace was seven hundred dollars extra.

Everybody had Early American decor. I had an American eagle from Sears over the fireplace—not brass, black (they were cheaper). The Bombecks had beams in the ceiling. I mean real-wood Early American beams, perfectly mitered. You kept looking for Martha Washington. Bill Bombeck made those beams all by himself. I envied those beams so much. It explains why my relationship with Bill throughout my adult life has been so difficult.

The spirit of those times has lived in the work of Erma Bombeck ever since 1961, and that is a remarkable thing when you realize what's happened to us since then. We were everything our parents prayed that we would be, our parents sacrificed for us, and by 1961 we had achieved more than they had ever dreamed. We were making more money than they had ever made. And then somebody killed our president and we lost a war and the Japanese took over automotive engineering and a president resigned in disgrace and we looked up to discover that we were prepared for a world that never materialized. But while cities were burning and all this was happening to us, there was one constant in our culture and it was Erma Bombeck. Her spirit never flagged. Her humor never waned. Her light shone out from millions of refrigerator doors, just one of the many venues Erma found herself in, and allowed her work to reach the hearts of countless readers around the world.

She became a historic figure of publishing and newspapering. It is not so much that she was the best; she was the *only*. There is no other time when the phrase is more appropriate to say than now: We shall never see the likes of her again. We shall never know again her brilliance, her insight, and especially her generosity. She is the modern Catholic woman. She is the married-once, faithful wife, who got more fun out of writing about infidelity than would be approved by the early Church, and she was without pretense. She was real and she brought us all down to earth—gently, generously, and with brilliant humor. She is a twentieth-century political figure, and when the scholars gather hundreds of years from now to learn about us, they can't know it all if they don't read Erma.

For all these reasons, I feel so blessed to have known this woman who made me a better person—not an easy task. I am so, so grateful to her. I join you in mourning her passing, but she will live. She will live forever.

1927	Born Erma Fiste in Dayton, OH, to a lower-middle-class family.
1941	Age 14, her career begins: She interviews Shirley Temple for premiere of *Since You Went Away*. The interview runs in the *Dayton Herald* and Erma is paid ten dollars.
1945	At college, her submissions to the college paper are uniformly rejected. She nearly fails Composition. Dejected, Erma begins writing a department store newsletter—joking about shoplifting, the lunch menu, and the clearance rack. Upon graduation, she moves back home to work for the *Dayton Journal-Herald,* covering women's issues.
1949	Marries high-school sweetheart Bill Bombeck.
1952	Her column, "Operation Dustrag," strikes a chord with postwar women.
1954	After unsuccessful attempts to conceive, the Bombecks adopt Betsy. Erma puts career on hold—then gives birth to two more children.
1964	Offers to pen a column for the *Kettering-Oakwood Times*. Her pay: $3/week. Her philosophy: hook them with a lead, hold them with laughter. When a rival newspaper spots her work, they offer her $50/week for two columns. By the end of the year, "At Wits End" is in syndication at 38 papers. Collected, the columns are later published as her first book
1969	500 papers carry Bombeck's column.
1975	Begins her stint on *Good Morning America*, chatting up celebrities like Zsa Zsa Gabor (whom she interviews in her king-size bed) and Phyllis Diller. The following year, she publishes her fourth and most successful book, *The Grass Is Always Greener Over the Septic Tank*.
1978	Travels the country in support of the Equal Rights Amendment. The quintessential housewife, she sees no contradiction: "I wish they could put this on my tombstone: She got Missouri for the ERA."
1989	Column, books, show, marriage, and motherhood—all begin to

weigh on her, and after 11 years on the show she calls it quits. Takes time off to write *I Want to Grow Hair, I Want to Grow Up, I Want to Go to Boise,* about children with cancer.

1991   Her kidneys begin to fail. Bombeck begins dialysis.

1996   After 5 years of waiting and daily treatments, Bombeck receives a kidney transplant. Lacing her characteristically humorous prose with a potent dose of anguish and compassion, she addresses it with her readers for the first time. The transplant doesn't take. Bombeck dies, age 69, having bequeathed a funny new feminism to American women.

EMILY DICKINSON

1830–1886

By SUSAN DICKINSON, *sister-in-law and neighbor*

Published in The Republican *(Springfield, MA) as an unsigned editorial, May 18, 1886*

T HE DEATH OF MISS EMILY DICKINSON, DAUGHTER OF THE late Edward Dickinson, makes another sad inroad on the small circle so long occupying the old family mansion. It was for a long generation overlooked by death, and one passing in and out there thought of old-fashioned times, when parents and children grew up and passed maturity together, in lives of singular uneventfulness unmarked by sad or joyous crises.

Very few in the village, except among the older inhabitants, knew Miss Emily personally, although the facts of her seclusion and her intellectual brilliancy were familiar Amherst traditions. There are many houses among all classes into which her treasures of fruit and flowers and ambrosial dishes for the sick and well were constantly sent, that will forever miss those evidences of her unselfish consideration, and mourn afresh that she screened herself from close acquaintance. As she passed on in life, her sensitive nature shrank from much personal contact with the world, and more and more turned to her own large wealth of individual resources for companionship, sitting thenceforth, as someone said of her, "in the light of her own fire." Not disappointed with the world, not an invalid until within the past two years, not from any lack of sympathy, not because she was insufficient for any mental work or social career—her endowments being so exceptional—but the "mesh of her soul," as Browning calls the body, was too rare, and the sacred quiet of her own home proved the fit atmosphere for her worth and work. . . .

Her talk and her writings were like no one else's, and although she never published a line, now and then some enthusiastic literary friend would turn love to larceny, and cause a few verses surreptitiously obtained to be printed. Thus, and through other natural ways, many saw and admired her verses, and in consequence frequently notable persons paid her visits, hoping to overcome the protest of her own nature and gain a promise of occasional contributions at least, to various magazines.

A Damascus blade gleaming and glancing in the sun was her wit. Her swift poetic rapture was like the long glistening note of a bird one hears in the June woods at high noon, but can never see. Like a magician she caught the shadowy apparitions of her brain and tossed them in startling picturesqueness to her friends, who charmed with their simplicity and homeliness as well as profundity, fretted that she had so easily made palpable the tantalizing fancies forever eluding their bungling, fettered grasp. So intimate and passionate was her love of Nature, she seemed herself a part of the high March sky, the summer day and birdcall. Keen and eclectic in her literary tastes, she sifted libraries from Shakespeare to Browning; quick as the electric spark in her intuitions and analyses, she seized the kernel instantly, almost impatient of the fewest words by which she must make her revelation. To her, life was rich, and all aglow with God and immortality. With no creed, no formulated faith, hardly knowing the names of dogmas, she walked this life with the gentleness and reverence of old saints, with the firm step of martyrs who sing while they suffer. How better note the flight of this "soul of fire in a shell of pearl" than by her own words?

> *Morns like these, we parted;*
> *Noons like these, she rose;*
> *Fluttering first, then firmer*
> *To her fair repose.*

1830	Born in Amherst, MA, to Edward and Emily Dickinson. Emily enjoys a normal childhood rounded out by girlfriends, parties, books, and a strong education.
1847	Enrolls in Mount Holyoke College but returns home a year later, shaken by their attempts to persuade her to join the Congregational Church. She resists declaring a faith for the rest of her life.
1851	Inspired by Ralph Waldo Emerson and Emily Brontë, she begins writing poetry. Sends 50 poems to *Republican* editor Samuel Bowles, but preferring traditional rhymes and meters, he prints only one.
1855	Meets Rev. Charles Wadsworth. They exchange largely spiritual letters, addressing each other as "Master" and "Daisy." Emily's emotional turbulences are later ascribed to her unrequited love, but crisis suits her imagination: Her poetry ripens. She turns out hundreds of poems a year, binding them in packets with string, untitled and undated.
1860	Begins her withdrawal from the world, after taking to heart a *Republican* article criticizing poets, calling their art an unhealthy response to loneliness.
1862	Writes critic Thomas Higginson for advice. Dickinson's eccentric phrasing, slant rhymes, and emotional intensity lead him to advise her against publication, driving her further into her private world. Eight years later, Higginson finally meets her. "I never was with anyone who drained my nerve power so much. Without touching her, she drew from me. I am glad not to live near her."
1868	Becomes fully reclusive. Dressing in white and never leaving the family homestead, she occasionally lowers baskets of treats, tied with a rope, from her second-floor bedroom to children below— careful never to show her face. Her transformation from "Belle of Amherst" to "Nun of Amherst" is complete.

1874   Father dies. There is speculation of an affair with her father's friend, Judge Otis Lord.

1882   Suffers an emotional collapse after first her mother, then Lord, die. She never recovers.

1886   Dies at 56 of a kidney disorder. Dickinson's casket is carried through a field of buttercups by six Irish workers. Afterward, her sister, Lavinia, discovers 1800 poems in her dresser drawer. Published with the help of Higginson, *Poems* sells out quickly— going through 16 editions in 8 years—and Dickinson is almost immediately vaulted into the pantheon of greatest American poets. On her death certificate, the Amherst town clerk wrote, "Occupation: At home."

ROBERT FROST

1874–1963

By PRESIDENT JOHN F. KENNEDY, *admirer and friend*

Delivered at dedication of Robert Frost Library,
October 26, 1963, Amherst, MA

A NATION REVEALS ITSELF NOT ONLY BY THE MEN IT produces but also by the men it honors, the men it remembers.

In America, our heroes have customarily run to men of large accomplishments. But today this college and country honor a man whose contribution was not to our size but to our spirit; not to our political beliefs but to our insight; not to our self-esteem but to our self-comprehension.

In honoring Robert Frost we therefore can pay honor to the deepest sources of our national strength. That strength takes many forms, and the most obvious forms are not always the most significant.

The men who create power make an indispensable contribution to the nation's greatness. But the men who question power make a contribution just as indispensable, especially when that questioning is disinterested. For they determine whether we use power or power uses us. Our national strength matters; but the spirit which informs and controls our strength matters just as much. This was the special significance of Robert Frost.

He brought an unsparing instinct for reality to bear on the platitudes and pieties of society. His sense of the human tragedy fortified him against self-deception and easy consolation.

"I have been," he wrote, "one acquainted with the night."

And because he knew the midnight as well as the high noon, because he understood the ordeal as well as the triumph of the human spirit, he gave his age strength with which to overcome despair. At bottom he held a deep faith in the spirit of man. And it's hardly an accident that Robert Frost coupled poetry and power. For he saw poetry as the means of saving power from itself.

When power leads man toward arrogance, poetry reminds him of his limitations. When power narrows the areas of man's concern, poetry reminds him of the richness and diversity of his existence. When power corrupts, poetry cleanses.

Art establishes the basic human truths which must serve as the touchstones of our judgment. The artist, however faithful to his personal vision of reality, becomes the last champion of the individual mind and sensibility against an intrusive society and an officious state.

The great artist is thus a solitary figure. He had, as Frost said, "a lover's quarrel with the world." In pursuing his perceptions of reality he must often sail against the currents of his time. This is not a popular role.

If Robert Frost was much honored during his lifetime, it was because a good many preferred to ignore his darker truths.

Yet in retrospect we see how the artist's fidelity has strengthened the fiber of our national life. If sometimes our great artists have been the most critical of our society, it is because their sensitivity and their concern for justice, which must motivate any true artists, make them aware that our nation falls short of its highest potential.

I see little of more importance to the future of our country and our civilization than full recognition of the place of the artist. If art is to nourish the roots of our culture, society must set the artist free to follow his vision wherever it takes him. We must never forget that art is not a form of propaganda, it is a form of truth. And as Mr. MacLeish once remarked of poets, "There is nothing worse for our trade than to be in style."

In free society, art is not a weapon and it does not belong to the sphere of polemics and ideology. Artists are not engineers of the soul. It may be different elsewhere. But in democratic society, the highest duty of the writer, the composer, the artist, is to remain true to himself and to let the chips fall where they may. In serving his vision of the truth, the artist best serves his nation. And the nation which disdains the mission of art invites the fate of Robert Frost's hired man—"the fate of having nothing to look backward to with pride and nothing to look forward to with hope."

I look forward to a great future for America—a future in which our country will match its military strength with our moral restraint, its wealth with our wisdom, its power with our purpose.

I look forward to an America which will not be afraid of grace and beauty, which will protect the beauty of our natural environment, which will preserve the great old American houses and squares and parks of our national past, and which will build handsome and balanced cities for our future.

And I look forward to an America which commands respect throughout the world not only for its strength but for its civilization as well.

And I look forward to a world which will be safe not only for democracy and diversity but also for personal distinction.

Robert Frost was often skeptical about projects for human improvement. Yet I do not think he would disdain this hope.

As he wrote during the uncertain days of the Second World War:

> *Take human nature altogether since time began . . .*
> *And it must be a little more in favor of man,*
> *Say a fraction of one percent at the very least . . .*
> *Or our hold on the planet wouldn't have so increased.*

Because of Mr. Frost's life and work, our hold on this planet has increased.

1874	Born in San Francisco, Frost is named after Gen. Robert E. Lee.
1883	Frost hears voices when alone; his mother says he shares her gift of "second hearing" and "second sight."
1892	Enrolls in Dartmouth, but bored with college life, he stays only one semester. Returns to Massachusetts to teach school. Two years later he publishes his first poem, "My Butterfly: An Elegy," in a literary journal—for $15.
1895	Marries classmate Elinor White. They have six children.
1896	Tries his hand at college again, this time Harvard, but again leaves minus a degree. Over the next decade Frost writes, teaches, and operates a farm in New Hampshire.
1912	Frost sells the farm and moves to England, where he can focus on writing.
1913	Publishes collection *A Boy's Will,* followed a year later by *North of Boston.* Both are typical Frost—mediations on dark, universal themes infused with irony. While in England, Frost meets numerous literary figures, including W. B. Yeats and Ezra Pound, but his friendship with Pound becomes strained: "He says I must write something more like verse libre or he will let me perish by neglect. He really threatens."
1915	Returns to America and buys a farm in New Hampshire. Accepts an offer to teach at Amherst for $2000/semester.
1924	Awarded Pulitzer Prize for his collection *New Hampshire*—the first of four.
1938	A taxing year: Wife dies. Frost collapses and resigns from teaching. Asks secretary Kathleen Morrison to marry him, but she refuses. There is much speculation about his emotional stability.
1940	Son Carol commits suicide. Frost: "I took the wrong way with him. I tried many ways and every single one of them was wrong." Two of his daughters eventually suffer mental breakdowns as well.
1949	U.S. Senate honors Frost on his 75th birthday.

1961   Recites "The Gift Outright" at President Kennedy's inaugura-
        tion. The following year, he and Kennedy have a falling-out over
        Frost's goodwill trip to the Soviet Union.

1962   An anonymous donor gives $3.5 million for the construction of
        the Robert Frost Library.

1963   Frost dies at 89. His ashes are interred at a family plot in
        Vermont.

DASHIELL HAMMETT

By LILLIAN HELLMAN, *longtime companion*

Delivered at funeral, January 13, 1961

Frank E. Campbell Funeral Home, New York City

A FEW WEEKS AGO, ON A NIGHT WHEN HE WAS HAVING A tough time, I said, "You're a brave man." I had never said such a thing before, and as he came out of that half doze the very sick have from minute to minute, he smiled and said, "Better keep words like that for the end." The end has come and he would not have wanted words today. This small funeral, this small tribute, I arranged for my sake. He was a man who respected words in books and suspected them in life; he believed that words sometimes took the place of thought and almost always took the place of action, and he deeply believed in both.

With very little school behind him, Dashiell Hammett had the greatest respect for knowledge of anybody I have ever known. He read enormously, sometimes five or six books a week, and anything that came to hand. There were the years when there were stacks of books on mathematics. And then on chess, teaching himself by memorizing the problems and mumbling them to himself; there was a year when he was interested in the retina of the eye, and another year when he bought a hearing aid and wandered in the woods trying to find out if it would make the sounds of birds and animals come clearer. Poetry, fiction, science, philosophy—any book that came to hand. He believed in the salvation of knowledge and intelligence, and he tried to live it out.

I have asked myself many times in these last thirty years why he seemed to me a great man. Perhaps because the combinations in his nature were so unexpected and so interesting. He didn't always think well of people and yet I've never known anybody else who gave away anything he had to anybody who needed it, or even wanted it, who accepted everybody with tolerance. He didn't, as you know, think well of the society we live in, and yet when it punished him he made no complaint against it and had no anger about the punishment. The night before he went to jail, he told me that no matter what anybody thought he had no political reason for the stand he took, that he had simply come to the conclusion that a man should keep his word.

He was sick the night he came out of jail, and it took me years to find out that wandering around the Kentucky town from which he was to catch the plane back to New York, he had met a moonshiner who had been in jail with him and was walking the streets with his wife because he couldn't find work. Dash gave him all the money he had in his pocket and he arrived in New York sick because he had kept no money to eat with. Many people would do just that, but most of us would have talked about it.

Dash wrote about violence, but he had contempt for it and thus he had contempt for heroics. And yet he enlisted in the Second World War at the age of forty-eight because he was a patriotic man, very involved in America. He went through three basic-training courses with men young enough to be his grandsons, and told me later that his major contribution to the war had been to sit in the Aleutians and convince the young that the lack of ladies didn't necessarily have anything to do with baldness or toothache.

He was a gay man, funny, witty. Most of his life was wide open and adventurous, and most of it he enjoyed. He learned and acted on what he learned. He believed in man's right to dignity, and never in all the years did he play anybody's game but his own. "Anything for a buck" was his sneer at those who did. In the thirty years I knew him I never heard him tell a lie of any kind, and that sometimes made me angry when I wasn't envying the courage it takes. He saw through other people's lies but he dismissed them with a kind of tolerant contempt. He was a man of simple honor and bravery. Blessed are they, I hope, who leave good work behind. And who leave behind a life that is so worthy of respect. Whoever runs the blessing department, may they have sense enough to bless a good man this last day he is on earth.

1894	Born in Maryland, the second of three children.
1908	When his father falls ill, "Dash" leaves school and works odd jobs—messenger, newsboy, stevedore, freight clerk, machine operator—until joining the Pinkerton Detective Agency in 1915 as a detective.
1918	Catches tuberculosis while serving in the army. Ill health plagues him for the rest of his life.
1921	Marries Josephine Dolan, a nurse he befriends during a hospital stay. When his ill health makes it impossible to continue detective work, a Pinkerton colleague encourages him to write detective stories.
1922	Publishes his first short story in *Black Mask* magazine. Drawing on his detective experiences, he creates believable private-eye narratives woven in an unsentimental, journalistic style.
1926	Begins an affair with his secretary—even as his wife gives birth to their second daughter.
1930	A packed year: *The Maltese Falcon* is a runaway hit, introducing the character Sam Spade into pop culture and launching Hammett's career. Hollywood producers eagerly buy his material, and he spends the proceeds profligately. Meets Lillian Hellman at a party hosted by Darryl F. Zanuck, beginning a turbulent love affair that lasts until his death. By now his marriage to Josephine is over, the tuberculosis is in remission, but his health remains precarious—due to hard-partying ways.

1934   Publishes *The Thin Man*. Bases the character of Nora Charles on Lillian, who is endlessly curious about his detective work.

1942   World War II: The 48-year-old Hammett enlists, serving as editor of an army newspaper in Alaska's Aleutian Islands.

1946   Hospitalized for alcoholism, Hammett quits drinking once and for all. Spends the following years attending to political causes—including a fund for jailed Communists. When he refuses to testify against Communist sympathizers, he is sent to jail on contempt charges. Upon release six months later, he is ill, blacklisted, and responsible for a $140,000 tax bill.

1959   Spends last few years with Lillian, reading and talking.

1961   Dies of inoperable lung cancer, penniless but prolific: Though his writing career lasted only 12 years, he wrote 6 novels, 90 short stories, and more than 100 book reviews. In spite of J. Edgar Hoover's attempts to prevent it, Hammett is buried at Arlington National Cemetery.

LILLIAN HELLMAN

1905–1984

By WILLIAM STYRON, *longtime friend*

Delivered at graveside funeral, July 3, 1984

Martha's Vineyard, MA

I'M BILL STYRON, AN OLD FRIEND OF LILLIAN'S, LIKE MANY of us here. She once told me that this would be the day that I yearn for more than anything in my life, speaking words over her remains, and she cackled in glee. "Ha-ha," she said, and I cackled back. She said, "If you don't say utterly admiring and beautiful things about me, I'm going to cut you out of my will." I said there could be no possible way that I could refrain from saying a few critical things, and she said, "Well, you're cut out already."

That was the way it went with us. I think we had more fights per man and woman contact than probably anyone alive. We were fighting all the time, and we loved each other a great deal for sure because the vibrations were there. But our fights were never really, oddly enough, over abstract things like politics or philosophy or social dilemmas; they were always over such things as whether a Smithfield ham should be served hot or cold, or whether I had put too much salt in the black-eyed peas.

And I suddenly realized that this anger that spilled out from the lady, and it was almost a reservoir of anger, was not directed at me or her other friends or even at the black-eyed peas, but was directed at all the hateful things that she saw as menaces to the world. When she hated me and the ham, she was hating a pig like Roy Cohn, and I think this is what motivated her; and when one understood that the measure of her anger was really not personal but cosmic, then one was able to deal with her.

I was privileged, I think the word is, to be the last person to take her out to dinner, a few days ago here in Chilmark at La Grange, and it was quite an ordeal. We sat down. She groped for the various things she had to grope for because, as you know, she was blind and quite radically crippled; and we had a conversation. We carved up a few mutually detested writers and one or two mediocre politicians and an elderly deceased novelist, whom she specifically detested, and we got into this sort of thing; and we then started talking about her age.

She said, "I don't know whether the 20th of June was my 74th or my 73rd." And I measured this, because she had been doing this all her life, not as a vanity—though that was fine, too, what's wrong with a little vanity—but as a kind of demonstration of the way that she was hanging on to life.

I suddenly realized as I was sitting there that she was painfully uncomfortable. She said she was cursed by God with having from birth a skinny ass; so I had to go and put things under her constantly. She said this bolstered her skepticism of the existence of God. And I told her something that she had always responded to, that it was made up with an ample and seductive bosom, and she smiled at that. It hit me that this woman was in agony, and there was something enormously wrenching about being seated with this almost fragment of a human being, suffering so much, gasping for breath; and yet I had a glimpse of her, almost as if she was a young girl again, in New Orleans, with a beau and having a wonderful time.

And as these memories came flooding back, I remembered that gorgeous cackle of laughter that followed some beautiful harpooning of a fraud or a ninth-rater; and it was filled with a hatred, but it was usually a hatred and anger that finally evolved into what I think she, like all of us, was searching for, some sort of transcendent idea which is love. And so, as we went out, I simply was in awe of this woman.

I had no final reflection except that perhaps she was in the end a lover, a mother, a sister, and a friend, and in a strange way a lover of us all.

1905	Born in New Orleans, LA. Childhood is spent shuttling between New York City and New Orleans, where her aunts run a boardinghouse.
1922	Studies at New York University, and later Columbia, but leaves minus a degree.
1925	Marries playwright Arthur Kober. Together they move to Hollywood, where Hellman reads scripts for MGM—dull work, but it puts her in contact with political and creative visionaries. A leftist, Hellman soon organizes her fellow script readers into a union.
1930	Begins intimate relationship with Dashiell Hammett, which lasts until his death. "We talked at each other until it was daylight. We were to meet again a few days later, and after that, on and sometimes off again for the rest of his life and thirty years of mine." Hellman divorces Kober in 1932.
1934	Her play *The Children's Hour* debuts on Broadway. Despite its controversial lesbian theme, the play runs for 700 performances.
1936	The FBI opens a file, tracking her leftist activities.
1939	Her second—and biggest—success: *The Little Foxes* debuts on Broadway. The subsequent filmed version starring Bette Davis receives nine Academy Award nominations. Hellman buys a farm with her earnings.
1951	While Hammett serves a 6-month sentence for refusing to cooperate with the House Un-American Activities Committee, Hellman is advised to leave the country. Sails to Europe with director William Wyler. Upon returning, she finds herself blacklisted—and her income begins to dwindle. Sells her farm.
1952	Called before the HUAC, she refuses to reveal the names of

Communist theater friends: "I cannot and will not cut my conscience to fit this year's fashions." Hellman is excused by the committee with the remark, "Why cite her for contempt? After all, she is a woman."

| 1962 | Excited over recent student activism, Hellman begins teaching at a number of Ivy League colleges. |

| 1969 | Pens autobiography, *An Unfinished Woman*. |

| 1984 | Dies of cardiac arrest, age 79, at home in Martha's Vineyard. Pointedly, her will establishes two literary funds—one for arts and sciences, one to further radical causes. |

THEODOR SEUSS GEISEL

1904-1991

By ROBERT L. BERNSTEIN, *publisher and close friend*

Delivered at memorial service, November 18, 1991

San Diego Museum of Fine Art, San Diego, CA

WE ARE ALL MORTAL. SO IT HAD TO HAPPEN. TED GEISEL had to leave this earth sometime. But he worked it out so that he came as close to being immortal as possible. While Ted is gone, he left Dr. Seuss behind him. As far as any of us can see ahead of us, Dr. Seuss will be around, getting young kids interested in reading, starting them and their parents thinking about the important things in the world, and giving them all a great time while doing it.

I met Ted when I arrived at Random House in 1957, and one of the first things I did was to get him to go on an autographing and publicity tour. That wasn't easy, because Ted wasn't sure that anybody would come out to see him. In Detroit we rented a helicopter and landed in the parking lot of a J. L. Hudson suburban store. Ted was amazed when the store had to stay open two hours past closing time, to allow all the kids to get his autograph.

In Chicago, in Marshall Field's, Ted started autographing, and he soon called me over, because just where he wanted to write his name, books were coming through with the autograph of a Chief White Cloud. We looked around, and there was an Indian in full regalia, walking up and down, autographing Ted's books with his name, Chief White Cloud, and passing out a card that read: "Chief White Cloud dances at Loew's Orpheum Sunday at three." Ted very gently suggested that perhaps the chief could have his own party, and the chief left.

A few days later in the Dayton Company in Minneapolis, I got a little bored, and I took two books from children standing in line and wrote "Chief White Cloud." The first one sailed by Ted, but when the second arrived, he looked up and yelled to me across the store: "Bob! The damned Indian has followed us all the way to Minneapolis."

I loved being with Ted anywhere, but my favorite times were when I would visit Ted and Audrey as Ted was about to finish a book. The minute I entered the house, he would rush me into his studio, where the pages were mounted on his cork wall. He would go over the pages with me and then anxiously ask me what I thought. While sometimes this can be a tough moment with an author, I was always eager and relaxed in approaching Ted's work. I just wondered what this wonderfully original man would have invented his time. While Ted somehow needed reassurance, I knew every book would be great. It really wasn't hard to realize that Ted was a genius.

Like many of you, I will miss Ted always—and always feel that I was lucky to know him as an author, as a very dear friend, and as a truly great man. I know if he were here he would want this afternoon to be a moment of celebration, as it has been; a moment of fond remembrance, as it has been. He would hope that we all spoke well of him. And I think he would be pleased to know that I've kept a few things that he wrote for special occasions, poems very few people have heard of. I would like to share my collection with you today.

I gave Ted a party in New York on his eightieth birthday. Several of us who were to speak on that occasion had prepared our remarks, but Ted greatly surprised us with his own contribution. I can almost hear his mild protest about my reading it today. Here it is. It has as its heading "A Short Epic Birthday Poem entitled 'On an occasion such as this I maintain that my late father is of much greater importance than even Robert L. Bernstein.'"

If my Daddy hadn't have
met up with my Mommy,
I'd have missed this fine party tonight.

If my Daddy had shacked up
with some lady else . . .
just supposing, for instance,
Miss Abigail Schemltz
or Patricia MacPhee . . .
or Louella McGee . . .
I would not have resulted. I wouldn't be me!
There'd just be no telling who the hell I might be!

For example, had he foolishly eloped to South Wooster
with some floozy named Florabell Frankenstein Flooster
I might now be writing for Simon and Schuster
And this party could never have been.

Nor could it have been
if he'd shacked up in Chelsea
with Carolyn Baumgarten Crinoline Kelsey
or wedded some frump named Felicity Frink
Then who would I be . . . ?
Oh, I shudder to think.

I'd quite likely be writing
under the name of Dr. Gussler
for the National Enquirer
or maybe even the Hustler.
In which case, Bob Bernstein,
though a most generous soul
wouldn't have touched tonight's banquet
with a fifteen-foot pole.

So I thank you, dear Daddy
for doing things right
or I wouldn't be here
with my good friends tonight.

The first I knew that Ted was ill was when he had to cancel his sched-uled appearance at the American Booksellers Association convention breakfast in 1988 in Anaheim. Several thousand booksellers had come to hear him. Determined not to disappoint them, he sent some verse, and he asked me to deliver it. When you hear it, I think you will be amazed at how fresh it sounds, three and a half years later. It is entitled "A Rather Short Epic Poem (size 6 and 7/8)."

Oh . . .
I would that I were in Anaheim
in this early morning room.
How I would that I were in Anaheim
with Maurice Sendak and Judy Blume
and with all you friendly Booksters
and beautiful Bookster-esses
to discuss, as old friends, the sad state of the world
and other lugubrious messes

But . . .
I languish far from Anaheim
with a bad case of the Hyper Sty-mar-ess
an optical malady caused by reading
much too much junk
about the Presidential Primaries.

And being unable to be here
and to do it myself today

I have asked Mr. Bernstein,
who is an excellent blesser
to bless you all and to say
that in a country where Illiteracy is on the rise
and the economy is slinking low
and Chastity is out of the window
it is comforting to know
that, though the frost is on the pumpkin
and civilization is on the skids
You guys are fearlessly working underground
smuggling books into the hands of kids!

The verse went over so well that the applause just wouldn't stop. As his stand-in, I tried to figure out what Ted would do. Then I recalled that in 1977 he had given a commencement address at Lake Forest College in Illinois. He and I had talked about the address for most of the year while he was working on it. He explained to me that kids hated commencement addresses and that he wanted to write the world's shortest address but it had to have a point.

Shortly before he gave it he called and, unusually pleased with himself, stated he had got the address down to one minute and fourteen seconds. I loved it and have carried it in my wallet since 1977. So I pulled it out and used it as an encore at the convention.

When Ted died I sent the address to the newspapers in Los Angeles and San Diego. Accordingly, many of you may have read it. Nevertheless, I'd like to close with it now. I somehow think it's the advice Ted would like to leave with all of us.

My Uncle Terwillinger on the Art of Eating Popovers

My uncle ordered popovers
From the restaurant's bill of fare.
And, when they were served, he regarded them
with a penetrating stare . . .

Then he spoke great Words of Wisdom
as he sat there on that chair:
"To eat these things," said my uncle,
"You must exercise great care.
You may swallow down what's solid . . .
BUT . . . you must spit out the air!"

And as you partake of the world's bill of fare,
that's darned good advice to follow.
Do a lot of spitting out the hot air.
And be careful what you swallow.

These were wise words. Ted left us so much that will be remembered and enjoyed for generations. Having him in my life was a privilege and a joy. I shall always miss him.

1904	Born in Springfield, MA.
1910	Frequents the zoo as a child. Since his father is Superintendent of Parks, "they'd let me in the cage with the small lions and the small tigers, and I got chewed up every once in a while." His zoological playmates later shape-shift into fantastical Loraxes, Whos, and Zooks of his Seuss books.
1925	Graduates from Dartmouth with a B.A. in English.
1927	Marries teacher Helen Palmer, who persuades him to focus on drawing. "Ted's notebooks were always filled with these fabulous animals," she later recalls. Begins drawing the humorous "Quick Henry, the Flit!" pesticide ads.
1937	His first children's book, *And to Think That I Saw It on Mulberry Street,* is rejected by 43 publishers. Finally published by a friend, it achieves moderate success.

1939	His first book for grown-ups, *The Seven Lady Godivas,* flops outright. Geisel is unperturbed. "Adults are obsolete children, and the hell with them."
1945	World War II: Geisel battles the Nazis by way of Hollywood. Assigned to Frank Capra's Signal Corps Unit, he writes and produces *Hitler Lives* for the army. Later released by Warner Bros., it goes on to receive an Oscar for Best Short Documentary.
1951	Receives another Oscar for his cartoon *Gerald McBoing-Boing.*
1956	With school-age illiteracy rates on the rise, Geisel's publisher throws down the gauntlet: Write a book using 250 simple words. Nine months later, Geisel unveils *The Cat in the Hat.* Mixing zany animals, homespun morals, and a dollop of whimsy, the book goes on to sell 7 million copies and establish Geisel as the world's best-selling children's author. Bonus: His pen name, Dr. Seuss, lends scientific cachet to his goofy zoology.
1960	A friend bets Geisel $50 he can't write a book using only 50 words. The result? *Green Eggs and Ham.*
1967	Helen dies. Geisel marries Audrey Diamond the following year.
1984	Wins a Pulitzer Prize for his contribution to children's literature.
1990	Prolific to the end, Geisel publishes *Oh, the Places You'll Go!* The book stays on the best-seller list for 80 weeks, becoming a popular graduation present.
1991	Dies in his sleep, age 87, in La Jolla, CA. Childless himself, he leaves an empire of literature for "children of all ages," having written and illustrated 44 books, sold more than 200 million copies, and been translated into 20 languages (and picking up two Emmy Awards, a Peabody, and three Oscars along the way).

MARK TWAIN

By REV. HENRY VAN DYKE, *longtime friend*

Delivered at funeral, April 24, 1910

The Presbyterian Brick Church, New York City

I SHALL SPEAK NO EULOGY FOR OUR DEAD FRIEND. THE friends of Samuel Langhorne Clemens, whom all the world knew as Mark Twain, meet in this quaint place for a moment to look upon his face in tenderness and gratitude before his body is carried to rest in God's acre by those he loved so truly. Our friend would sympathize with our sentiments if he knew we were here, not to grieve for him, but to help the living to have braver, truer, sweeter sentiments in the presence of God's mystery.

This is not the time nor the place for eulogy for the famous writer, the honored representative of American letters in the world of literature. We are here reminded of the frailty of mortal flesh and the brevity of our stay on earth. We think of Mark Twain not as a celebrity, but as a man whom we loved. We remember the reality that made his life worth living—his laughing enmity of all sham; his love for truth; his honesty; his honor.

We know how he met with adversity, toiling years to pay a debt of conscience, following the injunction to do all things honorably as well as all things honestly. We know how he loved his family and his fellowmen. We knew Mark Twain and we loved him.

Nothing is more false than to think that the presence of humor means the absence of seriousness. It was the showing up of the unreal sham, the untruth, that made Mark Twain's humor. He was serious in his humor. But we know that Mark Twain never laughed at the frail, the weak, the poor, and the humble. He used his humor, but for things good and wholesome. He made fun without hatred. He laughed many of the world's false claimants out of court. Under all his humor he made us feel the pathos of life's realities, for he exposed the sham.

Now that he is gone, we who loved him—and we all loved him who knew him—will miss him. We are glad to give thanks that he left such an honorable name. We are glad he won such fame in the world of letters. We are glad, after so many shocks in his life, that he has gone into rest and a fullness of the enjoyment that is due to his honorable life.

1835	Born Samuel Langhorne Clemens in the village of Florida, MO, to parents who "were neither very poor nor conspicuously honest," he later writes. His childhood is laced with vivid stories from Jenny, the family-owned slave.
1839	The Clemenses move to nearby town of Hannibal on the Mississippi River. Samuel develops a love affair with the river that continues throughout his life.
1849	Quits school, age 14.
1851	Discovers literary talents while working as a typesetter for his brother's newspaper, the *Hannibal Journal*. He contributes occasional articles and the following year publishes two sketches in the *Saturday Evening Post*.
1859	Earns his license to pilot steamboats on the Mississippi River, fulfilling a boyhood ambition, and amassing the details of river life that find their way into his books.
1861	With the Civil War, travel on the Mississippi River shuts down. Clemens heads west to Nevada, becoming a reporter for the

Virginia City Territorial Enterprise, earning $25/week. Begins signing his articles Mark Twain, a Mississippi River phrase meaning "two fathoms deep."

1864   Continues westward to California, where he hopes to strike it rich in gold. Jots down a story he overhears in the gold fields, "The Celebrated Jumping Frog of Calaveras County." It becomes a national sensation and heralds his uniquely American, gently mocking voice.

1869   Publishes his first book, *The Innocents Abroad,* recounting his recent adventures in Europe and Palestine.

1870   Marries Olivia Langdon. The couple settles in Hartford, CT, where they have three daughters, two of whom die young.

1876   Publishes *The Adventures of Tom Sawyer.*

1884   His masterpiece, *The Adventures of Huckleberry Finn,* is published. The same year Clemens founds a small firm that publishes such notables as Gen. Ulysses S. Grant, but the firm goes bankrupt, plunging Clemens into steep debt.

1895   Embarks on a round-the-world lecture tour to repay his debts.

1904   Olivia dies. Clemens begins to spend most of his time in New York City, making public appearances in his trademark white linen suit. Infected with a growing pessimism due to his personal losses, Twain evolves from humorist to gently sarcastic, cigar-wielding philosopher.

1907   Receives an honorary degree from Oxford University. "You shake the sides of the whole world with your merriment," the chancellor tells him.

1910   After flipping casually through a book and bidding his doctor good-bye, Clemens slips into a coma and dies. Buried alongside his wife and children in Elmira, NY, he leaves behind an unfinished autobiography and the prototype for big-hearted American narratives.

WALT WHITMAN

1 8 1 9 – 1 8 9 2

By ROBERT GREEN INGERSOLL, *admirer and friend*

Delivered at funeral, March 30, 1892

Harleigh Cemetery, Camden, NJ

My FRIENDS: AGAIN WE, IN THE MYSTERY OF LIFE, ARE brought face-to-face with the mystery of Death. A great man, a great American, the most eminent citizen of this Republic, lies dead before us, and we have met to pay a tribute to his greatness and his worth.

I know he needs no words of mine. His fame is secure. He laid the foundations of it deep in the human heart and brain. He was, above all I have known, the poet of humanity, of sympathy. He was so great that he rose above the greatest that he met without arrogance, and so great that he stooped to the lowest without conscious condescension. He never claimed to be lower or greater than any of the sons of men.

He came into our generation a free, untrammeled spirit, with sympathy for all. His arm was beneath the form of the sick. He sympathized with the imprisoned and despised, and even on the brow of crime he was great enough to place the kiss of human sympathy.

One of the greatest lines in our literature is his, and the line is great enough to do honor to the greatest genius that has ever lived. He said, speaking of an outcast: "Not till the sun excludes you do I exclude you." His charity was as wide as the sky, and wherever there was human suffering, human misfortune, the sympathy of Whitman bent above it as the firmament bends above the earth.

He was built on a broad and splendid plan—ample, without appearing to have limitations—passing easily for a brother of mountains and seas and constellations; caring nothing for the little maps and charts with which timid pilots hug the shore, but giving himself freely with recklessness of genius to winds and waves and tides; caring for nothing as long as the stars were above him. He walked among men, among writers, among verbal varnishers and veneerers, among literary milliners and tailors, with the unconscious majesty of an antique god.

He was the poet of that divine democracy that gives equal rights to all the sons and daughters of men. He uttered the great American voice; uttered a song worthy of the great Republic. No man ever said more for the rights of humanity, more in favor of real democracy, of real justice. He neither scorned nor cringed, was neither tyrant nor slave. He asked only to stand the equal of his fellows beneath the great flag of nature, the blue sky and stars.

He was the poet of Life. It was a joy simply to breathe. He loved the clouds; he enjoyed the breath of morning, the twilight, the wind, the winding streams. He loved to look at the sea when the waves burst into the whitecaps of joy. He loved the fields, the hills; he was acquainted with the trees, with birds, with all the beautiful objects of the earth. He not only saw these objects but understood their meaning, and he used them that he might exhibit his heart to his fellowmen.

He was the poet of Love. He was not ashamed of that divine passion that has built every home in the world; that divine passion that has painted every picture and given us every real work of art; that divine passion that has made the world worth living in and has given some value to human life.

He was the poet of the natural, and taught men not to be ashamed of that which is natural. He was not only the poet of democracy, not only the poet of the great Republic, but he was the poet of the human race. He was not confined to the limits of this country, but his sympathy went out over the seas to all the nations of the earth. He stretched out his hand and felt himself the equal of all kings and of all princes, and the brother of all men, no matter how high, no matter how low.

He has uttered more supreme words than any writer of our century, possibly of almost any other. He was, above all things, a man, and above genius, above all the snow-capped peaks of intelligence, above all art, rises the true man. Greater than all is the true man, and he walked among his fellowmen as such.

He was the poet of Death. He accepted all life and all death, and he justified all. He had the courage to meet all, and was great enough and splendid enough to harmonize all and to accept all there is of life as a divine melody.

You know better than I what his life has been, but let me say one thing. Knowing, as he did, what others can know and what they cannot, he accepted and absorbed all theories, all creeds, all religions, and believed in none. His philosophy was a sky that embraced all clouds and accounted for all clouds. He had a philosophy and a religion of his own, broader, as he believed—and as I believe—than others. He accepted all, he understood all, and he was above all.

He was absolutely true to himself. He had frankness and courage, and he was as candid as light. He was willing that all the sons of men should be absolutely acquainted with his heart and brain. He had nothing to conceal. Frank, candid, pure, serene, noble, and yet for years he was maligned and slandered, simply because he had the candor of nature. He will be understood yet, and that for which he was condemned—his frankness, his candor—will add to the glory and greatness of his fame.

He wrote a liturgy for mankind; he wrote a great and splendid psalm of life, and he gave to us the gospel of humanity—the greatest gospel that can be preached.

He was not afraid to live, not afraid to die. For many years he and death were near neighbors. He was always willing and ready to meet and greet this king called death, and for many months he sat in the deepening twilight waiting for the night, waiting for the light.

He never lost his hope. When the mists filled the valleys, he looked upon the mountaintops, and when the mountains in darkness disappeared, he fixed his gaze upon the stars.

In his brain were the blessed memories of the day, and in his heart were mingled the dawn and dusk of life.

He was not afraid; he was cheerful every moment. The laughing nymphs of day did not desert him. They remained that they might clasp the hands and greet with smiles the veiled and silent sisters of the night. And when they did come, Walt Whitman stretched his hand to them. On one side were the nymphs of the day, and on the other the silent sisters of the night, and so, hand in hand, between smiles and tears, he reached his journey's end.

From the frontier of life, from the western wave-kissed shore, he sent us messages of content and hope, and these messages seem now like strains of music blown by the "Mystic Trumpeter" from Death's pale realm.

Today we give back to Mother Nature, to her clasp and kiss, one of the bravest, sweetest souls that ever lived in human clay.

Charitable as the air and generous as Nature, he was negligent of all except to do and say what he believed he should do and should say.

And I today thank him, not only for you but for myself—for all the brave words he has uttered. I thank him for all the great and splendid words he has said in favor of liberty, in favor of man and woman, in favor of motherhood, in favor of fathers, in favor of children, and I thank him for the brave words that he has said of death.

He has lived, he has died, and death is less terrible than it was before. Thousands and millions will walk down into the "dark valley of the shadow" holding Walt Whitman by the hand. Long after we are dead the brave words he has spoken will sound like trumpets to the dying.

And so I lay this little wreath upon this great man's tomb. I loved him living, and I love him still.

1819	Born in Huntington, Long Island, the second of nine children.
1831	Age 12: Walt leaves school to work as a printer in Brooklyn. When a fire destroys most of the printing district in 1836, he moves back to Long Island to teach school.
1841	For the next decade, Whitman works as a journalist and printer. Publishes several conventional poems with no hint of the radical works to come.
1842	Invited to pen a temperance novel, Whitman agrees, having witnessed the effects of alcohol on family members. The resulting *Franklin Evans* sells more than 20,000 copies and is the greatest success Whitman enjoys during his lifetime. He later dismisses it as "rot."
1848	Having begun writing for the *Brooklyn Daily Eagle,* Whitman is fired for his antislavery sympathies.
1855	July 4: Self-publishes the first edition of *Leaves of Grass*—795 copies, 12 poems—espousing the equality of women, "the manly love of comrades," and the oneness of humanity with creation. Pariah or prophet? Public opinion divides sharply. A publicity hound, Whitman writes unsigned reviews of the book, then sends them to leading literati.
1856	Second edition of *Leaves* runs over 400 pages. Despite his growing fame, Whitman frequents bohemian hangouts—haunting the docks, ferries, and baths of lower Manhattan.
1860	Devotes himself to nursing wounded Civil War soldiers—first in New York hospitals, then in the battlefield hospitals of Virginia.
1865	Appointed to a clerkship in Bureau of Indian Affairs, only to be discharged due to his "indecent" *Leaves.* Meets and has a relationship with 18-year-old Peter Doyle, a Washington, D.C., streetcar conductor. Their affair lasts several years and becomes one of the touchstones of Whitman's life.
1873	Suffers a paralytic stroke. Goes to live with brother George in Camden, NJ.

1882   Purchases his first house with proceeds from *Leaves*. In following years, he suffers a series of strokes, but still receives young admirers coming to pay respects.

1892   Publishes ninth edition of *Leaves* (the "Deathbed Edition"). Dies at home, age 72. Instructs that his tomb door be left ajar at twilight so his spirit can stroll. Whitman on *Leaves*: "Who touches this book touches a man."

VIRGINIA WOOLF

1882 - 1941

By CHRISTOPHER ISHERWOOD, *literary colleague and friend*

Written on the occasion of her death

VIRGINIA WOOLF IS DEAD—AND THOUSANDS OF PEOPLE, far outside the immediate circle of her friends and colleagues, will be sorry, will feel the loss of a great and original talent to our literature. For she was famous, surprisingly famous when one considers that she was what is called "a writer's writer." Her genius was intensely feminine and personal—private, almost. To read one of her books was (if you liked it) to receive a letter from her, addressed specially to you. But this, perhaps, was just the secret of her appeal.

As everybody knows, Mrs. Woolf was a prominent member of what journalists used to call "the Bloomsbury Group"—which included Lytton Strachey, Vanessa Bell, Duncan Grant, E. M. Forster, Arthur Waley, Desmond MacCarthy, and Maynard Keynes. Actually, the "group" was not a group at all, in the self-conscious sense, but a kind of clan, one of those "natural" families that form themselves without the assistance of parents, uncles, and aunts, simply because a few sensitive and imaginative people become aware of belonging to each other, and wish to be frequently in each other's company. It follows, of course, that these brothers and sisters under the skin find it convenient to settle in the same neighborhood—Bloomsbury, in this case. It is a district just behind and beyond the British Museum. Its three large squares, Gordon, Bedform, and Tavistock, have something of the dignity and atmosphere of Cambridge college courts.

Open *To the Lighthouse, The Common Reader,* or *The Waves,* read a

couple of pages with appreciation, and you have become already a distant relative of the Bloomsbury family. You can enter the inner sanc-
tum, the Woolf drawing room, and nobody will rise to greet you—for
you are one of the party. "Oh, come in," says Virginia, with that gracious informality that is so inimitably aristocratic, "you know everybody, don't you? We were just talking about Charles Tansley . . . poor
Charles—such a prig. . . . Imagine what he said the other day. . . ."
And so, scarcely aware, we float into our story.

The Bloomsbury family held together by consanguinity of talent.
That you could express yourself artistically, through the medium of
writing, or painting, or music, was taken for granted. This was the real
business of life: It would have been indecent, almost, to refer to it.
Artistic integrity was the family religion, and in its best days it could
proudly boast that it did not harbor a single prostitute, potboiler, or
hack. Nevertheless one must live. Some of the brothers and sister had
very odd hobbies. Keynes, for example, whose brilliant descriptive pen
could touch in an unforgettable and merciless portrait of Clemenceau
on the margin, as it were, of an economic report to the Versailles
treaty-makers—Keynes actually descended into that sordid jungle, the
City, and emerged a wealthy man! And Virginia—the exquisite, clois-
tered Virginia—became a publisher. True, the thing happened by
gradual stages. It began as a sort of William Morris handicraft—with
Leonard and Virginia working their own press, and Virginia's delicate
fingers, one supposes, getting black with printer's ink. But all this was
ancient history, and the handpress was stowed away in the cellar under
dust-sheets before the day in the early thirties when I first walked
timidly up the steps of the house in Tavistock Square.

I find it impossible to write anything about her that will carry the
breath of life. Which century did she belong to? Which generation?
You could not tell: She simply defied analysis. At the time of our first
meeting, she was, I now realize, an elderly lady, yet she seemed, in
some mysterious way, to be very much older and very much younger

than her age. I could never decide whether she reminded me of my grandmother as a young Victorian girl, or my great-grandmother—if she had taken some rejuvenating drug and had lived a hundred and twenty years, to become the brilliant leader of an intensely modern Georgian salon.

One remembers, first of all, those wonderful forlorn eyes; the slim, erect, high-shouldered figure, strangely tense, as if always on the alert for some distant sound; the hair folded back from the eggshell fragility of the temples; the small, beautifully cut face, like a Tennysonian cameo—Mariana, or the Lady of Shalott. Yes, that is the impression one would like to convey—an unhappy, high-born lady in a ballad, a fairy-story princess under a spell, slightly remote from the rest of us, a profile seen against the dying light, hands dropped helplessly in the lap, a shocking, momentary glimpse of intense grief.

What rubbish! We are at the tea table. Virginia is sparkling with gaiety, delicate malice, and gossip—the gossip that is the style of her books and that made her the best hostess in London; listening to her, we missed appointments, forgot love affairs, stayed on and on into the small hours, when we had to be hinted, gently but firmly, out of the house. This time, the guest of honor is a famous novelist, whose substantial income proves that Art, after all, really can pay. He is modest enough—but Virginia, with sadistic curiosity, which is like the teasing of an elder sister, drags it all out of him: how much time New York publishers gave, how much the movie people, and what the king said, and the Crown Prince of Sweden—she has no mercy. And then, when it is all over, "You know, Jeremy," she tells him, smiling almost tenderly, "you remind me of a very beautiful prize-winning cow." "A cow, Virginia?" The novelist gulps but grins bravely at me, determined to show he can take it. "Yes . . . a very, very fine cow. You can go out into the world and win all sorts of prizes, but gradually your coat gets covered with burrs, and so you have to come back again into your field. And in the middle of the field is a rough old stone post, and you rub yourself against it to get the burrs off. Don't you think, Leonard"—she looks across at her husband—"that that's our real mission in life? We're Jeremy's old stone scratching post."

What else is there to say about her? Critics will place her among the four greatest English women writers. Friends will remember her beauty, her uniqueness, her charm. I am very proud to have known her. Was she the bewitched princess, or the wicked little girl at the tea party—or both, or neither? I can't tell. In any case she was, as the Spaniards say, "very rare," and this world was no place for her. I am happy to think that she is free of it, before everything she loved has been quite smashed. If I wanted an epitaph for her, taken from her own writings, I should choose this:

"It was done; it was finished. Yes, she thought, laying down her brush in extreme fatigue, I have had my vision."

1882	Born Adeline Virginia Stephen in London. A man of letters, Leslie Stephen educates his daughter at home. Virginia: "Think how I was brought up! No school, mooning along among my father's books, never any chance to pick up all that goes on in schools—throwing balls, ragging, slang, vulgarities, scenes, jealousies!"
1895	Mother dies. Virginia has a severe mental breakdown.
1904	Father dies. Virginia suffers a second mental breakdown and tries to commit suicide by jumping out a window. The Stephen siblings move to Bloomsbury, where Virginia becomes a book reviewer for the *Times Literary Supplement*.
1910	Bloomsbury Group begins to take form.
1912	Virginia marries political theorist Leonard Woolf and has her third mental breakdown, which lasts three years. During this time, she writes *The Voyage Out*.

1917	Woolfs buy a secondhand printing press and set up the Hogarth Press in their basement. Later they will publish T. S. Eliot, Freud, Isherwood, and all of Woolf's writings.
1925	Publishes *Mrs. Dalloway.* Hogarth Press moves from basement to London.
1926	Publishes *To the Lighthouse,* basing the central character, Mrs. Ramsay, on her mother. Establishes herself as one of the leading modern writers.
1939	War is declared on September 3. Woolfs prepare to commit suicide if Nazis invade.
1941	At start of another breakdown, Virginia fills her pockets with stones and wades into the River Ouse, leaving a suicide note for her husband: "I feel certain that I am going mad again: I feel we can't go through more of these terrible times. And I shan't recover this time. I begin to hear voices, and can't concentrate. So I am doing what seems the best thing to do. You have given me the greatest possible happiness. . . ."

JOHN F. KENNEDY

1917–1963

By CHIEF JUSTICE EARL WARREN

Delivered at memorial service, November 24, 1963

The Rotunda of the Capitol, Washington, D.C.

THERE ARE FEW EVENTS IN OUR NATIONAL LIFE THAT unite Americans and so touch the hearts of all of us as the passing of a president of the United States. There is nothing that adds shock to our sadness more than the assassination of our leader, chosen as he is to embody the ideals of our people, the faith we have in our institutions, and our belief in the fatherhood of God and the brotherhood of man.

Such misfortunes have befallen the nation on other occasions, but never more shockingly than two days ago.

We are saddened; we are stunned; we are perplexed.

John Fitzgerald Kennedy, a great and good president, the friend of all people of good will, a believer in the dignity and equality of all human beings, a fighter for justice, and apostle of peace, has been snatched from our midst by the bullet of an assassin. What moved some misguided wretch to do this horrible deed may never be known to us, but we do know that such acts are commonly stimulated by forces of hatred and malevolence, such as today are eating their way into the bloodstream of American life. What a price we pay for this fanaticism.

It has been said that the only thing we learn from history is that we do not learn. But surely we can learn if we have the will to do so. Surely there is a lesson to be learned from this tragic event. If we really love this country, if we truly love justice and mercy, if we fervently want to make this nation better for those who are to follow us, we can at least abjure the hatred that consumes people, the false accusations that divide us, and the bitterness that begets violence.

Is it too much to hope that the martyrdom of our beloved president might even soften the hearts of those who would themselves recoil from assassination, but who do not shrink from spreading the venom that kindles thoughts of it in others?

Our nation is bereaved. The whole world is poorer because of his loss. But we can all be better Americans because John Fitzgerald Kennedy has passed our way, because he has been our chosen leader at a time in history when his character, his vision, and his quiet courage have enabled him to chart for us a safe course through the shoals of treacherous seas that encompass the world.

And now that he is relieved of the almost superhuman burdens we imposed on him, may he rest in peace.

1917   Born in Brookline, MA, to Rose and Joe Kennedy—"Jack" is one of nine children. As a child he is prone to illness, falling prey to numerous diseases, from whooping cough to scarlet fever.

1932   In boarding school, a 15-year-old Jack subscribes to *The New York Times*. His father writes: "I will not be disappointed if you don't turn out to be a real genius, but I think you can be a really worthwhile citizen with good judgment and understanding."

1940   Graduates with honors from Harvard. Joins the navy the following year. When the Japanese ram his torpedo boat, splitting it in half, Kennedy leads the survivors to safety through perilous waters despite his own grave injuries. Awarded the Navy Medal.

1945   Bucking Bostonian prejudice against Irish Catholics, Kennedy campaigns for Congress and wins. Over the following decade, his star rises and he is eventually elected senator.

1953   Marries Jacqueline Lee Bouvier. They raise two children in the spotlight, Caroline and John Jr.

1954   While recovering from a back operation, Kennedy pens *Profiles in Courage,* which wins a Pulitzer Prize.

1960   Defeats Richard Nixon to become 35th president of the United States, winning by a margin of two-tenths of one percent.

1961   At 43, he is the youngest president to take office—and the first Roman Catholic. Pledging an ambitious political agenda of economic expansion, civil rights, world peace, and a war on poverty, Kennedy ushers a youthful spirit into the White House. Creates the Peace Corps to take American prosperity to Third World nations. "Ask not what your country can do for you," he declares in his inaugural address. "Ask what you can do for your country."

1962   Bay of Pigs invasion of Cuba backfires. Back home, Kennedy signs a Nuclear Test Ban Treaty, hoping to "press onward in quest of man's essential desire for peace."

1963   Assassinated while his motorcade winds through Dallas streets. The nation grieves openly. "Where were you when JFK was shot?" becomes part of American history. Eventually a commission headed by (eulogizer) Earl Warren concludes that assassin Lee Harvey Oswald acted alone, but the question is still openly debated. Marking his grave at Arlington National Cemetery, an eternal flame lit by Jackie still burns.

JOHN F. KENNEDY JR.

1960–1999

By SEN. EDWARD M. KENNEDY, *uncle*

Delivered at memorial service, July 23, 1999

The Church of St. Thomas More, New York City

ONCE, WHEN THEY ASKED JOHN WHAT HE WOULD DO IF he went into politics and was elected president, he said, "I guess the first thing is call up Uncle Teddy and gloat." I loved that. It was so like his father.

From the first day of his life, John seemed to belong not only to our family but to the American family.

The whole world knew his name before he did.

A famous photograph showed John racing across the lawn as his father landed in the White House helicopter and swept up John in his arms. When my brother saw that photo, he exclaimed, "Every mother in the United States is saying, 'Isn't it wonderful to see that love between a son and his father, the way that John races to be with his father.' Little do they know—that son would have raced right by his father to get to that helicopter."

But John was so much more than those long-ago images emblazoned in our minds. He was a boy who grew into a man with a zest for life and a love of adventure. He was a pied piper who brought us all along. He was blessed with a father and mother who never thought anything mattered more than their children.

When they left the White House, Jackie's soft and gentle voice and unbreakable strength of spirit guided him surely and securely to the future. He had a legacy, and he learned to treasure it. He was part of a legend, and he learned to live with it. Above all, Jackie gave him a place to be himself, to grow up, to laugh and cry, to dream and strive on his own.

John learned that lesson well. He had amazing grace. He accepted who he was, but he cared more about what he could and should become. He saw things that could be lost in the glare of the spotlight. And he could laugh at the absurdity of too much pomp and circumstance.

He loved to travel across this city by subway, bicycle, and Rollerblade. He lived as if he were unrecognizable—although he was known by everyone he encountered. He always introduced himself, rather than take anything for granted. He drove his own car and flew his own plane, which is how he wanted it. He was the king of his domain.

He thought politics should be an integral part of our popular culture and that popular culture should be an integral part of politics. He transformed that belief into the creation of *George*. John shaped and honed a fresh, often irreverent journal. His new political magazine attracted a new generation, many of whom had never read about politics before.

John also brought to *George* a wit that was quick and sure. The premier issue of *George* caused a stir with a cover photograph of Cindy Crawford dressed as George Washington with a bare belly button. The "Reliable Source" in *The Washington Post* printed a mock cover of *George* showing not Cindy Crawford but me dressed as George Washington, with my belly button exposed. I suggested to John that perhaps I should have been the model for the first cover of his magazine. Without missing a beat, John told me that he stood by his original editorial decision.

John brought this same playful wit to other aspects of his life. He campaigned for me during my 1994 election and always caused a stir when he arrived in Massachusetts. Before one of his trips to Boston, John told the campaign he was bringing along a companion but would need only one hotel room.

Interested, but discreet, a senior campaign worker picked John up at the airport and prepared to handle any media barrage that might accompany John's arrival with his mystery companion. John landed with the companion all right—an enormous German shepherd dog named Sam he had just rescued from the pound. He loved to talk about the expression on the campaign worker's face and the reaction of the clerk at the Charles Hotel when John and Sam checked in.

I think now not only of these wonderful adventures, but of the kind of person John was. He was the son who quietly gave extraordinary time and ideas to the Institute of Politics at Harvard that bears his father's name. He brought to the institute his distinctive insight that politics could have a broader appeal, that it was not just about elections, but about the larger forces that shape our whole society.

John was also the son who was once protected by his mother. He went on to become her pride—and then her protector in her final days. He was the Kennedy who loved us all but who especially cherished his sister, Caroline, celebrated her brilliance, and took strength and joy from their lifelong mutual admiration society.

And for a thousand days, he was a husband who adored the wife who became his perfect soul mate. John's father taught us all to reach for the moon and the stars. John did that in all he did—and he found his shining star when he married Carolyn Bessette.

How often our family will think of the two of them, cuddling affectionately on a boat, surrounded by family—aunts, uncles, Caroline and Ed and their children, Rose, Tatiana, and Jack; Kennedy cousins, Radziwill cousins, Shriver cousins, Smith cousins, Lawford cousins—as we sailed Nantucket Sound.

Then we would come home and before dinner, on the lawn where his father had played, John would lead a spirited game of touch football. And his beautiful young wife—the new pride of the Kennedys—would cheer for John's team and delight her nieces and nephews with her somersaults.

We loved Carolyn. She and her sister Lauren were young, extraordinary women of high accomplishment—and their own limitless possibilities. We mourn their loss and honor their lives. The Bessette and Freeman families will always be part of ours.

John was a serious man who brightened our lives with his smile and his grace. He was a son of privilege who founded a program called Reaching Up to train better caregivers for the mentally disabled.

He joined Wall Street executives on the Robin Hood Foundation to help the city's impoverished children. And he did it all so quietly, without ever calling attention to himself.

John was one of Jackie's two miracles. He was still becoming the person he would be, and doing it by the beat of his own drummer. He had only just begun. There was in him a great promise of things to come.

The Irish ambassador recited a poem to John's father and mother soon after John was born. I can hear it again now, at this different and difficult moment:

> *We wish to the new child*
> *A heart that can be beguiled*
> *By a flower*
> *That the wind lifts*
> *As it passes.*
> *If the storms break for him*
> *May the trees shake for him*
> *Their blossoms down.*
> *In the night that he is troubled*
> *May a friend wake for him*
> *So that his time may be doubled,*
> *And at the end of all loving and love,*
> *May the Man above*
> *Give him a crown.*

We thank the millions who have rained blossoms down on John's memory. He and his bride have gone to be with his mother and father, where there will never be an end to love. He was lost on that troubled night—but we will always wake for him, so that his time, which was not doubled, but cut in half, will live forever in our memory, and in our beguiled and broken hearts.

We dared to think, in that other Irish phrase, that this John Kennedy would live to comb gray hair, with his beloved Carolyn by his side. But like his father, he had every gift but length of years.

We who have loved him from the day he was born, and watched the remarkable man he became, now bid him farewell.

God bless you, John and Carolyn. We love you and we always will.

1960	Born in Washington, D.C., to Jacqueline and John F. Kennedy, weeks after President Kennedy wins the election.
1961	Nicknamed John-John by a reporter, he frequently interrupts White House meetings to greet his father in bathrobe and slippers.
1963	Kennedy is assassinated. Image of John-John saluting his father's casket becomes an indelible symbol of American grief over the slain president. The following year Jackie moves family to New York City, hoping to provide her children with a seminormal childhood. Fascination with the Kennedys continues unabated.
1983	Graduates from Brown. Moves back to Manhattan, where he dabbles in theater and social work.
1988	Named "Sexiest Man Alive" by *People* magazine.
1989	Graduates from NYU Law School and is hired by Manhattan District Attorney to prosecute white-collar fraud and street crime. After taking three years to pass the bar, Kennedy wins all of his cases—then resigns four years later.
1990	Begins five-year relationship with actress Darryl Hannah.

1995   With inheritance money, Kennedy launches *George* magazine, a
        glossy look at government. The magazine provides a way to go
        on record with political beliefs without running for office.
        Kennedy: "Once you run for office, you're in it—sort of like
        going into the military. You'd better be damned sure it is what
        you want to do and that the rest of your life can accommodate
        that. It takes a certain toll on your personality and on your family
        life. I've seen it personally."

1996   Marries Carolyn Bessette, former publicist for Calvin Klein, in
        secret ceremony off coast of Georgia.

1998   Receives pilot license.

1999   Flying to Hyannisport, Kennedy and Bessette sisters crash at sea.
        Years before, his father had pondered: "It is an interesting biolog-
        ical fact that all of us have in our veins the exact same percentage
        of salt in our blood that exists in the ocean. . . . We are tied to
        the ocean. And when we go back to the sea—whether it is to sail
        or to watch it—we are going back from whence we came." In a
        private ceremony, their ashes are scattered off the coast of
        Martha's Vineyard.

JACQUELINE KENNEDY ONASSIS
1929-1994

By SEN. EDWARD M. KENNEDY, *brother-in-law*

Delivered at memorial service, May 23, 1994

St. Ignatius Loyola Church, New York City

L AST SUMMER, WHEN WE WERE ON THE UPPER DECK ON the boat at the Vineyard, waiting for President and Mrs. Clinton to arrive, Jackie turned to me and said, "Teddy, you go down and greet the president."

But I said, "Maurice [Tempelsman] is already there."

And Jackie answered, "Teddy, you do it. Maurice isn't running for reelection."

She was always there—for all our family—in her special way.

She was a blessing to us and to the nation, and a lesson to the world on how to do things right, how to be a mother, how to appreciate history, how to be courageous. No one else looked like her, spoke like her, wrote like her, or was so original in the way she did things. No one we knew ever had a better sense of self.

Eight months before she married Jack, they went together to President Eisenhower's inaugural ball. Jackie said later that that's where they decided they liked inaugurations.

No one ever gave more meaning to the title of First Lady. The nation's capital city looks as it does because of her. She saved Lafayette Square and Pennsylvania Avenue.

Jackie brought the greatest artists to the White House, and brought the arts to the center of national attention. Today, in large part because of her inspiration and vision, the arts are an abiding part of national policy.

President Kennedy took such delight in her brilliance and her spirit. At a White House dinner, he once leaned over and told the wife of the French ambassador, "Jackie speaks fluent French. But I only understand one out of every five words she says—and that word is De Gaulle."

And then, during those four endless days in 1963, she held us together as a family and a country. In large part because of her, we could grieve and then go on. She lifted us up and, in the doubt and darkness, she gave her fellow citizens back their pride as Americans. She was then thirty-four years old.

Afterward, as the eternal flame she lit flickered in the autumn of Arlington Cemetery, Jackie went on to do what she most wanted—to raise Caroline and John, and warm her family's life and that of all the Kennedys. Robert Kennedy sustained her, and she helped make it possible for Bobby to continue. She kept Jack's memory alive, as he carried Jack's mission on.

Her two children turned out to be extraordinary, honest, unspoiled, and with a character equal to hers. And she did it in the most trying of circumstances. They are her two miracles.

Her love for Caroline and John was deep and unqualified. She reveled in their accomplishments, she hurt with their sorrows, and she felt sheer joy and delight in spending time with them. At the mere mention of one of their names, Jackie's eyes would shine brighter and her smile would grow bigger.

She once said that if you "bungle raising your children, nothing else much matters in life." She didn't bungle. Once again, she showed us how to do the most important thing of all, and do it right.

When she went to work, Jackie became a respected professional in the world of publishing. And because of her, remarkable books came to life. She searched out new authors and ideas. She was interested in everything.

Her love of history became a devotion to historic preservation.

You knew when Jackie joined the cause to save a building in Manhattan, the bulldozers might as well turn around and go home.

She had a wonderful sense of humor—a way of focusing on someone with total attention—and a little-girl delight in who they were and what they were saying. It was a gift of herself that she gave to others. And in spite of all her heartache and loss, she never faltered.

I often think of what she said about Jack in December after he died: "They made him a legend, when he would have preferred to be a man." Jackie would have preferred just to be herself, but the world insisted that she be a legend, too. She never wanted public notice—in part, I think, because it brought back painful memories of an unbearable sorrow, endured in the glare of a million lights.

In all the years since then, her genuineness and depth of character continued to shine through the privacy, and reach people everywhere. Jackie was too young to be a widow in 1963, and too young to die now.

Her grandchildren were bringing new joy to her life, a joy that illuminated her face whenever you saw them together. Whether it was taking Rose and Tatiana for an ice cream cone, or taking a walk in Central Park with little Jack as she did last Sunday, she relished being Grand Jackie and showering her grandchildren with love.

At the end, she worried more about us than herself. She let her family and friends know she was thinking of them. How cherished were those wonderful notes in her distinctive hand on her powder-blue stationery!

In truth, she did everything she could—and more—for each of us.

She made a rare and noble contribution to the American spirit. But for us, most of all she was a magnificent wife, mother, grandmother, sister, aunt, and friend.

She graced our history. And for those of us who knew and loved her—she graced our lives.

1929	Born Jacqueline Lee Bouvier in Southampton, MA. Learns to ride almost as soon as she can walk.
1944	Attends Miss Porter's Finishing School. Confides to a friend, "I'm sure no one will marry me, and I'll end up being a house-mother here." Three years later she is dubbed Debutante of the Year.
1952	Graduating from George Washington University, Jackie is hired as an inquiring photographer for a local paper. At a dinner party, she is introduced to Congressman John F. Kennedy. She marries him the following year. Their wedding is attended by 900 guests—and thousands of gate-crashing onlookers.
1957	Jackie gives birth to daughter Caroline Bouvier. Three years later, John Jr. is born.
1960	Kennedy elected 35th president of the United States. The mystique surrounding Jackie grows—she becomes known for her un-erring, elegant sense of style. From pillbox hats to white gloves, her fashion choices inspire an avalanche of public interest.
1961	Determined to restore the White House to its original splendor, Jackie hires a curator and transforms it into a living museum. She brings in a French chef, throws elegant dinner parties—inviting artists, intellectuals, and Nobel laureates—and leads the nation on a televised tour of the newly refurbished White House.
1963	John F. Kennedy is assassinated. Images of Jackie lunging across the open limousine are seared in national memory. Jackie establishes an eternal flame by his grave at Arlington and presents a dignified front to the nation. A week later, she bestows the name Camelot on the Kennedy presidency. (Before bed, Kennedy had often played the title song from the musical *Camelot* on a Victrola in their bedroom.)
1964	Jackie moves to New York City to raise her children privately.
1968	Becomes a target of scandal sheets by marrying shipping magnate Aristotle Onassis. When Onassis dies in 1975, she returns to New York, taking a job as editor at Doubleday. "One of the things I

like about publishing is that you don't promote the editor—you promote the book and the author."

1990   In her last years, Jackie lives quietly—spending time with family, preserving historic New York buildings, jogging in Central Park, and going about town with companion Maurice Tempelsman. She never grants interviews about her past.

1994   Jackie dies of cancer, age 65. Buried alongside President Kennedy at Arlington National Cemetery, she is remembered by John Jr. for her "love of words, the bonds of home and family, and her spirit of adventure."

Acknowledgments

This book was conceived in turbulent times—began after 9/11 and delivered just before the war with Iraq. In a world shaken by intolerance and discord, I found the following people to be reminders of the finer aspects of humanity. I'd like to thank them.

Peter Allen for his surgical wit and ever ready help; Shaye Areheart for her vision, and giving me my first foothold in publishing; Leila Astarabadi for her photos and warm-hearted friendship; Oak Atkinson for her highly infectious enthusiasm; Erica Barnes for 15 years of hijinx (starting with Garfield) and help editing; Lisa Caccavale for her kind introduction to publishing folk; Joe Cohen for his keen suggestions on structuring the proposal; Bert Fink for locating tributes to our musical gods; Brent Gallenberger for his canny advice on negotiating the publishing world; Victoria Tang Goffard, fellow B-school misfit, for her transcendent 2 A.M. help on everything from the Follies onwards; Google for being there; Karen Grey for her tough but fair editing style, and for sharing her muffins; Barbara Hall and Carrie Ford Hilliker for their vital Hollywood help; Mark Jacobs for his editing assistance, even whilst gallivanting in India; Barbara Marco for letting me commiserate, repeatedly (fellow authors, unite!); Kimley "W" Maretzo for helping me design a great proposal; Jay Mulvaney for a poignant title; Albert Naglieri for being right there, always, and for introducing me to Magnolia Bakery; Anne Marie O'Neill for helping me track down hermetic handlers; Tom-Tom and Michele Shpetner for their generous legal counsel; Starbucks for being a second, less lonely livingroom; Dan Strone for representing me with determination and wisdom; Ron Wall for being thoroughly himself, and for teaching me to disregard rules; and Susan White for her gracious assistance with timelines.

Special thanks to: All the contributors, who launched our icons into the afterlife on such powerful tailwinds; Lois Atkinson—a gentle, incisive editor and extraordinary cook; Lee Bantle for his unstinting love, and for making this world a much richer, gentler place; Paul Gavriani for his rigorous edits, L'il Bird alter ego, and making Fridays fun; Kim Kanner Meisner for her always gracious help in managing this project; Kimberly Needham for being the best research assistant; Robert Pennoyer for his generosity and techno-savvy; Barbara Reeder for her always wise counsel, ebullient friendship, and for introducing me to my agent; Kathryn Sermak for her cheerleading, transcribing, and cool marketing ideas; Gene Taggert for his generous way with words; Jess Taylor for his sharp suggestions, and demonstrating how to live with abandon.

And finally—my mother Shahin for her timeless love; my father Max for teaching me to see and love smaller things; and my sister Katayoun for sustaining me with really cool presents.

Thank you.

Credits and Permissions

Epigraph

Poem by Robinson Jeffers from *The Collected Poetry of Robinson Jeffers* edited by Tim Hunt, Volume 2. © 1938, renewed 1966 by Garth Jeffers and Donnan Jeffers; Editorial matter © 1988 by the Board of Trustees of the Leland Stanford Jr. University. Used with the permission of Stanford University Press, www.sup.org.

Maestros

Isadora Duncan: Eulogy by Max Eastman courtesy of *The Nation* magazine; Copyright © 1927 by *The Nation* magazine. Eulogy provided by Jeanne Bresciani.

Bob Fosse: Eulogy courtesy of Neil Simon. Copyright © 1987 by Neil Simon.

Keith Haring: Eulogy courtesy of Kay Haring.

Jemone Robbins: Eulogy courtesy of Mikhail Baryshnikov.

Gianni Versace: Eulogy courtesy of Madonna. Originally appeared in *Time* magazine.

Andy Warhol: Eulogy courtesy of John Richardson. Copyright © 1987 by John Richardson.

Visionaries

Susan B. Anthony: Eulogy courtesy of Susan B. Anthony House, with additional assistance on timeline.

Quentin Crisp: Delivered by Louis Colaianni at *An Evening for Quentin Crisp*, organized by Phillip Ward, Executor of Quentin Crisp Estate. A portion was previously broadcast on Pacifica Radio, Brian de Shazor host.

Che Guevara: Delivered by Fidel Castro, broadcast on Havana Domestic Television and Radio Services in Spanish. Abridged. Courtesy of Dave Homenuck.

Martin Luther King: Eulogy by Benjamin E. Mays courtesy of Bernice Mays Perkins. Abridged.

Karl Marx: Eulogy by Friedrich Engels courtesy of International Publishers Company.

Ryan White: Eulogy courtesy of Reverend Dr. Ray Probasco.

Malcolm X: Eulogy courtesy of Mr. Ossie Davis.

Wisecrackers

Lucille Ball: Eulogy courtesy of Diane Sawyer

Jack Benny: Eulogy courtesy of Bob Hope

Stan Laurel: Eulogy courtesy of Dick Van Dyke

Gilda Radner: Eulogy courtesy of Alan Zweibel, previously published in *Bunny Bunny—Gilda Radner: A Sort of Love Story,* (Applause Books). Copyright © 1994, 1997 by Alan Zweibel.

Charles Schulz: Eulogy courtesy of Cathy Guisewite. Copyright © 2000 by Cathy Guisewite.

Captains of Industry

Andrew Carnegie: Eulogy by John H. Finley courtesy of Carnegie Hero Fund Commission.

David Ogilvy: Eulogy courtesy of Jock Elliott.

John D. Rockefeller Jr.: Eulogy by Dr. Robert J. McCracken, courtesy of James McCracken.

Charles Tiffany: Eulogy by Annabel A. Goan courtesy of The Tiffany Archives.

Matinee Idols

Humphrey Bogart: Eulogy by John Huston courtesy of Angelica Huston.

Richard Burton: Eulogy by Emlyn Williams courtesy of The Beneficiaries of the Estate of the late Emlyn Williams and the Maggie Noach Literary Agency. Eulogy provided by the National Library of Wales (Rhydwen Williams 45) Copyright © 2003 by The Beneficiaries of the Estate of the late Emlyn Williams.

Bette Davis: Eulogy courtesy of James Woods, with help from Kathryn Sermak.

James Dean: Eulogy by Xen Harvey courtesy of Betty Harvey and The James Dean Memorial Gallery.

Jack Lemmon: Eulogy courtesy of Larry Gelbart. Copyright © 2001 by Larry Gelbart.

Walter Matthau: Eulogy courtesy of Charlie Matthau.

River Phoenix: Eulogy by William Richert printed with permission from Barry C. Lawrence. Copyright © 2002 by Barry C. Lawrence. Originally appeared in *The Search for River Phoenix, The Truth Behind the Myth*.

Mae West: Eulogy by Kevin Thomas, from "Mae West: At One with her Image" (*Los Angeles Times*: November 30, 1998). Copyright © 1980 by Los Angeles Times. Abridged. Reprinted by permission of the *Los Angeles Times*.

Explorers & High Fliers

Challenger Astronauts: Eulogy courtesy of President Ronald Reagan.

Amelia Earhart: Tribute by Muriel Morrissey courtesy of Amy M. Kleppner. Additional assistance by Sue Butler.

Thomas Edison: Eulogy by J. F. Owens courtesy of Edison National Historic Site.

Albert Einstein: Eulogy by Ernst Straus courtesy of Daniel and Louise Straus. Abridged.

Carl Jung: Eulogy by Sir Laurens van der Post courtesy of Analytical Psychology Club of New York. Copyright © 1961 by The Analytical Psychology Club of New York, Inc. Abridged.

Timothy Leary: Eulogy courtesy of Winona Ryder. Previously published in *Timothy Leary: Outside Looking In*. Ed. Robert Forte (Park Street Press, 1999).

Marshall McLuhan: Eulogy by John Culkin (founder of the Center for Understanding Media) is used with permission of T. C. McLuhan.

Tunesmiths & Troubadours

Chet Atkins: Eulogy by Garrison Keillor. Copyright © 2003 by Garrison Keillor. Reprinted by permission of Ellen Levine Literary Agency / Trident Media Group.

Irving Berlin: Eulogy courtesy of Samuel Goldwyn Jr.

Sammy Davis Jr.: Eulogy courtesy of Gregory Hines.

Duke Ellington: Eulogy by Stanley Dance courtesy of Francis Dance.

George Harrison: Eulogy courtesy of Eric Idle. Copyright © 2002 by Eric Idle.

Janis Joplin: Eulogy by Ralph Gleason courtesy of Jean Gleason. Abridged.

Lawrence Welk: Eulogy courtesy of Shirley Welk Fredricks.

Movie Moguls

Stanley Kubrick: Eulogy courtesy of Jan Harlan. Copyright © 1999 by Jan Harlan.

Irving 'Swifty' Lazar: Eulogy courtesy of Larry McMurtry.

David O. Selznick: Eulogy by Truman Capote courtesy of Alan U. Schwartz.

Billy Wilder: Eulogy courtesy of Larry Gelbart. Copyright © 2002 by Larry Gelbart.

Darryl Zanuck: Eulogy by Orson Welles originally appeared in Los Angeles Herald Examiner, January 13, 1980.

Wordsmiths

Erma Bombeck: Eulogy courtesy of Phil Donahue

Emily Dickinson: Eulogy by Susan Dickinson courtesy of Tevis Kimball, The Jones Library.

Dashiell Hammett: Eulogy by Lillian Hellman courtesy of Richard Poirier.

Lillian Hellman: Eulogy by William Styron courtesy of *The Vineyard Gazette*. Copyright © 1984 by Richard F. Reston. Originally appeared in *The Vineyard Gazette*.

Theodor Seuss Geisel: Eulogy by Robert Bernstein courtesy of Robert Bernstein and Audrey Geisel.

Virginia Woolf: Eulogy by Christopher Isherwood courtesy of Don Bachardy. Copyright © 1966 by Christopher Isherwood. Originally appeared in *Exhumations*, 1966, by Christopher Isherwood.

Camelot

John F. Kennedy Jr. and Jacqueline Kennedy Onassis eulogies courtesy of Senator Edward Kennedy.